a youth worker's commentary on JOHN, volume two

les christie & david nystrom

volume
two
John 9-21

JN

a youth
worker's
commentary
on
JOHN

les christie & david nystrom

ZONDERVAN.com/
AUTHORTRACKER
follow your favorite authors

ZONDERVAN

A Youth Worker's Commentary on John, Volume 2
Copyright © 2012 by Les Christie & David Nystrom

YS Youth Specialties is a trademark of YOUTHWORKS!, INCORPORATED and is registered with the United States Patent and Trademark Office.

This title is also available as a Zondervan ebook.
Visit www.zondervan.com/ebooks.

Requests for information should be addressed to:

Zondervan, *Grand Rapids, Michigan 49530*

Library of Congress Cataloging-in-Publication Data

Christie, Les John.
    A youth worker's commentary on John / Les Christie and David Nystrom.
       p. cm.
    Includes bibliographical references.
    ISBN 978-0-310-67033-9 (softcover)
    1. Bible. N.T. John—Study and teaching. 2. Bible. N.T. John—Criticism, interpretation, etc.
3. 3. Church work with youth. I. Nystrom, David P., 1959- II. Title.
    BS2616.C47 2011
    226.5'077—dc22   2011011146

Cover design: Chris Gilbert, Gearbox
Interior design: David Conn

Printed in the United States of America

12 13 14 15 16 /DCI/ 23 22 21 20 19 18 17 16 15 14 13 12 11 10 9 8 7 6 5 4 3 2 1

CONTENTS

ACKNOWLEDGMENTS

We are grateful to Jay Howver, former publisher of Youth Specialties, for his positive response to our book's initial proposal. We are appreciative of Greg Clouse, senior editor of Zondervan's book group, for coordinating all of the components that go into the publishing process. We are indebted to our editor, Doug Davidson, who took our original manuscript and shaped it with great care into a more cohesive book. Thanks also to Tammy Johnson for her thought-provoking cover design, to David Conn for his work on the interior design, to Chris Fann and Jen Howver for marketing the book, and to Laura Gross and Janie Wilkerson for their careful proofreading.

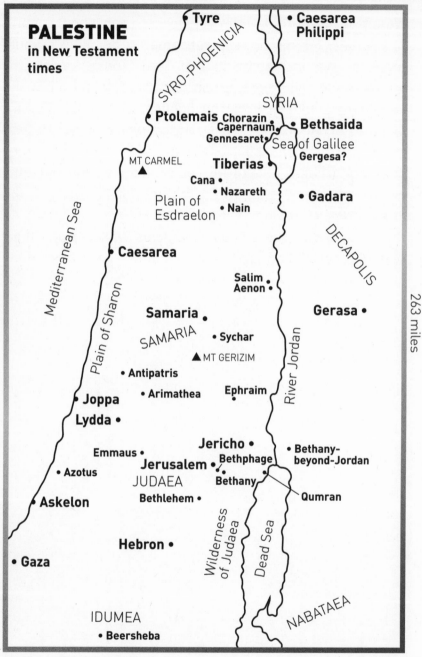

71 miles

PALESTINE
in New Testament
times

• Tyre

SYRO-PHOENICIA

• Caesarea
Philippi

SYRIA

• Ptolemais   Chorazin
Capernaum•   • Bethsaida
Gennesaret•
MT CARMEL   Sea of Galilee
▲   Gergesa?

• Tiberias

Cana •
• Nazareth   • Gadara
Plain of   • Nain
Esdraelon

Mediterranean Sea

• Caesarea

DECAPOLIS

Salim •
Aenon •

Plain of Sharon

Samaria •   Gerasa •

SAMARIA
• Sychar

River Jordan

▲ MT GERIZIM

• Antipatris

• Arimathea   Ephraim
•
• Joppa

Lydda •

Jericho •
Emmaus •   • Bethany-
Jerusalem • Bethphage   beyond-Jordan
• Azotus   •
JUDAEA   Bethany
Bethlehem •   Qumran

• Askelon

Wilderness of Judaea

Dead Sea

Hebron •

• Gaza

IDUMEA   NABATAEA

• Beersheba

From Tom Wright, *John for Everyone* **(Cambridge: University Press), by permission of SPCK.**

INTRODUCTION

This two-volume commentary on the Gospel of John is designed to reach and engage the hearts and minds of youth workers and their students. Our hope is that you will find it stimulating as you seek to unpack ancient biblical truth in today's world. Written with the busy youth worker in mind, it will save you time while preparing messages. You can use these books for personal reading and edification, but the commentary's primary purpose is to stimulate small-group discussions that will help you and your students grow in faith and knowledge of God and the Scriptures.

In the first volume of *A Youth Worker's Commentary on John*, we looked at the first eight chapters of John's Gospel. Here in Volume 2 we'll consider chapters 9 through 21. As in Volume 1, we'll walk you through the Gospel a few verses at a time, thoughtfully considering the context and meaning of each element in John's narrative. Then at the end of each section, you'll find a group of thought-provoking discussion questions to help you and your students connect the biblical text with your world.

As we mentioned in the Introduction to the first volume, the Gospel of John is relatively simple in terms of its grammatical structure and vocabulary, but it's also a deep and demanding book. This Gospel makes you think. The most humble believer can understand and profit from it, yet there are untold depths in this writing.

All four of the New Testament Gospels were originally anonymous. The title "The Gospel According to John" was most likely added to the Gospel by early Christians, and it represents the early church's understanding of the book's source. While tradition has said that the apostle John is the author of the Gospel, in the first volume we considered several other possibilities. Some believe the writing is the product of several people or several communities who associated themselves with John. Others have suggested John Mark, Thomas, or Lazarus as the possible writers. While many scholars have abandoned the idea that this Gospel was written by the apostle John, others accept the traditional view that John wrote the Gospel or was closely associated with it in some way.

Most scholars agree that the fourth gospel is of a comparatively late date. It is commonly held that it was written in the latter half of the first century (AD 60–90). The early church father Irenaeus believed that John wrote the Gospel during his residence in Ephesus. By the end of the first century, Christianity was no longer predominantly Jewish. The church was overwhelmingly Gentile from a Hellenistic background. Most of John's Gentile readers had never heard the term *Messiah*. The Gospel of John sought to proclaim the message of Jesus to a world dominated by Greek philosophy and language. (You'll find much more information about the origins, background, and structure of John's Gospel in the Introduction to Volume 1 of this commentary.)

The theme of John's Gospel is the deity of Jesus Christ. John 20:30-31 tells us: "Jesus performed many other signs in the presence of his disciples, which are not recorded in this book. But these are written that you may believe that Jesus is the Messiah, the Son of God, and that by believing you may have life in his name."

The Gospel of John provides a series of snapshots of people who became believers through their encounters with Jesus. In our first volume we met some memorable characters, including John the Baptist, Philip, Nathanael, Andrew, Peter, the disciple whom Jesus loved (perhaps John), Nicodemus, a Samaritan woman at a well, an invalid at a pool, a boy with five small barley loaves of bread, and a woman caught in adultery. Many of them will be heard from again in Volume 2, but we'll also get to know other unforgettable characters, including Lazarus, Mary and Martha, Thomas, Annas, Caiaphas, Pilate, Mary Magdalene, and Joseph of Arimathea.

How to Get the Most Out of This Book

In Volume 1 of *A Youth Worker's Commentary on John*, we included the NIV text and commentary for 38 episodes from the first eight chapters in the Gospel of John. In Volume 2 we'll take an in-depth look at 44 additional episodes, spanning the remaining 13 chapters in the Gospel of John.

We hope you'll move through the Gospel at a pace that best suits you and your group. You may want to do an episode a week for a few weeks, and then take a break from the Gospel of John and come back to it again later. Or, if you think your group could handle it, you could go through the entire two volumes over 82 weeks. Or, you may want to select particular episodes from different sections of the Gospel of John.

In each episode we'll take a rich look into the meaning of the text, including word studies, personal and historical studies, and discussion questions to help get you and your students thinking and talking. This book can be used for personal study, or it can be used as an invaluable aid for your message and lesson preparation. As you gain a solid understanding of the Gospel of John, including its historical context, rationale, and meaning, you'll see how to apply what you uncover to the needs and issues you and the teens in your group are dealing with.

When using the book in small-group discussions, we recommend having a student read aloud a small portion of the text or the entire passage you'll be tackling. Ask the group what key words stood out and have them highlight those words in their text, also noting any observations they might have. Then discuss some of the "Read Between the

Lines" questions at the end of each study. These questions will invite your students to dig more deeply into the text. You don't have to use every question; just pick a few that might appeal to you or your group. Toward the end of your session, move into the "Welcome to My World" questions that will invite students to apply what they've learned, bringing the study home to where they live, work, and play.

THE GOSPEL ACCORDING TO JOHN

Here's Mud in Your Eye

Birth is the beginning of the process of death. (Now, isn't that a pleasant way to start off this volume?) Thoughts about health and healing occupy a lot of our time because we tend to do all we can to keep our decaying bodies alive.

There are four types of healing:

1. *Natural healing* in which the body throws off an intruder by itself. The body compensates for the injury or illness and rebuilds or restores itself.
2. *Medical healing* using medical providers, drugs, and machinery.
3. *Psychological healing* using trained counselors to improve a person's mental health.
4. *Divine or miraculous healing* in which there is no possibility of the above three types of healing taking place. This healing violates the laws of nature.

This fourth type of healing is what we'll see at the beginning of John 9.

John 9:1

¹As he went along, he saw a man blind from birth.

As chapter 9 begins, Jesus has just slipped away from a crowd that was preparing to lift up stones in order to kill him (8:59) because of his "I AM" statements. Outside the temple—just a short time after declaring, "I am the light of the world" (8:12)—Jesus sees a man born blind who has never seen the light. Although his adversaries were surely pursuing him, Jesus takes the time to lend a hand to this blind man whom so many had overlooked. I'm so glad Jesus is never in a hurry, never too busy to care about others and their predicaments.

No one could say the healing in this passage was one of the first three types of healings, because the man who'd been born blind experienced immediate healing. The scene is similar to Acts 3:1-10, where Peter heals in the name of Jesus a man who'd been crippled since birth. Both men are beggars who are healed in the temple area.

The temple seems like a good place to beg. This blind man perhaps hoped the people going to and coming from the temple would be in a generous mood. In that culture charitable deeds were viewed as a way to gain favor with God and as a defense against wickedness.

The man's physical condition could be compared with the spiritual state of the unbelievers in 2 Corinthians 4:4— "The god of this age has blinded the minds of unbelievers, so that they cannot see the light of the gospel that displays the glory of Christ, who is the image of God." This man who'd been blind since birth did not seek out Jesus; how could he have seen him coming? Yet Jesus comes to the blind man just as Jesus comes to us—before we even consider coming to him.

> While I know myself as a creation of God, I am also obligated to realize and remember that everyone else and everything else are also God's creation.
>
> —Maya Angelou
>
> Each one of them is Jesus in disguise.
>
> —Mother Teresa

John 9:2-5

²His disciples asked him, "Rabbi, who sinned, this man or his parents, that he was born blind?"

³"Neither this man nor his parents sinned," said Jesus, "but this happened so that the works of God might be displayed in him. ⁴As long as it is day; we must do the works of him who sent me.

Night is coming, when no one can work. [5]While I am in the world, I am the light of the world."

The disciples' question may seem cruel at first. Many people in the first century—and even today—blame their afflictions on their own or their parents' sins. Exodus 20:5 seems to offer some reason for this belief: "I, the LORD your God, am a jealous God, punishing the children for the sin of the parents to the third and fourth generation of those who hate me." Yet this verse and Exodus 34:7 are primarily national in scope—focusing on how future generations of the nation of Israel will suffer due to the failures of those who precede them.

But the religious leaders also considered parental sins as having individual consequences on one's children. We see this today in cases where children suffer from the effects of a parent's abuse of alcohol or drugs, such as "crack babies" or those born with fetal alcohol syndrome. When a mother has gonorrhea, the infection can be passed to the child's eyes at birth and cause blindness—although we now have medication that can cure this. But Ezekiel 18:20 tells us, "The one who sins is the one who will die. The child will not share the guilt of the parent, nor will the parent share the guilt of the child." Each individual bears the consequences of his or her own sin. There is not always a direct link between suffering and personal sin.

The disciples are asking why this man should suffer if his parents are the ones who sinned. Many religious leaders of Jesus' day would have answered by talking about a prenatal sin, a sin *in utero*. They would say that a child could commit a sin in the womb and suffer for the rest of his or her life. This comes from a unique interpretation of Genesis 4:7—"Sin is crouching at your door; it desires to have you, but you must rule over it." They would say the "door" refers to the birth canal and this man must have been a bad, bad embryo! They would reinforce this notion by pointing to Genesis 25, which speaks of Jacob and Esau wrestling in their mother's womb.

Jesus says this particular guy was born blind so he could glorify God. He was a prepared vessel, a miracle waiting to happen. This does not mean God deliberately caused this man to be born blind. Jesus is saying to his disciples, "I don't want to get into a theological or philosophical argument; this happened to serve God's higher purpose. Here's a man who needs light, and I am the light of the world—so let's get at it." The "must" (9:4) indicates a sense of urgency.

Can you imagine the disciples having this discussion with Jesus right in front of this man? The disciples act as if the blind man isn't even there, but he must have heard every word—including their question about who sinned. They stopped not to talk to the man but to talk *about* him. Yet Jesus sees him as a human being in need of a healing touch from God. From his earliest childhood, this man has experienced only darkness. There was no Braille, no Jews with Disabilities Act in antiquity. He's spent his entire life begging. So Jesus compassionately reaches out to him.

When Jesus speaks of the night coming (9:4), he may be referring to the period after the crucifixion and before the resurrection. He may also be referring to the religious leaders' attempts to snuff out the light of Christianity. He says, "we must do the works of him who sent me." This "we" is inclusive—Jesus is talking about his disciples—including you and me.

John 9:6-7

⁶ After saying this, he spit on the ground, made some mud with the saliva, and put it on the man's eyes. ⁷ "Go," he told him, "wash in the Pool of Siloam" (this word means "Sent"). So the man went and washed, and came home seeing.

Commentators go crazy over these verses because this is one of the rare cases where Jesus uses a substance to heal someone. Usually Jesus just speaks or touches a person and healing occurs. But here he creates mud with his saliva. In antiquity, spittle was thought to have medicinal power. However, Jesus does not need mud or saliva.

There are only two other recorded incidents in which Jesus put saliva on a person to heal him. In Mark 7:33 Jesus heals a man with an impediment of speech and hearing by first putting his fingers into the man's ears and then spitting and touching the man's tongue. In Mark 8:23 Jesus takes a blind man outside the village, spits on the man's eyes, and then places his hands on the man.

Some have suggested that Jesus healed in this way in order to make use of the healing quality of saliva, or that he did it to tick off the religious leaders because the spitting incident may have been more offensive to devout Jews than breaking the Sabbath. But Jesus healed the man in this way simply because he wanted to do so. God is creative and uses variety in his healings. We want to put God in a formulaic box (five easy steps to healing), but God often surprises us.

Notice that Jesus does not ask this man if he wants to be healed. This is a work of pure grace.

One of the extraordinary things about this miracle is that Jesus does here what God does in Genesis 2—out of the dust of the earth, he creates. Jesus does not restore sight. He creates it. The man does what he is told and he can see. No fanfare, no lightning. God just created two new eyes.

We don't know why Jesus didn't go to the pool with the man, or why the man had to go to that specific pool. The Pool of Siloam is a small rock-cut pool (20 x 30 feet) located inside the south wall of the city. King Hezekiah built it in 701 BC in case the city was seized. The pool was fed by Hezekiah's tunnel or aqueduct from the Gihon spring in the Kidron

Valley (2 Kings 20:20; 2 Chronicles 32:30). To build the tunnel, excavators had to cut through 583 yards of solid rock. The tunnel was only two feet wide in some places, with an average height of six feet. The builders cut from both ends and met in the middle. It was an amazing engineering feat.

The word *Siloam* means "sent" in Hebrew. The water from the large spring outside the city was sent to this little pool inside the city walls. The high priest would draw water from this pool for the Feast of Tabernacles. (See the commentary on 7:39 in Volume One for more about this.) It was the only source of spring water in the city.

The message in this healing is that those who long to see—physically or spiritually—must go to Jesus, the One sent by God. Giving sight to the blind was predicted as a messianic activity in Isaiah 29:18; 35:5; and 42:7.

John 9:8-12

8 His neighbors and those who had formerly seen him begging asked, "Isn't this the same man who used to sit and beg?" 9 Some claimed that he was.

Others said, "No, he only looks like him."

But he himself insisted, "I am the man."

10 "How then were your eyes opened?" they asked.

11 He replied, "The man they call Jesus made some mud and put it on my eyes. He told me to go to Siloam and wash. So I went and washed, and then I could see."

12 "Where is this man?" they asked him.

"I don't know," he said.

Imagine seeing for the first time—seeing mountains, trees, and people. The healed man must have been dancing with excitement. But his neighbors seem reluctant to celebrate with him; they do not smile, rejoice, or clap for joy.

This man was a beggar, and then as now, beggars get treated as if they are invisible. Most people don't make eye contact with beggars. When the man's neighbors see him, some think he's the man they'd often seen begging; others think he just looks like that man. He tells them, "I am the man." The man actually uses the words *ego eimi,* meaning "I am"—a phrase Jesus uses multiple times in John's Gospel (see Volume 1 of this commentary for more about this.) This incident shows that John isn't referring to Jesus' divinity every single time this phrase is used.

It's clear that the healed man knows little, if anything, about Jesus. He humbly acknowledges that he doesn't know where the man who healed him has gone.

READ BETWEEN THE LINES

- Define "miraculous healings."
- Why did Jesus choose to heal this particular man?
- What biblical evidence is there for—or against—the belief that trials are the direct result of sin?
- How does Jesus answer the disciples' question about who sinned?
- What does Jesus mean by "the night is coming"?
- What did Jesus tell the man to do? Why?
- What do you think it would be like to see for the first time?
- How do the neighbors react to the healing?
- What is the significance of the term the blind man uses when he says, "I am"?
- What does this man know about Jesus?
- Why do you think giving sight to the blind is the miracle that occurs most often in the Gospel? How does this tie in with Jesus being the light of the world?

WELCOME TO MY WORLD

- What types of healings have I, and those I know, personally experienced?
- What is the relationship between sin and suffering?
- How have I or my friends used sicknesses, tragedies, weaknesses, or disabilities to bring glory to God?
- How am I similar to this blind man? (See Ephesians 4:18 and 2 Corinthians 4:4.)
- How am I "sent"?
- How do I react when I see someone begging on the sidewalk?
- If I were blind, what would I miss seeing the most?
- What are some of the "blind spots" in my life?

The Pharisees Investigate the Healing

John 9:13-16

13 They brought to the Pharisees the man who had been blind. 14 Now the day on which Jesus had made the mud and opened the man's eyes was a Sabbath. 15 Therefore the Pharisees also asked him how he had received his sight. "He put mud on my eyes," the man replied, "and I washed, and now I see."

16 Some of the Pharisees said, "This man is not from God, for he does not keep the Sabbath."

But others asked, "How can a sinner perform such signs?" So they were divided.

When this formerly blind man's neighbors brought him to the Pharisees, he must have been smiling from ear to ear. There are several possible explanations for why the man's neighbors brought him before the Pharisees:

1. The neighbors did not understand what had happened and hoped the Pharisees could explain it.
2. The neighbors may have heard of the plots against Jesus, so they brought the healed man to show the Pharisees how wrong they'd been about Jesus.
3. The neighbors knew the miracle had been done on the Sabbath, so they wanted to see how the Pharisees would respond.

By healing on the Sabbath, Jesus is violating the rabbinic teachings (or "yoke") that had been put in place during the time between the writing of the Old and New Testaments. These teachings were based on the Ten Commandments, but the rules themselves were not biblical. For example, the biblical commandment to honor the Sabbath led to a long list of activities that were forbidden on the Sabbath. Here are just a few examples:

- You could not cut your fingernails, toenails, hair, or beard.

- If your lamp ran out of oil, you could not put fresh oil in the lamp. You had to sit in the darkness. Carrying new oil was working. In fact, you were forbidden to turn lamps on or off on the Sabbath. (Even today some orthodox Jews have lights set by an automatic controller for the Sabbath.)

- You could not make clay or knead mud—a tradition Jesus violated by making the mud and placing it on the man's eyes.

- You could not heal a person on the Sabbath, which Jesus also violated. While pacifying a problem was acceptable, completely healing someone was forbidden.

The Pharisees question the former blind man about what has happened, and he gives them a simple answer. Some of the Pharisees didn't seem to care that a man born blind was now able to see. They were only concerned that a rule had been broken. So they seek to break down the man's testimony.

These Pharisees insist, "This man is not from God, for he does not keep the Sabbath." They are a little like folks who insist on following the 25 mph speed limit even if you need to drive faster than that to avoid the path of a runaway truck! These Pharisees contend that Jesus couldn't be God because he doesn't meet the standards they have established for godly behavior. But others ask: How can a sinner do such miraculous signs? The group stands divided, so they ask to hear more from the man born blind.

John 9:17-23

¹⁷ Then they turned again to the blind man, "What have you to say about him? It was your eyes he opened."

The man replied, "He is a prophet."

¹⁸ They still did not believe that he had been blind and had received his sight until they sent for the man's parents. ¹⁹ "Is this your son?" they asked. "Is this the one you say was born blind? How is it that now he can see?"

²⁰ "We know he is our son," the parents answered, "and we know he was born blind. ²¹ But how he can see now, or who opened his eyes, we don't know. Ask him. He is of age; he will speak for himself." ²² His parents said this because they were afraid of the Jewish leaders, who already had decided that anyone who acknowledged that Jesus was the Messiah would be put out of the synagogue. ²³ That was why his parents said, "He is of age; ask him."

The former blind man calls Jesus a prophet. It was probably the most significant title he could think of. But the neighbors remain skeptical until the blind man's parents arrive.

These Pharisees are not on a search for truth. They are ignoring all the evidence to build a weak case against Jesus. The parents of the former blind man answer the Pharisees questions very cautiously because the religious authorities hold a powerful weapon over the parents' heads. The parents were afraid of being excommunicated (12:42; 16:2). So rather than answer the questions directly, they put the responsibility back on their son, insisting that he should speak for himself since he is of age.

Excommunication was a dreaded punishment. There were two levels:

- *Nidduy*, where you'd be severely talked to and then excommunicated for 30 days; and

- *Herem*, where you'd be permanently excommunicated.

If you were excommunicated, you would have no part of the social, legal, and religious life of the community. Even your family would treat you as if you were dead. You could not buy food at a local store. No Jew within the community could do business with you. If you died, the family would not have a funeral for you. You would be forbidden to attend religious services, branded as a traitor, and not allowed to make sacrifices or read the Torah. If you were permanently excommunicated, you usually relocated to another town.

I did not become a Christian until the summer before my junior year of high school. It was Buckley Simmons, my buddy on the wrestling team, and my youth pastor, Jim Irby, who introduced me to Jesus. Buckley and his family attended a little church in West Los Angeles pastored by Harry Bucalstein. "Mr. B," as we liked to call him, was a wonderful man of God. You may be able to tell by his name that he was Jewish. He had come to know the Lord when he was 16. His family had warned him that if he became a Christian, they would force him to leave their home. He did and they did. He ended up spending the next few years in an orphanage. His family bought a burial plot and put a gravestone at the site with his name, his birth date, and the date of his death (the day he became a Christian). He spent his life boldly proclaiming the truths of Jesus. He later became president of an organization that reached into the Jewish community. I always admired him because I knew it had cost him a great deal to be a follower of Jesus.

—Les

John 9:24-27

24 A second time they summoned the man who had been blind. "Give glory to God by telling the truth," they said. "We know this man is a sinner."

25 He replied, "Whether he is a sinner or not, I don't know. One thing I do know. I was blind but now I see!"

26 Then they asked him, "What did he do to you? How did he open your eyes?"

27 He answered, "I have told you already and you did not listen. Why do you want to hear it again? Do you want to become his disciples too?"

"Give glory to God" is a solemn charge to the former blind man to tell the truth about what has happened (Joshua 7:19). The religious leaders want him to glorify God by saying that God alone (not Jesus) was responsible for his healing. They are convinced that Jesus is a Sabbath breaker and, therefore, a sinner.

This guy has a simple testimony. He's not interested in getting into the Pharisees' debate. He tells them he does not know whether Jesus is a sinner or not; but he does know that he was once blind and now he sees.

The Pharisees are relentless. The man gets weary of their questions and sarcastically asks if they also want to be Jesus' disciples. The earliest readers of John's Gospel knew the answer to his question—and they must have been chuckling at the man's tenacity.

John 9:28-29

28 Then they hurled insults at him and said, "You are this fellow's disciple! We are disciples of Moses! 29 We know that God spoke to Moses, but as for this fellow, we don't even know where he comes from."

The religious leaders are incensed and begin throwing insults at the formerly blind man. They tell him, "You are this fellow's disciple! We are disciples of Moses!" They are saying you have to choose, that one cannot be a disciple of both Jesus and Moses. Yet we know that Moses looked forward to the arrival of Jesus. In John 5:45-47, Jesus stated, "If you believed Moses, you would believe me, for he wrote about me. But since you do not believe what he wrote, how are you going to believe what I say?" Moses pointed to the grace and truth that comes in its fullness through Jesus.

Jewish Christians today (often referred to as "Jews for Jesus" or "Messianic Jews") claim they have not given up their Judaism. According to Michael Medved in "How Not to Win the Jewish Vote," an opinion piece in *USA Today* (November 21, 2011), these believers are often severely criticized by other Jews and considered outcasts for trying to be both Jewish and Christian. It's ironic that while a person may become an atheist and yet still consider himself or herself Jewish, belief in Jesus is considered to be irreconcilable with Judaism. However, as professor and author Gary Burge points out, "The rabbi Paul would have considered himself no less a Jew even though he believed in Jesus."

John 9:30-34

30 The man answered, "Now that is remarkable! You don't know where he comes from, yet he opened my eyes. 31 We know that God does not listen to sinners. He listens to the godly person who does his will. 32 Nobody has ever heard of opening the eyes of a man born blind. 33 If this man were not from God, he could do nothing."

34 To this they replied, "You were steeped in sin at birth; how dare you lecture us!" And they threw him out.

This former blind man now gives the religious leaders a theological lesson. He responds to their statement in 9:29—"we don't even know where he comes from"—by suggesting that Jesus may have come from God. (This Gospel often uses irony; see 4:12; 7:35, 42; 8:22; 11:50).

There are no accounts in the Old Testament of a person being healed of blindness from birth. But there are numerous statements in the Old Testament predicting that the coming Messiah would bring sight to the blind (Isaiah 29:18; 35:5; 42:7). Apparently, these Pharisees were either blind to these passages, or they chose to ignore them.

These religious leaders don't have a response for the former blind man turned theologian, so they insult him and throw him out. It seems the man may have been excommunicated—the very thing his parents feared.

READ BETWEEN THE LINES

- Why do you think the neighbors bring the man to the Pharisees?
- Why does Jesus heal on the Sabbath?
- What were the people's responses to the Pharisees' questions?
- How does the formerly blind man describe Jesus?
- What keeps his parents from making a definitive statement?
- What does it mean to be excommunicated?
- Why did they accuse Jesus of being a sinner?
- What question does the healed man ask the Pharisees?
- How did Moses point to Jesus?
- What theological lesson does the former blind man teach the religious leaders?

- What was their response?
- How does the former blind man's attitude toward the Pharisees change during these verses?

WELCOME TO MY WORLD

- What keeps many Christians today from confidently expressing their knowledge of Jesus?
- Are there "Pharisees" in my world? What are they like?
- How is the former blind man's response before antagonistic inquisitors an example for us?
- What rules for behavior do I have? Are these rules biblical?
- What would I have said if I were one of the parents being questioned by the Pharisees?
- Do I have a testimony? What is it?
- How do I respond to people who question my beliefs?

Spiritual Blindness

John 9:35-38

35 Jesus heard that they had thrown him out, and when he found him, he said, "Do you believe in the Son of Man?"

36 "Who is he, sir?" the man asked. "Tell me so that I may believe in him."

37 Jesus said, "You have now seen him; in fact, he is the one speaking with you."

38 Then the man said, "Lord, I believe," and he worshiped him.

This man whom Jesus healed has been abandoned by his parents and excommunicated by the religious leaders. Jesus seeks him out because he wants to see this man's complete conversion. Jesus asks, "Do you believe in the Son of Man?" (See 1:51.) Salvation is divinely initiated but requires a faith response.

This story reminds us that the more time we spend walking with Jesus, the more we'll understand and appreciate who he is. Check out the way the healed man's various statements about Jesus reflect the progression of his faith:

- John 9:11—He is a man who "made some mud and put it on my eyes."
- John 9:17—He is "a prophet."
- John 9:38—He is "my Lord."

People either pick up stones or bow down when they come to Jesus. This former blind man realizes that God is at work in Jesus—so much so that the man calls him "Lord" and worships him. By allowing this man to worship him, Jesus once again establishes his deity.

This is not just the story of a blind man who regains his physical sight. This is the story of how a man becomes rightly related to his God and "sees" completely for the first time in his life. Jesus did not merely give him sight—he gave him life.

John 9:39-41

39 Jesus said,[a] "For judgment I have come into this world, so that the blind will see and those who see will become blind."

40 Some Pharisees who were with him heard him say this and asked, "What? Are we blind too?"

41 Jesus said, "If you were blind, you would not be guilty of sin; but now that you claim you can see, your guilt remains."

John 9:39 reads almost as if it's the opposite of John 3:16. Jesus came to bring life, yet those who refuse salvation, peace, grace, and mercy have brought judgment upon themselves—they end up blind. The Pharisees could not imagine themselves as being spiritually blind, nor that anyone would even consider them to be blind.

God eventually hardens the hearts of those who willfully refuse to see, closing their eyes so they remain blind. John 12:40 tells us, "He has blinded their eyes and hardened their hearts, so they can neither see with their eyes, nor understand with their hearts, nor turn—and I would heal them." This is what happened with Pharaoh in the Old Testament. Pharaoh hardened his own heart and, as a result, God also hardened Pharaoh's heart (Exodus 4:21; 7:3; 9:12; 10:1, 20, 27; 11:10; 14:4, 8). First Timothy 4:2 speaks of "hypocritical liars, whose consciences have been seared as with a hot iron." Some people have a skewed sense of right and wrong. Jesus tells these religious leaders their guilt remains— which means it is still at work in their lives like an active virus. (See also John 12:37-41.)

---

a John 9:39 Some early manuscripts do not have *Then the man said . . . Jesus said.*

What would it be like to never feel guilty for things you've done or said or thought? No spiritual pain. Or what would it be like not to feel any physical pain? I used to think it would be so cool not to feel physical pain. Imagine being able to slam your finger in a car door and feel no pain.

It is my understanding that people with leprosy don't feel pain at the extremities of their bodies. Their fingers and toes become numb to pain. However, this is not as good as it sounds. A leper can scrape his foot and not know it. The foot will become infected and may have to be removed surgically. The numbness sometimes even affects the face. In such cases, a leper could accidentally throw extremely hot water on his face without realizing just how hot it is and end up burning and disfiguring his face. Physical pain tells us something is wrong with our bodies, and we need to get medical help quickly.

In the same way, our consciences (spiritual pain, guilt) tell us when we need spiritual help. That guilty feeling we have is often an indication that something in our life is out of whack. When we sin and feel no guilt, we are in serious trouble.

—Les

These religious leaders don't realize they are spiritually blind. This possibility has never crossed their minds. Jesus says that because they claim to "see," their sin remains. Jesus cannot help those who refuse to admit they have any need or those who think they have it all together and stubbornly refuse to admit their blindness. They have become complacent and self-satisfied. In Matthew 15:14 Jesus tells his disciples to "Leave them; they are blind guides. If the blind lead the blind, both will fall into a pit." (See also Proverbs 12:15; 26:12; and Isaiah 5:21.)

> The only thing worse than being blind is having sight but no vision.
> —Helen Keller

READ BETWEEN THE LINES

- Why did Jesus seek out the former blind man?
- How does this man's understanding of Jesus and his faith grow over the course of these verses?
- What twist does Jesus put on being blind?
- What does Jesus mean by "the blind will see" and "those who see will become blind"?
- In what ways are the Pharisees blind?
- Why does their guilt remain?
- This story ends with the religious leaders seeming to grow more blind and the blind man gaining more than physical sight. What are your thoughts?

WELCOME TO MY WORLD

- How have my friends responded to Jesus' seeking them out?
- What does it mean to worship Jesus?
- Do I know people who are willfully blind?
- What happens to those who are willfully blind?
- How are physical pain and spiritual pain similar and different?
- Do I know people who feel no guilt?
- What are the blind spots in my life?
- How has my understanding of Jesus changed since I began my spiritual journey?

- Are my eyes open and am I looking for the truth of God?

- Do I have any perceptions about God or theology that have had to change in light of Scripture?

- What would it be like to stand in front of Jesus and worship him?

- Does God care more about physical sight or spiritual sight? Why?

The Good Shepherd and His Sheep

The same group that was with Jesus throughout chapter 9 seems to be with him still in chapter 10 because the healing of the blind man is referred to again in John 10:21. However, it's clear that some time has passed by the time we reach verse 22, which speaks of the Feast of Dedication (also called Hanukkah or the Feast of Lights). This festival comes almost three months after the Feast of Tabernacles referenced in John 7:2.

In chapter 10 we read of Jesus as the Good Shepherd, an image presented with hidden spiritual meanings. Most of us have never spent time with a shepherd. However, it was a perfect illustration for people in the first century. David and Moses, two of the greatest leaders in the Old Testament, were both shepherds. The life of the shepherd was hard. The shepherd was a raw-boned, leather-skinned, weather-beaten man out in the field. Lions, bears, wolves, thieves, and robbers were all real dangers to him and his sheep.

> Looking out the window of a tourist bus while traveling in Israel, I thought I saw a shepherd and his sheep. Our guide told us the man was not a shepherd but a butcher. When I asked how he could tell, he said a shepherd leads his sheep, while the butcher drives or pushes his sheep. What a tremendous description of leadership. Jesus leads us. He goes before us.
>
> **—Les**

Shepherds in Israel would raise their sheep and keep them for the purpose of gathering their fleece. Sheep were rarely killed for their meat. The shepherds regularly sheared the heavy coats of the sheep. And the shepherd would be with his sheep for decades.

John 10:1-2

[1] "Very truly I tell you Pharisees, anyone who does not enter the sheep pen by the gate, but climbs in by some other way, is a thief and a robber. [2] The one who enters by the gate is the shepherd of the sheep."

Jesus begins with the familiar "Very truly I tell you" (translated in some Bibles as "Amen, amen" or "Verily, verily"). Jesus uses this expression when he's deeply serious about what he is about to say. The scene he describes is so familiar to his listeners that they must have found it easy to imagine. It would be like me explaining something that happened to me at Starbucks; you could easily see it in your mind.

There's lots of history behind these verses. In Israel herding sheep was a major form of livelihood. If a man owned sheep, he or one of his sons would normally take the sheep out to pasture each day. Then, as night fell, the sheep would be led back to a shelter in the center of the village, where a hireling or gatekeeper would be on duty during the night. The sheep pen may have bordered a home or building surrounded by a waist-high stone wall topped by briars. The shepherd would lead the sheep to the door of the shelter. Then the hireling or porter was in charge of the sheep until the shepherd returned in the morning. Anyone who did not enter through the gate was likely a thief and a robber. (The word translated "thief" is *kleptes*, from which we get our word *kleptomaniac*.

In this metaphor, the sheep pen represents Israel (or possible secondary meanings could include the church or heaven). The gate or door is Jesus. The thief and robbers are the self-appointed religious leaders. Matthew 7:15 warns, "Watch out for false prophets. They come to you in sheep's clothing, but inwardly they are ferocious wolves." In the Old Testament, Ezekiel 34 similarly speaks of people who call themselves shepherds but aren't necessarily true shepherds; they are more concerned about feeding themselves instead of their sheep. They abuse the sheep and the sheep are scattered. God had warned Israel's faithless religious leaders that he would come to do the job of shepherding himself (Jeremiah 23; Zechariah 11). Here we see the fulfillment of these passages in Jesus (God in the flesh) becoming the Shepherd. God's sheep thrive and are content and satisfied (Psalm 23:1).

John 10:3

³ "The gatekeeper opens the gate for him, and the sheep listen to his voice. He calls his own sheep by name and leads them out."

"The gatekeeper" may refer to John the Baptist or, more likely, God the Father who opens the gate for Jesus. With Jesus we are not just a number. He knows every one of us (our name, our history, our personality, our joys and problems). Sheep would follow closely the leading of the shepherd. The shepherd would remove stones, bend back the briars, select the least difficult paths, and drive away the wild beasts and robbers. Similarly, we are to follow closely to Jesus as he stays close to us. Jesus doesn't lead his sheep from a mile ahead, but he walks with us. No matter how difficult your path seems, if you look closely you can always see the footprints of Jesus beside you.

> Among the animal kingdom sheep seem to have come out on the short end. From all accounts they are of limited intelligence. When it comes to finding food, they are definitely uncreative. As creatures of habit, they will follow paths through desolate places even though not far away is excellent forage. Sheep are also given to listless wandering. They are definitely at the

lower end of the intelligence scale. There are even accounts of their walking into an open fire! Shepherds confirm that they are timid and stubborn. They can be frightened by the most ridiculous things, though at other times *nothing* can move them. They are absolutely defenseless. There is no way a sheep can defend itself. Furthermore, of all the animals subject to husbandry, they take the most work.

—R. Kent Hughes, *John: That You May Believe,* 263

Sheep are dirty and helpless animals. They must be led; they will stray if left to themselves. Shepherds must move the sheep around regularly, or else the sheep will eat all the grass down to the dirt. They aren't like cattle, which will eat only a portion of the grass in a field. That's one of the reasons for the cattle-and-sheep wars in the prairies of the Old West in the United States. The sheep would destroy the land meant for cattle grazing.

John 10:4-6

⁴ "When he has brought out all his own, he goes on ahead of them, and his sheep follow him because they know his voice. ⁵ But they will never follow a stranger; in fact, they will run away from him because they do not recognize a stranger's voice." ⁶ Jesus used this figure of speech, but the Pharisees did not understand what he was telling them.

Sheep are utterly dependent on the shepherd. A shepherd will make a unique sound, call, or song with his voice. The sheep quickly become accustomed to their shepherd's particular voice tone and inflections and can distinguish it from any other shepherd's voice. Two shepherds' sheep might be intermingled; but when one shepherd makes his particular sound, his sheep will respond to his voice and follow only him. If a stranger should come among them and use the same words and phrases, the sheep wouldn't react in the same way. Sheep won't follow a stranger's voice.

Those hearing Jesus describe the behavior of sheep may have wondered why he was telling them something so familiar and obvious. The Greek term translated "figure of speech" is *paroimia* and can mean "proverb," "story," or "illustration." John does not use the Greek term *parabole* (parable) as found in the other three Gospels.

John 10:7-10

7 Therefore Jesus said again, "Very truly I tell you, I am the gate for the sheep. 8 All who have come before me are thieves and robbers, but the sheep have not listened to them. 9 I am the gate; whoever enters through me will be saved.ª They will come in and go out, and find pasture. 10 The thief comes only to steal and kill and destroy; I have come that they may have life, and have it to the full."

Recognizing that his listeners weren't getting his message, Jesus tells them again, this time describing another role of the shepherd. When the shepherds of Israel had to take their flocks far away from home to find good grazing land and greener pastures, they might be gone for days or weeks. When darkness fell, the shepherd would have to build a small shelter for his sheep or find a natural enclosure. He might seek out the end of a canyon, or a cliff face sheltered by some brush or trees. Sometimes the shepherd would lead the sheep into a cave for the night, and then he'd lie down at the entrance to the cave with the sheep inside. In that way the shepherd himself became the gate. The shepherd would guard his sheep with his life.

---

a John 10:9 Or *kept safe*

Psalm 23 tells us "The LORD is my shepherd, I lack nothing. . . . Even though I walk through the darkest valley, I will fear no evil, for you are with me; your rod and your staff, they comfort me." The shepherd would stretch his rod across the entrance to the sheepfold before the sheep entered. As each sheep came to the entrance, the shepherd would inspect it lovingly, looking for scars, thorns, cuts, and injuries before allowing it to pass. The shepherd would then anoint the sheep with soothing, healing oil. In Psalm 121:8 we read, "The LORD will watch over your coming and going—both now and forevermore."

> To feel loved, to belong, to have a place and to hear one's dignity and worth often affirmed, these are to the soul what food is to the body.
>
> —Anne Ortlund

The term *gate* would resonate not only with John's Jewish readers, but also with his Greek readers. In Greek literature Homer and others frequently spoke of entering heaven by a gate. Jesus is claiming to be that gate. Jesus also reminds them that he and he alone is the gateway to a life that is overflowing. This life can be found nowhere else. "All who have come before," is referring not to the Old Testament saints and prophets, but to those who came pretending to be the Messiah, as well as those religious leaders who cared nothing about the spiritual welfare of the people.

> The phrase *have it to the full* (10:10) is derived from a Greek word that has the connotation of overabundance. It would be as if you ordered a soft serve ice cream and the person behind the counter started filling your cone and then forgot about it,

allowing the ice cream to spill out over the edges of the cone and onto the floor.

When I was in college, a friend and I would walk to the local Dairy Queen for malts. Just for fun, we'd say to the person behind the counter, "I would like a malt. Only what I want you to do is put more malt powder into my malt than you have ever seen, and then double it." This is what abundant life means. It means more than you could imagine. It is life the way it is meant to be—life as only God can give you.

—David

John 10:11-12

11 "I am the good shepherd. The good shepherd lays down his life for the sheep. 12 The hired hand is not the shepherd and does not own the sheep. So when he sees the wolf coming, he abandons the sheep and runs away. Then the wolf attacks the flock and scatters it."

In calling himself "the good shepherd," Jesus is contrasting himself with many false shepherds—including Israel's wicked kings, corrupt priests, false prophets, and pseudo-messiahs. But his most likely target is the Pharisees and other leaders in Jerusalem. Jesus is the Good Shepherd because he's willing to sacrifice his life for his sheep. The term *good* can also mean "beautiful." This may be a better term for us, since *good* strikes modern readers as being moralistic. Yet we are attracted to Jesus not because of his looks but because of who he is.

Jesus is the only true gate to salvation. Those who hop the fence will kill and ravage the flock. False shepherds are in it only for what it will get them—whether it be money, ego satisfaction, power, prestige, or glory. Similarly, a hired hand is not committed to the sheep in the same way the shepherd is. If a sheep were injured or attacked by a beast and killed, the hired hand had to bring back a piece of the sheep to prove that he tried to save it, or else he would be dismissed. Exodus 22:13 explains, "If it was torn to pieces by a wild animal, the neighbor shall bring in the remains as evidence and shall not be required to pay for the torn animal."

A good shepherd, on the other hand, would gladly defend his sheep—and even lay down his life for them. In *The Land and the Book* (Harper and Brothers, New York, 1886), William M. Thomson writes, "Last spring a shepherd fought three robbers until he was hacked to pieces with their knives and died among the sheep he was defending." There was a tremendous attachment between a shepherd and his sheep. Jesus was willing to die for his sheep, as would a good shepherd.

John 10:13-18

13 "The man runs away because he is a hired hand and cares nothing for the sheep."

14 "I am the good shepherd; I know my sheep and my sheep know me— 15 just as the Father knows me and I know the Father—and I lay down my life for the sheep. 16 I have other sheep that are not of this sheep pen. I must bring them also. They too will listen to my voice, and there shall be one flock and one shepherd. 17 The reason my Father loves me is that I lay down my life—only to take it up again. 18 No one takes it from me, but I lay it down of my own accord. I have authority to lay it down and authority to take it up again. This command I received from my Father."

Jesus is willing to lay down his life for his sheep. He is also going to expand his flock (Israel) by welcoming additional sheep. The other sheep referred to in this passage will include Jewish Christians who'd been scattered because of the persecution, non-Jews, Samaritans, Gentiles—and you and me. Twenty centuries ago Jesus had us in mind. He is telling his followers that these "outsiders" should no longer be viewed as the enemy. Jesus is describing Jewish believers and Gentile believers worshiping Christ together.

No one takes Jesus' life from him. He is on a divine timetable. He is in control and decides when it is time to die. On the cross he yielded up himself and voluntarily laid down his life for his sheep. It wasn't that he couldn't escape. If he'd wanted to, there were legions of angels ready to remove him from the cross (Matthew 26:53).

Jesus laid down his life that we might live. The Shepherd became a Lamb. In the Old Testament, faithful Jews brought a lamb to the temple to have their sins forgiven for a year. The priests would carefully inspect the lambs for any spots or blemishes. It was not the worshipper who was judged; it was the lamb. Pilate said about Jesus, "I find no basis for a charge against this man" (Luke 23:4). Even Judas who betrayed Jesus said, "I have sinned, for I have betrayed innocent blood" (Matthew 27:4). Worthy is the Lamb. We receive blessings only because of the Lamb.

John 10:19-21

¹⁹ The Jews who heard these words were again divided. ²⁰ Many of them said, "He is demon-possessed and raving mad. Why listen to him?"

²¹ But others said, "These are not the sayings of a man possessed by a demon. Can a demon open the eyes of the blind?"

The Pharisees have been listening intently all this time. Jesus tells them not only are they unfit to lead the sheep, but also they aren't even sheep because they cling to their spiritual blindness and refuse to follow him.

As the scene ends, the crowd is again divided over Jesus. Some say he is demon-possessed. (In ancient times insanity and demon possession were frequently linked.) Others know Jesus isn't demon-possessed because of his ability to open the eyes of the blind.

READ BETWEEN THE LINES

- What comes to mind when you think of a shepherd?
- What are sheep like?
- What is the relationship between a shepherd and his sheep?
- Who are the thieves and robbers?
- How is Jesus not like the thieves and robbers?
- How is a shepherd also a gate?
- What two "I am" statements does Jesus make in this passage?
- What does it mean that there is only one flock and one Shepherd?
- Was Christ's death an accident?
- What motivates false shepherds?
- Who are the "other sheep"?
- Why is Jesus the ultimate Lamb?

WELCOME TO MY WORLD

- How do shepherds and butchers differ in the way they move sheep? How does that apply to my life and how I interact with others under my care?
- How are we like sheep?
- How do we listen to God's voice today?
- What other voices are calling to us today?

- Who are the thieves, robbers, and hirelings today?
- How well does Jesus know each of us?
- How can we differentiate between the Good Shepherd's voice and the voices of imitators?
- How am I doing at allowing Jesus to be my Shepherd?
- How am I leading the sheep entrusted to my care?
- How does it make me feel knowing that I'm among the "other sheep" that Jesus was talking about?

Further Conflict Over Jesus' Claims

John 10:22-26

22 Then came the Festival of Dedication[b] at Jerusalem. It was winter, 23 and Jesus was in the temple courts walking in Solomon's Colonnade. 24 The Jews who were there gathered around him, saying, "How long will you keep us in suspense? If you are the Messiah, tell us plainly."

25 Jesus answered, "I did tell you, but you do not believe. The works I do in my Father's name testify about me, 26 but you do not believe because you are not my sheep."

Approximately two-and-a-half months have passed between the incident in verses 1-21 and the scene set in verse 22.

The Festival of Dedication is also called Hanukkah or the Feast of Lights. This feast occurs in late December and lasts eight days. Hanukkah was a minor festival started during the intertestamental period (the time between the writing of the Old and New Testaments). It celebrates Israel's victory over the wicked Seleucid ruler Antiochus Epiphanes who ruled from 175–164 BC. He desecrated the temple in Jerusalem (167 BC) and later sacrificed a pig on the altar. He wouldn't let the people own or read the Scriptures. He turned the outer courts of the temple into brothels for prostitution.

Antiochus Epiphanes desecrated the holiest of places in Jerusalem. According to the Mishnah (the oral traditions written down), there are ten degrees of holiness:

- The Land of Israel is holier than any other land.
- The walled cities (of the Land of Israel) are more holy.
- Within the wall (of Jerusalem) is yet more holy.

---

b John 10:22 That is, Hanukkah

- The Temple Mount is even more holy.
- The *hel* is more holy.
- The Court of Women is even holier.
- The Court of Israelites is more holy.
- The Court of Priests is more holy.
- Between the *ulam* (outer porch of the temple) and the altar is more holy.
- The *hekhal* [the part of the temple between the outer altar, where most sacrifices took place, and the Holy of Holies] is yet holier.
- The Holy of Holies is more holy than all of them, for only the high priest on Yom Kippur at the time of the *Avodah* service [sacrificial offerings by the high priest on Yom Kippur] can enter therein. (*Mishnah, Kelim* 1, 6–9; quoted in Levine, *Jerusalem: Portrait of the City in the Second Temple Period (538 b.c.e.–70 c.e.),* 246–247).

After years of guerrilla warfare, the priest Mattathias and his son Judas Maccabaeus led a group of Jews to revolt against Antiochus Epiphanes. They were able to retake Jerusalem and rededicated the temple in the Jewish month of Chislev (November to December) in 165 BC. The Festival of Dedication celebrates this victory and rededication of the temple (2:13-15). This is the last festival before the Passover when Jesus will lay down his life.

John mentions that it's winter. Some believe that John's mentions of weather or temperature are statements about the spiritual condition of the people in the stories. This reference to winter may be referring to the chilly manner in which some people responded to Jesus' message or to their sense of impending doom.

The scene takes place at Solomon's Porch—a covered walkway just inside the temple courtyard. The cover was supported by 40-foot stone columns. During the winter with its wind, rain, and cold, Solomon's Porch was a great place to be. Each year, the Jewish people constructed a huge patio that looked like it had been built for giants. There would be conversations and dialogue under this large canopy.

The people who are gathered around Jesus ask him if he is the Messiah. Jesus reminds them of what he has already told and shown them many times—that he is the Christ, although he doesn't use this term because of their misunderstanding of it. The people believed the Messiah would be a political leader like Judas Maccabaeus—someone who'd lead a zealot-led revolt, seeking to conquer the Roman authority. Jesus *is* the Messiah, but he hasn't come in the ways they expect. He comes not as a military leader or a conquering king, but as a suffering servant.

Earlier in John's Gospel, Jesus clearly told them that he has unity with the Father (5:17ff) and has heavenly origins (6:32ff). His works and words confirm to anyone who is watching closely that he is the Messiah. Again, he brings up the subject of sheep, letting the religious leaders know they are not his sheep:

John 10:27-30

27 "My sheep listen to my voice; I know them, and they follow me. 28 I give them eternal life, and they shall never perish; no one will snatch them out of my hand. 29 My Father, who has given them to me, is greater than all[c]; no one can snatch them out of my Father's hand. 30 I and the Father are one."

In these verses Jesus gives four characteristics of his sheep:

1. "My sheep listen to my voice." Jesus' sheep are sensitive to his voice. Christians often use phrases similar to "God reminded me . . ." or "God showed me . . ."

---

c John 10:29 Many early manuscripts *What my Father has given me is greater than all*

2. "They follow me." Jesus' sheep are obedient. They do what Jesus says.
3. "I give them eternal life." Jesus' sheep know their future is set. When they die, they will be absent from the body but present with the Lord (2 Corinthians 5:8).
4. "No one can snatch them out of my Father's hand." Jesus' sheep are assured that they can never be separated from God's love and care.

In declaring, "I and the Father are one," Jesus is stressing the perfect union between Father and Son. He isn't just saying that he has joined his efforts with God's efforts. He's talking about a bond of love between the two—a unity of nature, will, and purpose. The great philosopher and theologian Augustine points out that they are one in essence or one in kind.

The mystery of the Trinity is that Father, Son, and Spirit are three distinct persons who are each fully God—and together they are the One God. Deuteronomy 6:4 declares, "Hear, O Israel: The LORD our God, the LORD is one." The word translated "one" is the Hebrew word *echad*, which means singularity and plurality coexisting simultaneously. The same term can be used to describe grapes, as in "one cluster with many grapes." It is also used to describe a man and woman coming together in marriage.

John 10:31-33

31 Again his Jewish opponents picked up stones to stone him, 32 but Jesus said to them, "I have shown you many good works from the Father. For which of these do you stone me?"

33 "We are not stoning you for any good work," they replied, "but for blasphemy, because you, a mere man, claim to be God."

Here they go again, picking up stones to kill Jesus (5:17-18; 8:58-59). Evidently, they get the message—this time. They know exactly what Jesus is saying. He is claiming to be God. Jesus believes in one God, and he says he is that One. This would be blasphemy and rightfully punishable by stoning if it were not true (Leviticus 24:23). Jesus never once says, "Oh, my bad! I think you misunderstood what I was saying." Jesus repeatedly claims to be God.

They have ignored all the evidence he's shown them so far. In effect, Jesus tells them, "If you don't believe me, believe the works. You may not like what I've said; but if you think that what I've done in front of you is of God, then you have to conclude that my words are true. The miracles I've performed are exactly what God would have done."

John 10:34-39

34 Jesus answered them, "Is it not written in your Law, 'I have said you are "gods"'d? 35 If he called them 'gods,' to whom the word of God came—and Scripture cannot be set aside— 36 what about the one whom the Father set apart as his very own and sent into the world? Why then do you accuse me of blasphemy because I said, 'I am God's Son'? 37 Do not believe me unless I do the works of my Father. 38 But if I do them, even though you do not believe me, believe the works, that you may know and understand that the Father is in me, and I in the Father." 39 Again they tried to seize him, but he escaped their grasp.

Some of Jesus' opponents were concerned that he, a mere man, was claiming to be God. Jesus gives a unique defense, citing a passage from the Old Testament that has baffled many people. This section moves into some deep theological

---

d John 10:34 See Psalm 82:6

waters; in fact, it's among the most challenging pieces of Christology in the entire New Testament.

Jesus asks his listeners, "Is it not written in your Law, 'I have said you are "gods"'?" Jesus is referring to Psalm 82:5-7 where God speaks and says:

> "The 'gods' know nothing, they understand nothing. They walk about in darkness; all the foundations of the earth are shaken."
>
> "I said, 'You are "gods"; you are all sons of the Most High.'
>
> But you will die like mere mortals; you will fall like every other ruler."

The psalmist's use of the word *gods* shouldn't be understood as indicating a belief in other gods. The Jews were monotheistic—*mono* meaning "one," and *theistic* meaning "God." This understanding of one God is underlined throughout the Hebrew Scriptures. Isaiah 43:10 says,

> "'You are my witnesses,' declares the LORD, 'and my servant whom I have chosen, so that you may know and believe me and understand that I am he. Before me no god was formed, nor will there be one after me.'"

Similarly, Isaiah 44:6 reads, "This is what the LORD says—Israel's King and Redeemer, the LORD Almighty: I am the first and I am the last; apart from me there is no God."

So who are these "gods" referenced in the psalm that Jesus quotes? Most commentators believe the psalmist is referring to those who have authority and power. One Jewish explanation of Psalm 82 says that God delegated authority to angelic beings, entrusting them with responsibility for defending those whom God himself would defend (such as those who are weak, orphaned, poor, oppressed, or needy). Yet these angelic beings have shown partiality to groups that

God himself would not, such as the unjust and the wicked. Although these agents of God have been unfaithful, he still calls them "gods." Yet they haven't fulfilled what God intended them to be. Jesus, on the other hand, always does exactly what the Father would do. They share a unity of purpose; the Son has a unique relationship of oneness with the Father.

Another possible explanation of Psalm 82 comes from Deuteronomy 32:37-38, where it's revealed that God has placed over every people group a guardian or steward. Human beings mistakenly worshiped these leaders as gods, but they are not God. So when these beings accept that worship, they participate in sin. Many of them have abused their station.

One more possibility is that Psalm 82 may be referring to the corrupt judges of the Old Testament who were called "gods" because they held the power of life and death. Jesus is saying, "You had no argument with these judges being called 'gods.' So if these mere human judges can use this term, how much more acceptable is it for me to apply the term to myself as God's unique agent on earth?" Jesus is using the technique of *qal wahomer*—a typical rabbinic way of proving a point by moving from the lesser to the greater argument. Jesus is saying that if Israel can be called "god" in some sense in Scripture, then how much more appropriate is this title for the one who is truly the Son of God? Jesus used this method in Luke 16:31; John 3:12; 5:47; 6:27; and 7:23 as well.

John 10:40-42

40 Then Jesus went back across the Jordan to the place where John had been baptizing in the early days. There he stayed, 41 and many people came to him. They said, "Though John never performed a sign, all that John said about this man was true." 42 And in that place many believed in Jesus.

Jesus escapes again because it is not yet his time to die. He moves away from Jerusalem and the conflict, heading back to a familiar place where John the Baptist had been ministering. Jesus has a lot of fond memories here. This is where he was baptized and heard the voice from heaven declare, "This is my Son, whom I love; with him I am well pleased" (Matthew 3:17). The people there know what John the Baptist said about Jesus; they are now aware that what John said is coming true. This is the final time that John the Baptist is mentioned in the Gospel of John. And what a great ending to chapter 10: "And in that place many believed in Jesus."

Not only did God become a Man, and the Man became a Lamb, but Psalm 22:6 tells us that the Lamb became a worm. Why? The Hebrew word for worm, *tolaath*, is translated two ways in the Old Testament: either as scarlet or as worm. To obtain the color specified for the garments of the priests and the curtains of the tabernacle throughout the Book of Exodus, *tolaaths*, or worms, were ground up, thereby producing a scarlet dye in which cloth would be dipped. When bearing its young, the female *tolaath* would climb a tree and fasten herself to a branch, where, the process of giving birth, she would explode, leaving a spot of blood on the tree. Truly, Jesus was right when he declared, I am a *tolaath*, for as our High Priest, He is clothed in the dye of His own blood; the spots of blood left on the tree of Calvary being the only way we could be born again. No wonder Isaiah declares, Though your sins be as scarlet (*tolaath*), they shall be white as snow (1:18). *Great* is the mystery. God became a Man, became a Lamb, and became a worm.

—*Jon Courson's Application Commentary: New Testament*, 530

READ BETWEEN THE LINES

- What does the Festival of Dedication celebrate?
- What are these people pressuring Jesus to do?

- Why does Jesus say these people are not his sheep?
- Why does John let us know it's winter?
- What are the characteristics of Jesus' sheep?
- Why did the people pick up stones to throw at Jesus?
- How is Jesus doing the works of the Father?
- How are Jesus' words and deeds proving his position?
- Why did people on the other side of the Jordan respond so differently?

WELCOME TO MY WORLD

- In what spiritual season of life am I? What about my friends?
- What other voices call out to me in this world?
- Has anyone hurled verbal stones at me or my friends for being a Christian?
- What works are Christians doing in the world today in the name of the Father?
- How do I feel knowing that Jesus knows me?
- How can I improve in following the Good Shepherd?
- How secure and confident am I about the future?

The Death of Lazarus

There have already been six miracles in John's Gospel:

1. Turning water to wine (2:1-11)
2. Healing of the nobleman's son (4:43-54)
3. Restoring an infirmed man (5:1-9)
4. Multiplying the loaves and fish (6:1-5)
5. Walking on the water (6:16-25)
6. Healing a man born blind (9:1-41)

Now here comes miracle number seven, the final miracle in John's Gospel before the resurrection. Seven is the perfect number and the climactic miracle.

We know from the other Gospels that Jesus raised others from the dead, including Jairus's daughter (Matthew 9:18-26; Mark 5:41-42; Luke 8:40-56) and a widow's son (Luke 7:11-17). However, each of those occurred shortly after death. Lazarus, as we will see, has already been dead for four days and is entombed in his grave. Rot and decay have already set in. The phrase used in the King James translation of 11:39 is, "he stinketh."

John 11:1-2

¹ Now a man named Lazarus was sick. He was from Bethany, the village of Mary and her sister Martha. ² (This Mary, whose brother Lazarus now lay sick, was the same one who poured perfume on the Lord and wiped his feet with her hair.)

Lazarus wasn't one of the 12 disciples, but Jesus deeply loved him. His name comes from the Hebrew name *Eleazer*, which means "one whom God helps." This is not the same Lazarus who is a beggar in the parable recorded in Luke 16. The emphasis in John's passage is not on Lazarus but on Jesus and his resurrection power. Lazarus just happens to be the guy who is raised.

The story occurs in Bethany, which means "house of the poor." Two different towns named Bethany get mentioned in John's Gospel. This is not the same Bethany mentioned in John 1:28 and 10:40-42. The Bethany in John 11 is a little village east of the Mount of Olives, just two miles from Jerusalem. John makes it clear that Jesus often visited the home of Lazarus and his sisters, Mary and Martha. This was a place where Jesus could unwind; it was a place to relax (Matthew 21:17; 26:6).

Martha appears to be the older of the two sisters. John alludes to Mary's anointing of Jesus' feet here, but we'll tackle that story in chapter 12, where John tells the full story. Some have suggested that John's mention of this story before he's told it in full may indicate that the stories in the Gospel may have been reordered over the years. Others suggest that John assumed his readers would already be familiar with the story of Mary anointing Jesus, since that event is recorded in Matthew 26 and Mark 14.

> In the Gospel we often find explanatory comments inserted into the running narrative of the story. They explain names (1:38; 42) and symbols (2:21; 12:33; 18:9); they correct possible misapprehensions (4:2; 6:6); they remind the readers of related events (3:24; 11:2) and reidentify for them the characters of the plot (7:50; 21:20).
>
> —Raymond E. Brown, *An Introduction to the Gospel of John*, 290

John 11:3-6

³ So the sisters sent word to Jesus, "Lord, the one you love is sick."

⁴ When he heard this, Jesus said, "This sickness will not end in death. No, it is for God's glory so that God's Son may be glorified through it." ⁵ Now Jesus loved Martha and her sister and Lazarus.

⁶ So when he heard that Lazarus was sick, he stayed where he was two more days,

These sisters know Jesus has healed strangers, so they are certain Jesus will want to heal someone close to him. The implication is that the sickness is very serious.

Notice that the women don't ask Jesus to come to Bethany or do anything. That's simple faith. They don't give God a lot of instructions or try to bribe him into acting by talking about how much Lazarus loves Jesus. If it were our love for Jesus that activated his blessing, we'd all be in sad shape. Jesus acts not because we love him, but because he loves us.

The other thing that impresses me about Mary and Martha is they went immediately to the source of life. In the Old Testament, Moses cried out to the Lord when the people on the wilderness journey murmured (Exodus 15:25; 17:4). He didn't form a committee to discuss his concerns. Hezekiah is another good example. When Hezekiah received a threatening letter from King Sennacherib of Assyria, Hezekiah laid it out before the Lord (Isaiah 36–38). When John the Baptist was beheaded, his disciples went right to Jesus.

We are told in 1 Peter 5:7 to "Cast all your anxiety on him because he cares for you." The word for love here is *phileo*, which means "brotherly love." Jesus had a warm human affection for Lazarus. While it's sometimes hard for us to understand this, Jesus was both fully human and fully God. He knew what it was like to desire companionship. When Jesus said, "This sickness will not end in death," the disciples probably understood him to mean that Lazarus wasn't going to die.

God gets glory when a person is healed, but God can also be glorified in the situations when there isn't physical healing. When God is glorified, God's people receive joy. And suffering often produces a stronger servant. Look at the apostle Paul. He dealt with some unspecified infirmity throughout his life (2 Corinthians 12:7-9). God received glory through Paul's sickness, not Paul's good health. First Corinthians 10:31 tells us, "So whether you eat or drink or whatever you do, do it all for the glory of God."

After being told that Lazarus is sick, Jesus stays where he is for two more days. God often makes us wait. When we're waiting on God, there is almost a guarantee that blessing is on the way—but it may come in a package we don't expect. Two passages in Isaiah remind us of this. Isaiah 30:18 reads, "Yet the LORD longs to be gracious to you; therefore he will rise up to show you compassion. For the LORD is a God of justice. Blessed are all who wait for him!" Similarly, Isaiah 40:30-31 states, "Even youths grow tired and weary, and young men stumble and fall; but those who hope in the LORD will renew their strength. They will soar on wings like eagles; they will run and not grow weary, they will walk and not be faint."

Jesus loves not only Lazarus, but also Lazarus's sisters. It is not a lack of love that keeps Jesus from going to them. Human love is often in a hurry; divine love isn't. The Lord is never late, although he often delays. When someone is late, it means he or she should have been somewhere earlier. But when we delay, we may be intentionally coming later. Jesus' delay in going to Bethany would bring more faith to the disciples and Mary and Martha, more glory to God, and a more fantastic testimony to those who'd witness what's about to happen.

John 11:7-13

7 and then he said to his disciples, "Let us go back to Judea."

8 "But Rabbi," they said, "a short while ago the Jews there tried to stone you, and yet you are going back?"

9 Jesus answered, "Are there not twelve hours of daylight? Anyone who walks in the daytime will

not stumble, for they see by this world's light. [10] It is when a person walks at night that they stumble, for they have no light."

[11] After he had said this, he went on to tell them, "Our friend Lazarus has fallen asleep; but I am going there to wake him up."

[12] His disciples replied, "Lord, if he sleeps, he will get better." [13] Jesus had been speaking of his death, but his disciples thought he meant natural sleep.

Jesus has just escaped from Judea with his life. So his suggestion that they should return there must have gone over really well with the disciples! At the Feast of Tabernacles the religious leaders had tried to arrest him (7:32, 44), and the rumor was they were out to kill him (7:25). Later, the crowd tried to stone him on two different occasions (8:59; 10:31). At Hanukkah, they tried to have him arrested (10:39).

Jesus tells his disciples that God prescribed the bounds of his life. The religious leaders who are out to get Jesus cannot shorten his life, nor can the disciples lengthen his time with them by their own concern. The application for us is that none of us will die a single second before the work that God wants to accomplish through us is complete. We don't have to fear death. So until God says it's time, I'm not going!

In verse 10 Jesus talks about people stumbling when they try to walk at night because there is no light. People would cease working at night. But it seems Jesus is also suggesting that we need to let our lives be guided by his Light. We need to stay close to Jesus, seeking to see the situations in our lives with his eyes—even if it means long periods of time when we cannot see anything happening. If we hang in there, we'll come out okay in the end. What God sees as a "good thing" and what we see as a "good thing" may not always be the same.

Jesus' reference to "our friend Lazarus" seems to indicate that his disciples loved Lazarus too. Jesus announces that Lazarus has fallen asleep—a euphemism in ancient Judaism for death—but the disciples think he is saying that Lazarus is merely taking a nap. The disciples figure it's good Lazarus is sleeping, believing this means he will probably get better. You know, a cup of chicken soup, some hot tea, a little rest, and he'll be fine.

John 11:14-16

14 So then he told them plainly, "Lazarus is dead, 15 and for your sake I am glad I was not there, so that you may believe. But let us go to him." 16 Then Thomas (also known as Didymus[a]) said to the rest of the disciples, "Let us also go, that we may die with him."

Jesus makes it clear that Lazarus is dead—and that he (Jesus) is glad! You may think this sounds heartless. But Jesus knows what's going to happen next. Jesus can see the big picture; he knows the end of the story. For Jesus, death is much like sleep, and Lazarus must be awakened. For Jesus, death does not have the finality that it does for everyone else.

The fact that Jesus knows Lazarus has died (the messenger said only that he was sick) reveals Jesus' omniscience. He knew this miracle would cause the disciples' faith to take a huge leap forward. They needed to know that Jesus has power over death since they would soon see him die on the cross.

> Every new step of faith I take makes my old steps look like unbelief.
>
> **—Unknown author**

---

a John 11:16 *Thomas* (Aramaic) and *Didymus* (Greek) both mean *twin*.

John is the only Gospel writer to give us insight into the life of Thomas whose Greek name, Didymus, means "twin." In the Synoptic Gospels, Thomas is mentioned only when all of the disciples are listed. But John gives Thomas a lot more attention. He's mentioned not only here, but also three additional times in John. He asks a question in the upper room (14:5), he has momentary doubts regarding the appearance of Jesus after the resurrection (20:24), and he's fishing while Jesus cooks breakfast in the final scene in this Gospel (21:2).

I sometimes think of Thomas as being a bit like Eeyore from *Winnie the Pooh*. Thomas is loyal to Jesus but a little slow to understand at times. It's as if Thomas is saying, "Okay, if Jesus is going to go back to Jerusalem to die, we may as well do the same." I admire Thomas's love, devotion, and courage; I can't say much for his faith. His love for Jesus is so strong that he would die for him, but his faith is so weak that he thinks that's what will happen. It's hard to know whether Thomas is being completely sincere or somewhat sarcastic here. However, Thomas knew the key was to stay close to Jesus, close to the Light.

I don't know if I'd be willing to die for Jesus. I hope I would. But most of us aren't even willing to live for him. If we say we love Jesus but live only for ourselves, then we are living a lie.

> We all know we're going to die; what's important is the kind of men and women we are in the face of this.
>
> —Anne Lamott, *Bird by Bird: Some Instructions on Writing and Life*

READ BETWEEN THE LINES

- What do you know about the name *Lazarus*? What is his relationship with Jesus?
- Why is Bethany significant to Jesus?

- How did the sisters phrase their concern about their brother?
- Why did Jesus wait two days?
- Why were the disciples hesitant to go back to Judea?
- What did Jesus mean by his comments about light?
- Why was Jesus glad Lazarus had died?
- What was Thomas's reaction?

WELCOME TO MY WORLD

- How is death like sleeping?
- How do I feel about death?
- Have I ever experienced a friend or family member who's been sick and near death? How did I feel? What did I do?
- What events have caused me to take a step or a leap forward in faith?
- When have I prayed and felt as though God wasn't answering my prayer?
- What can I learn from the sisters' approach to Jesus regarding their need?
- Have I ever felt that Jesus was calling me to do something risky?
- When has God answered my prayer in an unexpected way?

Jesus Comforts the Sisters of Lazarus

John 11:17-19

17 On his arrival, Jesus found that Lazarus had already been in the tomb for four days. 18 Now Bethany was less than two miles[b] from Jerusalem, 19 and many Jews had come to Martha and Mary to comfort them in the loss of their brother.

The two-day delay before Jesus arrives in Bethany did not cause Lazarus' death. Lazarus most likely died right after the messenger left to find Jesus. When Jesus arrives, Lazarus had been dead four days. The time that had passed since Lazarus died would only increase the significance of the miracle.

Jewish literature tells us that Jews believed the spirit or soul of a person would stay near the body for up to three days along with the chance that the person might come back to life. But after four days, the face would be too unrecognizable, and people were confident the spirit or soul had departed (*Genesis Rabbah* 100.7; *Leviticus Rabbah* 18.1). By the time Jesus arrives, everyone believes Lazarus is irrevocably, irreversibly dead. John wants us to know that this isn't going to be a mere resuscitation; Lazarus will be brought back from the dead fully restored.

John mentions that Bethany is less than two miles from Jerusalem. This fact may be included to help us understand how a large group of mourners could travel there so easily from the larger city of Jerusalem. John may also be emphasizing this point to help his readers understand the disciples' hesitancy to go to Bethany; they knew the crowd and religious leaders who wanted to stone Jesus would be nearby.

Do you realize that everything we do in this life (apart from serving God) is ultimately meaningless? There are no

---

b John 11:18 Or about 3 kilometers

pockets in a burial shroud. And no one ever saw a hearse pulling a trailer full of the deceased's earthly possessions. This truth is emphasized throughout the Scriptures. Check out 1 Timothy 6:7—"For we brought nothing into the world, and we can take nothing out of it." Ecclesiastes 2:18-19 reads:

> I hated all the things I had toiled for under the sun, because I must leave them to the one who comes after me. And who knows whether that person will be wise or foolish? Yet they will have control over all the fruit of my toil into which I have poured my effort and skill under the sun. This too is meaningless.

And Job 1:20-21 says:

> At this, Job got up and tore his robe and shaved his head. Then he fell to the ground in worship and said: "Naked I came from my mother's womb, and naked I will depart. The LORD gave and the LORD has taken away; may the name of the LORD be praised."

The good news is that death doesn't have to end all of our hopes and dreams. Believers can face death with joyous anticipation instead of anxiety, fear, and dread.

Martha and Mary are surrounded by friends at their home. In that day when there was a death in a Jewish family, several things might occur:

- There was a mourning period of up to 30 days. The first seven days were the most intense, and they were called *shibah* in Hebrew. Mourners stayed for a week to comfort the family.

- Professional mourners were paid to wail, moan, and show sadness at a funeral. They might even have clay vessels that they'd fill with tears. They got paid according to the number of tears they shed.

- There was a tradition that those attending the funeral would form a large procession and walk to the tomb and gather around it. The men and women would walk separately. When they got to the tomb, speeches were made.
- Only bread, lentils, and hard-boiled eggs were served to the guests. This was to ensure that people came for the funeral, not just for the food. It was also to make sure the funeral didn't turn into a party.
- There would be wailing and crying (Mark 5:38; Acts 8:2) along with the beating of their chests (Luke 18:13).
- The family might hire flute players (Matthew 9:23-24).

John 11:20-22

20 When Martha heard that Jesus was coming, she went out to meet him, but Mary stayed at home. 21 "Lord," Martha said to Jesus, "if you had been here, my brother would not have died. 22 But I know that even now God will give you whatever you ask."

According to the account in Luke 10:40-42, Martha seems to be the more busy and active of the two sisters, the one doing all the hostess jobs. Martha is the no-nonsense, practical, older sister, while Mary is the quieter one, more contemplative about what is happening around her. Jesus loves and welcomes both the Marthas and the Marys in this world.

Martha comes out to meet Jesus, which was not uncommon in Jewish culture. Her words are strong, clipped, and definitive. Many assume that Martha is scolding Jesus in this passage, but this is not so. Her statement is half faith and half grief. It's a statement of faith in that she believes Jesus could have helped Lazarus if he'd gotten there before Lazarus died. She believed Jesus had to be in close proximity to her brother in order to heal him. We know this isn't the case because we've already read about Jesus healing the nobleman's son in chapter 4. Martha thinks she knows what Jesus is capable of doing—and what he cannot do. She is like so many of us. We limit Jesus to the ways in which we think he works. Do we trust Jesus enough to let him do what he needs to do?

Martha seems to have some understanding of Jesus and his relationship with the Father. Jesus had to ask the Father because he voluntarily subordinated himself to become a little lower than the angels (Psalm 8:4-5).

John 11:23-24

23 Jesus said to her, "Your brother will rise again."
24 Martha answered, "I know he will rise again in the resurrection at the last day."

When Jesus says Lazarus will rise, Martha thinks he is referring to the final resurrection. Martha knew her Old Testament pretty well. Psalm 16:9-10 states, "Therefore my heart is glad and my tongue rejoices; my body also will rest secure, because you will not abandon me to the realm of the dead, nor will you let your faithful one see decay." Job 19:25-26 declares, "I know that my redeemer lives, and that in the end he will stand on the earth. And after my skin has been destroyed, yet in my flesh I will see God." The traditional Jewish view was that there would be a general resurrection on the last day of judgment, and people would rise from their graves and would recognize one another. Martha believed God could handle raising Lazarus on the last day, but she couldn't imagine God raising Lazarus after only four days! It sounds a little silly, but are we that much different from Martha?

The Pharisees had developed a belief in the resurrection of the physical body. This is rooted in Daniel 12:2—"Multitudes who sleep in the dust of the earth will awake: some to everlasting life, others to shame and everlasting contempt."

This belief was widely held by the Jews of the first century. The Sadducees strongly disagreed with this belief. Acts 23:8 notes the intensity of their disagreement over this and other questions.

John 11:25-27

25 Jesus said to her, "I am the resurrection and the life. The one who believes in me will live, even though they die; 26 and whoever lives by believing in me will never die. Do you believe this?"

27 "Yes, Lord," she replied, "I believe that you are the Messiah, the Son of God, who is to come into the world."

Jesus may have taken Martha into his arms as he whispered these words tenderly into her ear. Jesus is saying he can resurrect anyone at any time. John 11:25 is another one of the powerful "I AM" statements in John's Gospel. Jesus will soon cheat death himself—and he will provide a way for us to do the same.

> In Genesis 2:16-17, God declares very clearly to Adam and Eve, "When you sin, you will die." That is because God is life, and when we walk away from God, we walk away from life. Paul tells us in the Book of Romans, the wage for sin is death. I love the analogy that Paul uses there. He says we have earned death, but he says the gift of God is eternal life. Death is earned; life is given. That we have all earned death because of sin. Had there not been sin, there would not be death.
>
> **—Mark Driscoll, Sermon Notes**

Jesus' statement in verse 25—"The one who believes in me will live, even though they die"—is talking about physical death and how Christ will raise our bodies on the last day. The similar statement at the beginning of verse 26—"and whoever lives by believing in me will never die"—is talking about the fact that the believer never dies spiritually. If we can trust Jesus in the light, then we can continue trusting him as we jump into the darkness of death. He'll still be there.

Martha began her words to Jesus by looking at the past: "If you had been here . . . " And then she looked to the future, saying, "I know he will rise again in the resurrection at the last day." But Jesus is suggesting that this future can be brought into the present. The kingdom of heaven can begin now. Jesus prayed, "Your kingdom come, your will be done, on earth as it is in heaven" (Matthew 6:10). Resurrection is not just a future event, Jesus tells Martha. It is found in a Person, and he is standing in front of you, inviting you to trust in him.

What a tremendous statement Martha makes! "I believe that you are the Messiah, the Son of God, who is to come into the world." And yet she still doubts his power. You may be thinking, *If she already believes in Jesus, then why does she have doubts?* I don't know why. Don't you ask yourself the same question at times? Why do we believers continue to doubt? Maybe it's because Satan is still active in this world.

READ BETWEEN THE LINES

- Why are we told about the nearness of Bethany to Jerusalem?
- What is the significance of the "four days"?
- What happens at a Jewish funeral?
- Contrast Mary and Martha. How are they similar? Different?
- What does Martha know about Jesus' relationship with God?
- How do you think Martha's words made Jesus feel?

- What is Jesus saying about the kingdom when he says, "I am the resurrection"?
- How did Jesus enlarge Martha's faith?
- If Martha believed Jesus was the Messiah, why did she still have doubts?

WELCOME TO MY WORLD

- Compare first-century funerals with funerals today. What's similar? What's different?
- Am I more like Martha or Mary?
- How would I have responded to Jesus if I'd been in Mary's or Martha's shoes?
- How do we limit God's power and ability?
- Do I believe Jesus' words in John 11:25-26?
- What is of most value to me?
- Why do I still have doubts in spite of my belief?
- How does my faith compare to Martha's?
- How has my faith been stretched recently?

Jesus Goes to the Tomb

John 11:28-32

28 After she had said this, she went back and called her sister Mary aside. "The Teacher is here," she said, "and is asking for you." 29 When Mary heard this, she got up quickly and went to him. 30 Now Jesus had not yet entered the village, but was still at the place where Martha had met him. 31 When the Jews who had been with Mary in the house, comforting her, noticed how quickly she got up and went out, they followed her, supposing she was going to the tomb to mourn there.

32 When Mary reached the place where Jesus was and saw him, she fell at his feet and said, "Lord, if you had been here, my brother would not have died."

Martha refers to Jesus as "the Teacher." This is significant because the description is given by a woman. Most rabbis would not teach women, but Jesus taught them frequently. By his teachings and his pattern of life, Jesus reveals the character and will of God. Our world commonly makes distinctions and assigns value to those distinctions. Jesus makes it clear that both men and women are treasures in the sight of God. *You* too are a treasure in God's sight.

This passage also names these women as the heroes of the story. This was tremendously rare in the writing of the ancient world. It would have been unexpected and scandalous. Jesus often surprises people and overturns their expectations.

Imagine falling at the feet of Jesus in worship as Mary does. What a tremendous demonstration of love and adoration! We see Mary do the same thing in Luke 10. Mary falls at the feet of Jesus in both good and bad times. She is a great example for us all.

John 11:33-37

33 When Jesus saw her weeping, and the Jews who had come along with her also weeping, he was deeply moved in spirit and troubled. 34 "Where have you laid him?" he asked.

"Come and see, Lord," they replied.

35 Jesus wept.

36 Then the Jews said, "See how he loved him!"

37 But some of them said, "Could not he who opened the eyes of the blind man have kept this man from dying?"

Mary's tears are honest. There is nothing wrong with grief. When Jesus sees the family and friends weeping (in the Greek it is a loud wailing and crying, which was common in this culture), his spirit is deeply moved and troubled. In the original language the words *deeply moved* suggest a groaning that's difficult to convey adequately in English. The literal meaning is "to snort like a horse." The exact Greek translation is not "loud wailing" but "silently bursting into tears." There is a feeling of anger, outrage, fury, and pain. But even more than anger, it is a feeling of deep offense. Andreas Köstenberger adds that the term may refers to Jesus' anticipation of what he is going to do as he braces himself for his impending assault on death.

This show of emotion in "Jesus wept" illustrates Jesus' humanity. Jesus was not just a divine being pretending to be human. The term *wept* means "to burst into tears." Jesus is experiencing and participating in the grief all around him. These were tears of spontaneous love for his friend Lazarus and the sisters.

> This display of emotion was in sharp contrast to the Greco-Roman world of the Stoics, who sought to be indifferent to pleasure or pain; they were determined never to submit or to yield; they were resolved to overcome their emotions and desires. The Hebrews, however, were a very passionate people; they did not hide or suppress their emotions.
>
> —Marvin R. Wilson, *Our Father Abraham: Jewish Roots of the Christian Faith*, 139

This verse shows the tenderness and human warmth of Jesus. The Creator of the universe weeps at the grave of a friend. Isaiah 53:4 tells us, "Surely he took up our pain and bore our suffering."

I am tired of hearing that John 11:35 is the shortest verse in the Bible. I think all the talk about how brief it is keeps us from noticing that it is also one of the most profound verses in the entire Gospel. Perhaps John made it short to make it stand out.

One of my (Les) students, Ben Aleshire, commented, "When people display sadness and grief over the loss of a loved one, there will be others who look at them for a lack of faith. This is a very coldhearted approach to the Christian walk, and in many ways it can be dangerously prideful."

> I am convinced there is a place in the family of God for tears. There have been only two times in my life when I have experienced the type of deep pain and sorrow that I believe Jesus expresses in this passage. Let me tell you about one of those moments.
>
> I had been the youth minister at Eastside Christian Church in Orange County, California, for 22 years. I was taking part in a board meeting, and when the organizational chart for the next year was handed out, my name was not on it. It was an awkward

moment for all of us. So many people in that room had become my close friends. Several had grown up in the youth group and had gone on to become adult leaders of this large church. I had several job opportunities before me, but the thought of leaving this church began to well up inside of me. Suddenly, across the room I could hear a couple members of the board begin to cry quietly. The chair of the board asked me privately if I could say something to cheer up the group. I couldn't. They tried to go on with the usual business but couldn't.

Suddenly, and to my surprise, what came out of my mouth was a deep sorrowful moan. It is difficult to describe. It certainly caught me off guard. I was a little embarrassed. Maybe some of you reading this have felt this type of deep emotional pain. The chair of the board asked people to gather around me and pray for me and for my family and for one another. It was a very moving time for all of us. You know, I never heard my Lord rebuke me for those tears. It was the closest I've come to experiencing the groaning Jesus expressed at the death of his friend Lazarus.

—Les

Some have asked why Jesus cried if he knew what he was going to do. There are many possibilities. He may simply have been caught up in the moment, grabbed by the situation and the pain his loved ones were experiencing. Jesus could have separated himself from their pain, knowing that he would raise Lazarus. But Jesus wasn't like the Greek gods who were said to be separate from the people and had no emotions or empathy for humans. Jesus allowed himself to feel the emotions of the moment. We have a God who cares.

Perhaps when Jesus sees the powerful impact of death, it is painful to him because he knows this wasn't part of God's original design. He may have been indignant over what sin had done to all those involved.

Another possible explanation for this outpouring of emotion is that Jesus knew he had to bring Lazarus back from being in the presence of God the Father in order to show his glory. This meant Lazarus would have to die again at a later time. Or perhaps Jesus was disturbed by the excessive sorrow of the mourners and by Martha and Mary's limited faith.

In any case what a powerful statement the onlookers standing near Jesus make: "See how he loved him!"

> When Paul says he doesn't want us to grieve like people who have no hope (1 Thessalonians 4:13) he doesn't mean that he doesn't want us to grieve at all; he means that there are two sorts of grief, a hopeless grief and a hopeful grief. Hopeful grief is still grief. It can be very, very bitter.
>
> —Tom Wright, *John for Everyone, Part Two, Chapters 11–21*, 10

READ BETWEEN THE LINES

- Why did Martha leave Jesus to go find her sister?
- What kind of relationship did Mary and Martha have?
- Martha calls Jesus "the Teacher." What does this tell you about her relationship with Jesus?
- Why did Jesus cry?
- What was the response of those who saw Jesus cry?
- How is Jesus different from the Greek gods?

WELCOME TO MY WORLD

- How is Mary a great example to us?
- How does this story and Jesus' responses to Mary and Martha challenge the role and treatment of women in that society?

- How would Jesus respond to women today?
- How does my church react to women in ministry?
- What has Jesus taught me?
- Are there times when I've felt like Martha—knowing Jesus has the ability to do something but feeling he may not be willing to do something for me right now?
- Mary said to Jesus, "If you had been here . . ." What "If . . ." statements have I made?
- How do I handle grief?
- When have I experienced a deep groaning in my spirit? How do I think God responds in those moments?

Jesus Raises Lazarus From the Dead

John 11:38-40

[38] Jesus, once more deeply moved, came to the tomb. It was a cave with a stone laid across the entrance. [39] "Take away the stone," he said.

"But, Lord," said Martha, the sister of the dead man, "by this time there is a bad odor, for he has been there four days."

[40] Then Jesus said, "Did I not tell you that if you believe, you will see the glory of God?"

Once again, Jesus is deeply moved. In *What the Gospels Meant,* Garry Wills offers this explanation for Jesus' agony, "He faces his own death as he wrenches Lazarus free from death. When Lazarus's sisters called for him while their brother was dying, he knew he was returning to the killing zone."

The tomb where Lazarus was buried did not have a door at the entrance but a wheel-shaped stone that was rolled down a slight incline to cover the front of the opening. To enter the tomb, you'd have to stoop to get inside, but then you'd be able to stand up. The tomb was most likely a cave carved out of the soft natural limestone of the hillside. It would have been approximately ten feet by six feet by six feet. Inside the tomb, there was a stone bench running around the perimeter; this is where the body would be laid for preparation for burial.

In hot countries dead bodies would be washed, wrapped in spice-soaked linens, and buried as soon as possible to avoid decay and stench. The Jews didn't mummify or embalm dead bodies as the Egyptians did. Those preparing Lazarus's body would have bandaged him tightly from the armpit to the toes using strips of linens about a foot wide. The legs and arms were wrapped separately—again, unlike the Egyptians—and then the entire body was wrapped in a shroud or large sheet. Spices of a gummy consistency were placed between the wrappings and the folds to serve as a preservative and mask the smell of decomposition. Coins may have been placed on the eyes, and a square piece of cloth would be wrapped around the head to cover the face, and tied under the chin to keep the lower jaw from sagging.

After the body was prepared, it would not be put in a coffin or cremated. It would have been placed on one of the shelves, or burial niches, carved into the walls of the tomb and left there to decompose. After a body decomposed (months or possibly a year or more later), the bones would be gathered and placed in a limestone box (an *ossuary*). And the ossuary would then be kept on the tomb floor.

Jesus' statement in verse 40—"Did I not tell you that if you believe, you will see the glory of God?"—does not suggest that the miracle is dependent on Martha's belief. He is saying that what Martha carries into the miracle is what she will get out of it. If she believes, then she will see the glory of God. Lazarus would have risen even if Martha didn't believe; but in order to see God's glory, she would have to believe. Martha needed to keep her eyes on Jesus. This miracle is for the glory of God.

Technically, Lazarus's resurrection is not like what Jesus experienced—where he came from the tomb with a heavenly body that could pass through walls. Jews believed the resurrection was what happened at the end of time; the resurrected body would be a different kind of body prepared for heaven. But it was also more than a mere resuscitation. Imagine what it must have been like for Lazarus as he awakens from death. As he comes out of the tomb, he still has a mortal, corruptible body that will die again. But on another day in the future, Lazarus will rise again with a resurrected body. Death is not the end.

John 11:41-42

41 So they took away the stone. Then Jesus looked up and said, "Father, I thank you that you have heard me. 42 I knew that you always hear me, but I said this for the benefit of the people standing here, that they may believe that you sent me."

Jesus prays before raising Lazarus as a way of demonstrating that his authority comes from the Father. What is about to happen will let people know that Jesus is God's agent.

In this prayer Jesus announces the unity of the Father and Son. Jesus wants to be in his Father's will, to be a part of that intimate mysterious union. But Jesus doesn't have to—

- Ask God the Father for power to raise Lazarus. Jesus has the power.
- Ask God the Father for the right to do it. Jesus has the right.
- Ask God the Father what he wants Jesus to do. Jesus already knew what to do. Jesus knew that he was God, yet he was distinct from the Father. However, Jesus and the Father agree on everything.

John 11:43-44

43 When he had said this, Jesus called in a loud voice, "Lazarus, come out!" 44 The dead man came out, his hands and feet wrapped with strips of linen, and a cloth around his face.

Jesus said to them, "Take off the grave clothes and let him go."

This is the moment of truth. If Lazarus doesn't come out of the tomb, then Jesus is finished. The people gathered at the tomb must have been stricken with terror. Did Jesus really have the power to reverse death, to re-create fresh skin and all the internal organs?

Jesus doesn't yell loudly because death was looked upon as a deep sleep and the noise would wake Lazarus up. No, the reason Jesus shouts is to shake up the people standing there so that when Lazarus comes out, they will know who caused it to happen. This also differs from the wizards, witches, warlocks, and magicians of that day who muttered their spells and incantations.

Augustine once pointed out that it's a good thing Jesus called Lazarus by name. If he had just said, "Come out!" then all of Hades might have emptied itself! Every grave in the earth might have split open. On a future date this is exactly what will happen.

Imagine Lazarus lying in this dark cave when suddenly his cold, lifeless body warms up. The crowd of mourners must have first seen a rustling of movement in the tomb, and then a figure came to the doorway. Imagine him stepping out of the tomb while still wearing his burial clothes.

Jesus tells the mourners to take off Lazarus's grave clothes. When they did this, they would have found fresh skin—live and warm to the touch. Lazarus was raised and restored. Just like those who removed the grave clothes, we can participate in the activities of God. We can become God's agents.

For us, the raising of Lazarus dramatizes the life of the baptized Christian. We have all died spiritually and risen again, even in this life. Paul states in Romans 6:3-4, "Don't you know that all of us who were baptized into Christ Jesus were baptized into his death? We were therefore buried with him through baptism into death in order that, just as Christ was raised from the dead through the glory of the Father, we too may live a new life."

READ BETWEEN THE LINES

- What does the tomb of Lazarus look like?
- How did the Jews prepare a body for burial?
- Is this miracle conditional on Martha's belief?
- How will Martha be able to see the glory of God?
- Why did Martha object to removing the stone from the tomb?
- Why did Jesus lift up his eyes?
- What was the purpose of Jesus' prayer?
- Why did Jesus call out in a loud voice?
- Was this miracle for Lazarus and his family? Or was it for a larger group of people?

WELCOME TO MY WORLD

- What is the worst odor that I can remember smelling?
- How would I have reacted if I'd been there to see Lazarus come out of the tomb?
- Would I have been willing to take off Lazarus's grave clothes?
- Who has assisted me in taking off my "grave clothes" (the things that hinder my spiritual walk)?
- When has God brought about a miracle in my life?

The Plot to Kill Jesus

John 11:45-48

45 Therefore many of the Jews who had come to visit Mary, and had seen what Jesus did, believed in him. 46 But some of them went to the Pharisees and told them what Jesus had done. 47 Then the chief priests and the Pharisees called a meeting of the Sanhedrin.

"What are we accomplishing?" they asked. "Here is this man performing many signs. 48 If we let him go on like this, everyone will believe in him, and then the Romans will come and take away both our temple and our nation."

Many who saw what Jesus did put their faith in him. Faith, in order to be meaningful, must be placed in the right object. Faith in faith is meaningless. Belief without something or someone to believe in makes no sense. Faith is nothing unless it is placed in Jesus Christ.

While most large Jewish communities had a Sanhedrin (local court), the supreme Sanhedrin was in Jerusalem (1:19). In response to the stories about the raising of Lazarus, this supreme body called an official meeting. Yet it's quite possible they never even discussed the raising of Lazarus at that meeting. Jesus said in Luke 16:31—"If they do not listen to Moses and the Prophets, they will not be convinced even if someone rises from the dead." These religious leaders in the Sanhedrin were more concerned that Jesus was a threat to their own places of power and status in the community.

This is the only time in all four Gospels that the word *Romans* is specifically mentioned. The Sanhedrin leaders know that if Jesus gets a big following and becomes a political Messiah, then Rome—with its legions of soldiers just a few miles north in Syria—will come down, squash the rebellion, and take away the religious leaders' power by scattering them. These guys were protecting their own interests.

One of the few things the two primary groups within the Sanhedrin (Sadducees and Pharisees) could agree on is that they both want to get rid of Jesus. This is similar to how Pilate and Herod (who had long been enemies) will one day work together to see that Jesus is crucified (Luke 23:11-12). The Sadducees and Pharisees don't deny that Jesus does miracles. They simply oppose him.

John 11:49-53

49 Then one of them, named Caiaphas, who was high priest that year, spoke up, "You know nothing at all! 50 You do not realize that it is better for you that one man die for the people than that the whole nation perish."

51 He did not say this on his own, but as high priest that year he prophesied that Jesus would die for the Jewish nation, 52 and not only for that nation but also for the scattered children of God, to bring them together and make them one. 53 So from that day on they plotted to take his life.

Caiaphas is a sly, egotistical opportunist and a manipulator bent on getting what he wants by hook or by crook (John 18:12-14, 24, 28; Matthew 26:57; Luke 3:2; Acts 4:5-7). The text says he was the high priest that year. Originally, the high priest was to serve for his lifetime (Numbers 35:25). However, the high priesthood had become a position that changed at the discretion of the Romans, because the Romans did not want any Jewish leader to become too powerful. Still, Caiaphas was able to hold the office for 18 years (AD 18–36). His corrupt father-in-law Annas (18:13) had held it for nine years (AD 6–15).

For 10 years Caiaphas had worked with the Roman governor Pilate to forge an uneasy peace. Rome allowed the Jewish provinces to operate in relative freedom as long as the peace was kept and the status quo remained in place. Caiaphas was the leader of the Sadducees who did not believe in resurrection. So he had a problem with a dead man walking around. Caiaphas argues that if Jesus is allowed to live, then this Messiah frenzy among the crowds will continue. Things will start getting out of control—and then the Romans will step in and take control. In that case the religious leaders might lose their power and positions. But if they kill Jesus, this troublemaking "messiah," the Romans will let them live and they will have saved their nation.

The truth is that Caiaphas sees Jesus as a threat to his popularity. So he uses the oldest trick in the political book. He presents two extremes and says they must make a choice: It's either the nation or Jesus. Caiaphas isn't interested in justice, guilt, or innocence. He is interested only in political expediency. Craig Blomberg has pointed out the irony of Caiaphas's statement that anyone who can bring someone back to life is too dangerous to be allowed to live.

However, the very steps these men took to save their nation eventually betrayed their nation. The Jewish leaders rejected the Messiah in favor of peace with Rome. Just 40 years later, in AD 70, the Roman army destroyed the temple and the city of Jerusalem. John's Gospel was written not long after that happened. Therefore, no one reading this Gospel at that time would have missed the irony. Killing Jesus did not prevent the Romans from destroying the temple. John's first-century readers would have known that Jesus wasn't growing a political revolution. He came to bring humankind and God back together. He came to die on a cross.

Caiaphas's statement that "it is better for you that one man die" was made in ignorance, but God made those words a prophecy. Caiaphas's statement became true in a way he could never have imagined. God had basically elevated Caiaphas to the stature of Balaam's donkey (Numbers 22:21-35).

When Caiaphas spoke of "the scattered children of God," he was probably thinking of the Jews in the dispersion who'd be gathered together in God's kingdom at the end times. But Jesus died not only for the Jewish nation of Israel, but also for the Gentiles (non-Jews).

From this day forward, every meeting of the religious leaders is focused on plotting this messianic murder. The six trials that are described later in the Gospel (18:12–19:16) are all a sham. These men decided on this very night what they would do with Jesus.

The raising of Lazarus is included only in the Gospel of John. In John's account, the raising of Lazarus seems to be the catalyst that prompts the religious leaders to make plans to kill Jesus. The other Gospels focus on Jesus' cleansing of the temple shortly before the Passover as being the key event that causes the religious leaders to plot against Jesus.

John 11:54-57

54 Therefore Jesus no longer moved about publicly among the people of Judea. Instead he withdrew to a region near the wilderness, to a village called Ephraim, where he stayed with his disciples.

55 When it was almost time for the Jewish Passover, many went up from the country to Jerusalem for their ceremonial cleansing before the Passover. 56 They kept looking for Jesus, and as they stood in the temple courts they asked one another, "What do you think? Isn't he coming to the festival at all?" 57 But the chief priests and the Pharisees had given orders that anyone who found out where Jesus was should report it so that they might arrest him.

This is the end of Jesus' public ministry—and it's the third and final Passover recorded in the Gospel of John. Many people at this time were making the annual trek to Jerusalem. For some sins, you had to come a month early in order to purify yourself for the Passover.

Everything is coming together as the hostility toward Jesus continues to build. The religious leaders have tried to arrest him and even to stone him to death, but he has miraculously avoided their attempts on his life. The time wasn't right. Jesus has been waiting for the right opportunity, the right time. There would be no better time than the Passover, the time when a lamb is killed to celebrate and remember God's promise of freedom.

READ BETWEEN THE LINES

- Why did some people go to the Pharisees after Lazarus was raised?
- What is the religious leaders' reaction to the miracle?
- Why was the Sanhedrin concerned about the Romans?
- Why aren't the religious leaders discussing the miracle?
- What do you know about Caiaphas?
- How does he solve the problem the religious leaders are having with Jesus?
- What did he, unknowingly, prophesy?
- What was the focus of the meetings of the Sanhedrin for the next several days?

WELCOME TO MY WORLD

- In what kinds of things do people put their faith?
- Who are some Caiaphas-like characters that I've met in my life?

- How do I feel when people put aside their beliefs, truth, and justice for the sake of politics?
- What would I have done if I were a member of the Sanhedrin?
- How has the Lord confronted me lately?
- Have I ever found myself acting like Caiaphas?

Jesus Anointed at Bethany

The first 11 chapters of this Gospel move quickly, covering selected events in the adult life of Jesus and stopping to zoom in on Jesus' interactions with certain characters. The tempo of the Gospel slows dramatically after chapter 11. Chapters 12 through 21 cover Jesus' final week on earth. Compared to the other three Gospels, John spends a lot of time on this last week:

- Of the 28 chapters in Matthew, 8 have to do with the last week
- Of the 16 chapters in Mark, 6 are devoted to the last week
- Of the 24 chapters in Luke, 6 have to do with the last week
- Of the 21 chapters in John, 10 are devoted to the last week (almost half)

As chapter 12 begins, a short period of time has passed since Lazarus was raised from the dead. Jesus spends the final week of his ministry doing things he felt were of paramount importance.

John 12:1-2

1 Six days before the Passover, Jesus came to Bethany, where Lazarus lived, whom Jesus had raised from the dead. 2 Here a dinner was given in Jesus' honor. Martha served, while Lazarus was among those reclining at the table with him.

It is Friday evening, a week before Jesus will be crucified. A large crowd would be coming to Jerusalem for the Passover, the greatest of the annual Jewish feasts.

Bethany is the town where Mary, Martha, and Lazarus live, and it's also the place where Jesus demonstrated his power over death. Martha is serving a dinner in Jesus' honor, and Lazarus is there; but the dinner is not in their home. According to the accounts in Matthew 26:6-13 and Mark 14:3-9, this anointing occurs in the home of Simon the Leper, another man who has evidently been cured by Jesus. It's worth noting that Matthew and Mark do not specifically say that Mary was the one who anointed Jesus—in their accounts the woman who anoints Jesus is not named. But other details suggest that these Gospels are referencing the same events recorded in this passage of John. There is an another anointing recorded in Luke 7:36-50 that some argue is this same story; yet it has few parallels to this story and takes place in a completely different setting (the home of a Pharisee also named Simon, a common name back then, who could not have been a leper).

Martha is always serving others. In the familiar story found in Luke 10:38-42, Martha is serving Jesus in her own home, and she's complaining because her sister Mary is just hanging out with Jesus. Jesus tells Martha that Mary is doing the better thing. Here, Martha is once again serving, and it's not even at her home. Have you ever met people like that—terrific people who are eager to step up and help wherever and whenever they're needed?

There were at least 16 people in this home. The purpose of the dinner was to honor Jesus, remembering how he'd raised Lazarus from the dead. A banquet like this would typically start as early as mid-afternoon and go on past midnight.

John 12:3

[3] Then Mary took about a pint[a] of pure nard, an expensive perfume; she poured it on Jesus' feet and wiped his feet with her hair. And the house was filled with the fragrance of the perfume.

John tells us that Mary anoints Jesus' feet with an expensive, sweet-smelling oil called nard or spikenard. The perfume was

---

a John 12:3 Or about 0.5 liter

derived from the root or spike of a plant imported from Northern India. The nard plant was brought by caravan over the Himalayan Mountains using camels. Pliny, the Latin writer, described nard as having a sweet scent and a red color. It's a thick substance. It cost a fortune. It's something you'd want to keep and use very sparingly. According to the similar account in Matthew's Gospel, Mary brought the perfume in an alabaster jar (26:7) and broke the jar so as not to save any of it. The aroma of the perfume would have filled the house.

I don't think Mary's pouring this on Jesus' feet was a calculated activity. She ran and found the most precious item she owned and poured it on Jesus. The rest of the people at the table must have been shocked. Mary breaks several cultural rules here:

- She seems to have done this during the evening meal, which is unusual. Jewish women never reclined at the table with men, especially during supper. They usually served the meal.

- She takes down her hair in public, which no Jewish woman would ever do. It would have been considered indecent and immodest. Only her husband was to see her hair.

- She touches his feet (which was considered degrading). Mark 14:3 tells us she put the perfume on his head.

- Wiping the feet of Jesus with her hair (considered a woman's crown and glory) took away all of her dignity.

- The perfume normally would have been kept for her dowry. She now has no dowry.

The two things that hit me about Mary in this scene are her extravagance (using large amounts of expensive perfume) and her humility (attending to a person's feet was usually the job of the lowest servant). She didn't mind falling at Jesus' feet. She worshipped him. She was lost in praise, oblivious to her surroundings. Mary is similar to King David who worshipped by dancing before the Lord (2 Samuel 6:20-22).

Broke it?! How shocking. How controversial. Was everybody doing it? Was it a vase-breaking party? No, she just did it all by herself. What happened then? The obvious: all the contents were forever released. She could never hug her precious nard to herself again. . . . The need for Christians everywhere (nobody is exempt) is to be broken. The vase has to be smashed! Christians have to let the life out! It will fill the room with sweetness, and the congregation will all be broken shards, mingling together for the first time. . . . If you know one another as broken people, you're ready to get on with a church service.

—Anne Ortlund, *Up With Worship: How to Quit Playing Church*, 21, 23

John 12:4-8

4 But one of his disciples, Judas Iscariot, who was later to betray him, objected, 5 "Why wasn't this perfume sold and the money given to the poor? It was worth a year's wages.b" 6 He did not say this because he cared about the poor but because he was a thief; as keeper of the money bag, he used to help himself to what was put into it.

7 "Leave her alone," Jesus replied. "It was intended that she should save this perfume for the day of my burial. 8 You will always have the poor among you,c but you will not always have me."

Just as David got criticism for worshipping and dancing before the Lord, Mary gets similar treatment from some of those gathered in this home (Matthew 26:8-9; Mark 14:4-5). Here, we see one disciple attempting to prohibit the worship

---

b John 12:5 Greek *three hundred denarii*

c John 12:8 See Deuteronomy 15:11.

of another disciple. Christians express their worship of Jesus in diverse ways. Jesus allows us all to worship him with our own unique styles and personalities.

What a contrast: The warmth and love of Mary compared to the cold, calculating hatred of Judas. This is the most tragic human who has ever lived. Remember how in John 6:70-71, Jesus said, "Have I not chosen you, the Twelve? Yet one of you is a devil!" Judas stands out clearly as a person who has money on the brain. These words in John 12 are the first recorded words of Judas in the Gospel of John. He sounds so noble, but Judas was a fake. He didn't care about the poor; he was a thief. Jesus unmasks Judas with his rebuke.

Verse 7 is a difficult verse to translate and understand. Jesus rebukes those who criticize Mary, saying the perfume was intended for the day of his burial. Perhaps Mary realizes that Jesus is going to die soon. (He's told them enough times!) Maybe she fears she may not have an opportunity to anoint the body after his death, so she does it now. Mary also may have realized something the others did not get yet: Jesus would not stay in that grave. Perhaps in this way Mary is similar to Caiaphas, who prophesied earlier in the Gospel of John without even realizing it.

Jesus tells those at the dinner to get their priorities straight. They have only six more days with Jesus being physically present; the poor will be with them forever. Deuteronomy 15:11 affirms, "There will always be poor people in the land." Jesus isn't putting down the poor or saying concern for the poor is unimportant. Jesus himself was poor—he didn't have a place to lay his head. And he was concerned about those who did not have enough to meet their needs. In Luke 18:22 Jesus tells the rich young ruler, "You still lack one thing. Sell everything you have and give to the poor, and you will have treasure in heaven." In Acts 20:35 the church remembered Jesus as saying "It is more blessed to give than to receive." And in Luke 12:33 Jesus urges his flock: "Sell your possessions and give to the poor."

At this point Judas still has a choice in front of him. He could cast himself at Jesus' feet in tears, confess his sin, and seek mercy at the throne of grace. But instead his pierced pride swelled up, and his heart was hardened. According to Mark 14:10-11, Judas leaves Bethany that very night to meet with the Jewish leaders in Jerusalem, and he sold Jesus for 30 pieces of silver.

John 12:9-11

9 Meanwhile a large crowd of Jews found out that Jesus was there and came, not only because of him but also to see Lazarus, whom he had raised from the dead. 10 So the chief priests made plans to kill Lazarus as well, 11 for on account of him many of the Jews were going over to Jesus and believing in him.

The crowds gathering in Jerusalem for the Passover feast continue to seek out Jesus. Some are followers, but many are just curious thrill-seekers, mere spectators. And now the crowds are coming to see not only Jesus, but also Lazarus. Lazarus is a freak of nature—no one had ever died and been buried, only to be raised to life four days later. Now the Jewish authorities have a formerly dead man roaming around and gaining even more crowds for Jesus.

The increasing crowds around Jesus are threatening the Jewish authorities for two reasons. Politically, if everyone gathers around Jesus, there's the possibility of a rebellion or insurrection. If this occurs, Rome will quickly squash it, and these Jewish leaders will be thrown out of power.

But there is also a theological concern. For years, the Sadducees have said there is no such thing as resurrection. Yet here's this guy who was resurrected from the dead.

Rather than change their thinking, they plan to destroy the evidence. I have often wondered if the religious leaders killed Lazarus that day, or soon after.

We don't hear from Lazarus again. In fact, it's interesting that John never records a single word that came out of the man's mouth. You'd have thought that he would have had a lot of interesting stories to tell about his death and the surprise of being brought back to life. But John doesn't offer any such stories. Lazarus must have been a quiet type of guy.

> Caiaphas had said, "it is better for you that one man die . . ." (11:50). But one was not enough; now it had to be two. Thus does evil grow.
>
> —Leon Morris, *The Gospel According to John*, 517

READ BETWEEN THE LINES

- Why does John spend so much time on the last week of Jesus' life?
- What is the significance of the Passover to the last week in the life of Jesus?
- What was the purpose of this dinner?
- Where do you think Mary got the nard? Is she from a wealthy family? Was it an heirloom?
- Why did Mary anoint Jesus?
- Was this an extravagant waste?
- What cultural rules did Mary violate with her actions?
- Contrast Mary and Judas.
- Is Jesus putting down the poor? Is he criticizing those who work among the poor?
- Why did the chief priests want to kill Lazarus as well as Jesus?

WELCOME TO MY WORLD

- Whom do I know that is similar to Mary?
- Have I ever done something extravagant for God?
- If I had a year's salary to spend on a gift, what would I buy and for whom?
- Where does my church spend the money it takes in? Do extravagant church buildings and cathedrals honor Jesus? Is our "nard" put to good use? At what point does it become misuse?
- So many of us often delay expressing our love for people until after they've died. Today is a great day to convey our love to those we care for. Whom do I need to call or visit?
- How would I live if I knew this were my final week on earth?
- How would I have reacted if I'd seen Mary doing what she did?
- Have I ever seen someone do something during worship that made me feel uncomfortable? How did I respond?
- What is one extravagant thing I could do for God this week?
- When was the last time I received criticism for doing something for God?

Jesus Comes to Jerusalem as King

John 12:12-13

[12] The next day the great crowd that had come for the festival heard that Jesus was on his way to Jerusalem. [13] They took palm branches and went out to meet him, shouting,

"Hosanna![d]"

"Blessed is he who comes in the name of the Lord!"[e]

"Blessed is the king of Israel!"

Many people from all over the known world are coming to Jerusalem because of the Passover. The Old Testament required Jews to come to Jerusalem for three Festivals each year: Passover, Pentecost, and Tabernacles. Passover had the largest attendance. According to the first-century Jewish historian Josephus, as many as 250,000 lambs would be slain for anywhere from 200,000 to 1 million people. (The non-holiday population in Jerusalem was about 100,000.) The crowds would have been too large for the city to accommodate, so many would have camped along the hillsides or stayed in neighboring villages.

Palm branches symbolize strength, as well as the salvation that a conqueror brings. Both Romans and Jews used them in victory parades. When Judas Maccabaeus defeated the pagan invaders and cleansed the temple in 164 BC, his followers entered the city waving palm branches in celebration. Here, the crowds wave palm branches to welcome Jesus—but the branches indicate that the people don't understand his mission. They are hailing Jesus as a political

---

d John 12:13 A Hebrew expression meaning "Save!" which became an exclamation of praise

e John 12:13 See Psalm 118:25, 26

conqueror, savior, and deliverer who would release them from the oppression of Rome.

Many in the crowd had come to see Jesus. Their expectations of what might happen were at a fever pitch. With this large a crowd, it would be the perfect time for a revolt. The crowd began shouting, "Hosanna!" It's an expression of praise that can mean "help us" or "save us now." This is not praise as much as it is a request. They aren't talking about spiritual salvation but political revolution. Few in the first century thought of Messiah as a divine title.

The Hebrews would memorize Psalms 113 through 118, a section of Scripture called the Hallel. The words—"Blessed is he who comes in the name of the Lord! Blessed is the King of Israel!"—comes from Psalm 118:25-26, a psalm that looks forward to the coming Messiah. The crowd may have misunderstood the nature of Jesus' Lordship (they were expecting a military deliverer), but they were singing the right Psalm in welcoming him as Messiah. In the past Jesus refused to accept this title, but here he does—and they are thrilled.

Another interesting prophecy that some people tie to this event is Daniel 9:25, "Know and understand this: From the time the word goes out to restore and rebuild Jerusalem until the Anointed One, the ruler, comes, there will be seven 'sevens' and sixty-two 'sevens.'" That's (7 x 7) + (62 x 7) or (49 + 434) which equals 483 Jewish years (360 days in each year). The decree was made in 445 BC by Artaxerxes. Using the complex calculations of that time, the year the prophecy was to be fulfilled would have been the year Jesus rode into Jerusalem.

John 12:14-16

14 Jesus found a young donkey and sat on it, as it is written:

15 "Do not be afraid, Daughter Zion; see, your king is coming, seated on a donkey's colt."[f]

---

f John 12:15 See Zechariah 9:9

16 At first his disciples did not understand all this. Only after Jesus was glorified did they realize that these things had been written about him and that these things had been done to him.

At this time of the year, Herod would be coming into town with his entourage. He was a wealthy man who'd come to Jerusalem for the major celebrations. As governor, Pilate would also be coming into town from his home on the coast in Caesarea. Pilate would come with a procession of Roman soldiers and chariots. What a contrast to Jesus entering the city on a donkey. Talk about humility!

Mark's Gospel tells us that Jesus stops in the village of Bethphage, where he borrows a donkey to ride into the city (11:1-6). His entrance on a donkey's colt fulfills a prophecy from Zechariah 9:9 that was written 600 years before Jesus' birth: "Rejoice greatly, Daughter Zion! Shout, Daughter Jerusalem! See, your king comes to you, righteous and victorious, lowly and riding on a donkey, on a colt, the foal of a donkey." A king riding on a donkey's colt meant he comes in peace, yet the crowd ignores this sign and continues to proclaim Jesus as the conquering king.

A king riding on a white charger meant he comes in war. Revelation 19:11 reads, "I saw heaven standing open and there before me was a white horse, whose rider is called Faithful and True. With justice he judges and wages war." The next time Jesus comes, it will be to judge and make war.

Palm Sunday sermons usually stress that Jesus' entry into Jerusalem was a time of triumph and great honor. But by the time Jesus rode into Jerusalem on the back of a donkey, he'd already been branded an outlaw by the religious leaders seeking to kill him! Jesus' entry into Jerusalem is not so much a coronation as it is an act of supreme courage. His example should encourage Christians of every age to be witnesses for him no matter the consequences.

Jesus' entry into Jerusalem is also a story of pious misunderstanding. Even his disciples didn't understand the meaning of this event until after the resurrection. We'd do well to remember that Jesus always arrives on his own terms—not necessarily in the way we'd want him to come. Teresa of Avila and John of the Cross both said we should pursue Jesus for what *he* wants to form in us, not for what we want him to form in us.

John 12:17-19

17 Now the crowd that was with him when he called Lazarus from the tomb and raised him from the dead continued to spread the word. 18 Many people, because they had heard that he had performed this sign, went out to meet him. 19 So the Pharisees said to one another, "See, this is getting us nowhere. Look how the whole world has gone after him!"

The people are hailing Jesus as a conquering hero. They know he raised Lazarus from the dead. The crowd is thinking that anyone who can raise a dead person to life can certainly handle the Roman government. Like the thrill-seekers who followed Jesus' after he fed the 5,000, the group hailing Jesus includes a lot of spectators who are just hoping to see another miracle. Jesus had a lot of superficial people following him. He still does.

At the end of the previous chapter of John's Gospel, the Pharisees had ordered that anyone who knew where Jesus was should report it so they could arrest him (11:57). But the crowd isn't turning Jesus in. One of the Pharisees exaggerates, "Look how the whole world has gone after him!"

READ BETWEEN THE LINES

- What are the expectations of the crowd?
- What is the significance of the palm branches?
- Why are they shouting "Hosanna" and quoting from Psalms 113–118?
- Why is Jesus riding a donkey colt?
- What was the significance of Jesus raising Lazarus from the dead compared to all of the other miracles he performed?
- Why did the Pharisee comment, "Look how the whole world has gone after him!" How are the Pharisees feeling?

WELCOME TO MY WORLD

- What was my favorite parade? What did I enjoy about it?
- If Jesus were to ride in a huge parade today, how would the crowds respond?
- How do our churches and communities use Jesus for their own political and social agendas?
- If Jesus showed up at my youth group this week, what would I shout out?
- When I think of the word *king*, what comes to my mind?
- For what do I need to praise God today?

Jesus Predicts His Death

John 12:20-22

20 Now there were some Greeks among those who went up to worship at the festival. 21 They came to Philip, who was from Bethsaida in Galilee, with a request. "Sir," they said, "we would like to see Jesus." 22 Philip went to tell Andrew; Andrew and Philip in turn told Jesus.

The term *Greeks* here doesn't necessarily mean people from Greece; it refers to Gentiles from any part of the Greek-speaking world. These individuals are most likely proselytes, meaning they've chosen to become Jews. This was common, even in the Old Testament. King Solomon set aside a special section of his temple for Gentile believers.

They also could have been "God-fearers" (Acts 10:2, 22; 13:16, 26) who were seeking God but hadn't converted to Judaism for some reason. Perhaps they were like the centurion who paid to have a synagogue built (Luke 7:1-5), the eunuch baptized in Acts 8:6-40 (who wasn't eligible to become a Jew), or Cornelius in Acts 10. All of these were among the "other sheep" whom Jesus referred to earlier (10:16).

We don't know why the Greeks chose to approach Philip. Philip and Andrew were both Jews with Hellenistic names, so maybe that's what attracted them (although many Jews had Greek names). Maybe they were aware that Philip was from Bethsaida, which was close to the Gentile region known as the Decapolis. Philip also may have spoken Greek.

This is the only Gospel account that mentions these no-named Greeks. In a sense, their approaching Jesus represents the fact that Jesus now belongs not just to the Jews, but to the entire world. The apostle Paul is writing about the Gentiles in Romans 9:25, "I will call them 'my people' who are not my people; and I will call her 'my loved one' who is not my loved one." However, Romans 9:27 reminds us that a remnant of Israel will be saved. Paul sensed this when he wrote in Romans 10:1, "Brothers and sisters, my heart's desire and prayer to God for the Israelites is that they may be saved."

Philip doesn't take the Greeks directly to Jesus. Philip may have known that Jesus was busy at the temple and didn't want to disturb him. Maybe he remembered what Jesus said in Matthew 10:5-6, "Do not go among the Gentiles or enter any town of the Samaritans. Go rather to the lost sheep of Israel." Instead, Philip takes them to Andrew, certain that he will know what to do. Andrew is mentioned only four times in the book of John; each time he brings someone to Jesus.

John 12:23-26

23 Jesus replied, "The hour has come for the Son of Man to be glorified. 24 Very truly I tell you, unless a kernel of wheat falls to the ground and dies, it remains only a single seed. But if it dies, it produces many seeds. 25 Anyone who loves their life will lose it, while anyone who hates their life in this world will keep it for eternal life. 26 Whoever serves me must follow me; and where I am, my servant also will be. My Father will honor the one who serves me."

Verse 23 should include some sort of fanfare with trumpets blowing and a huge fireworks display because it represents a big shift in John's Gospel. In contrast to previous statements that Jesus' hour has not yet arrived (2:4; 7:30; 8:20), this is the first time John records Jesus saying, "The hour has come" (13:1; 17:1). The time has come for the Son of Man (1:51) to be glorified. The crowds may have been thinking Jesus was about to wipe out the Romans and set up his earthly kingdom. But they will soon discover that this is the hour when Jesus will be glorified through his crucifixion, resurrection, and ascension. In Isaiah 52:13 we read, "See, my servant will act wisely; he will be raised and lifted up and highly exalted."

The people around Jesus are probably thrilled to hear him say it's time for him to be glorified. You can imagine them thinking: *Finally!!!* But the words that follow must have completely confused them. They suddenly realize Jesus is talking about dying. He must go to the cross. The kind of political Messiah they sought could not keep people from hell, nor give them the kind of life Jesus is offering—eternal life.

Jesus uses a lesson from nature that would be more familiar to these Greeks than Old Testament prophecy. Even if you don't know a lot about agriculture, you probably know that a seed placed in the ground dies so that a plant can grow from it. Jesus is saying he must die so that others can live.

Jesus uses a love/hate exaggeration in the wisdom saying of verse 25. If you humble yourself, abandon your old life, and follow Jesus, you will save your life. But if you love your life too much, then you're holding on to it too tightly. Stop focusing on yourself. Jesus should be your first priority. We must attach ourselves to the Teacher. Our love of God must make all other loves seem like hatred.

The Father will honor those who humble themselves and serve Jesus. People honor one another, but human honor pales in comparison to being honored by God, the Creator of the universe.

John 12:27-29

27 "Now my soul is troubled, and what shall I say? 'Father, save me from this hour'? No, it was for this very reason I came to this hour. 28 Father, glorify your name!"

Then a voice came from heaven, "I have glorified it, and will glorify it again." 29 The crowd that

was there and heard it said it had thundered; others said an angel had spoken to him.

The moment that Jesus has been anticipating throughout the Gospel of John has now arrived—and his response may surprise us. He says, "My soul is troubled." Here is clear evidence that the *Word* really did become flesh. Jesus is wrestling in his own heart and mind as he faces death. He knows there is pain and danger ahead. The perfect tense of the word *troubled* indicates that this is an ongoing struggle for Jesus. Don't ever think Jesus was detached from that body on the cross and merely looking down from heaven. He was there. He felt everything on that cross—not only the human pain of his physical suffering and abandonment, but also the weight and guilt of every sin ever committed.

Jesus could have said, "Father, save me from this hour," but he stayed true to his purpose. In Matthew 26:53, Jesus states, "Do you think I cannot call on my Father, and he will at once put at my disposal more than twelve legions of angels?" Instead of focusing his prayer life on avoiding the path before him, he desires to give glory to God the Father by going through it. Jesus prays in Gethsemane, "Father, if you are willing, take this cup from me; yet not my will, but yours be done" (Luke 22:42).

We read in Hebrews 12:2, "For the joy set before him he endured the cross, scorning its shame." The joy for Jesus is not in dying, but in what his death will accomplish. He doesn't pray that God will remove the cross but that the Father will be glorified. The world will be rescued by Jesus being lifted up "Just as Moses lifted up the snake in the wilderness" (3:14).

> The Johannine Jesus is no docetic actor in a drama, about to play a part which he can contemplate dispassionately because it does not really involve himself. "The hour has come for the

Son of Man to be glorified," it is true, but for the Son of man this involves arrest, binding, striking on the face, scourging, mocking, crucifixion and death—all to be endured in grim earnest. Hence his inward disquiet; hence his spontaneous prayer to be saved from "this hour." But scarcely has the prayer left his lips than it is retracted. All that must be endured was the very reason for his coming to this hour; he must go through with it.

—F. F. Bruce, *The Gospel and Epistles of John*, 265–266

There are only two other times in the New Testament where God speaks audibly to confirm Jesus' identity. God spoke at Jesus' baptism (Matthew 3:16-17) and at his transfiguration (Matthew 17:3-5). Both times God said, "This is my Son, whom I love; with him I am well pleased." In this case, the voice speaks of Jesus being glorified. God has glorified his own name in Jesus' miracles and teachings; God will glorify his name again in Jesus' death and resurrection.

Hearing the heavenly voice, some of the crowd thought it had thundered. Thunder was tied to the power and greatness of God (1 Samuel 12:18; Job 37:5) and was heard on Mount Sinai (Exodus 19:16-19). Regardless of the crowd's interpretation, the sound was clearly supernatural.

John 12:30-33

30 Jesus said, "This voice was for your benefit, not mine. 31 Now is the time for judgment on this world; now the prince of this world will be driven out. 32 And I, when I am lifted up^g from the earth, will draw all people to myself." 33 He said this to show the kind of death he was going to die.

The disciples hear the voice; Jesus says it's for them. Remembering this voice will be a source of encouragement when Jesus is hanging on the cross and it looks like all is lost.

g John 12:32 The Greek for *lifted up* also means *exalted*.

Jesus says this is the time for judgment. But remember that John 3:17-18 clearly states, "For God did not send his Son into the world to condemn the world, but to save the world through him. Whoever believes in him is not condemned." That's the triumph of the cross: Jesus died to release us from condemnation. Later in the chapter, Jesus says, "For I did not come to judge the world, but to save the world. There is a judge for the one who rejects me and does not accept my words; the very words I have spoken will condemn them at the last day" (12:47b-48). The "world" Jesus came to save includes all who are in rebellion against God. However, those who reject Jesus have already been judged.

When you evaluate the music of Mozart and Bach, they're not on trial as much as you are. Their cases are closed; they've proved to be two of the world's greatest composers. The way we judge and respond to their music says more about us than it does about them. In the same way, how each of us responds to Jesus passes a verdict not on him, but on us.

There is another triumph in the cross: Satan, the prince of this world, is defeated (14:29-31). Satan was an angel who rebelled against God (Isaiah 14:4-7; Revelation 12:7-9) and constantly worked in opposition to both God and those who love and obey God. Satan tempted Eve in the garden and persuaded the first humans to sin (Genesis 3:1-7); Satan also tempted Jesus in the wilderness but did not persuade him (Matthew 4:1-11). At first glance the cross appears to be Satan's greatest triumph, but it becomes his greatest defeat. Satan is "driven out"—as he will be again and again in the biblical drama:

- Revelation 12:9-10—Satan is tossed out of heaven.
- Revelation 20:2-3—Satan is cast into the bottomless pit for 1,000 years.
- Revelation 20:10—Satan is thrown into the lake of fire forever.

The phrase "when I am lifted up from the earth" could be understood two ways. It could refer to Jesus being raised up on the cross; it could also refer to Jesus' ascension into heaven where he is calling all to join him there. So another triumph of the cross is that all people will be drawn to Christ—regardless of race, class, age, nationality, gender, or any other distinction.

John 12:34

34 The crowd spoke up, "We have heard from the Law that the Messiah will remain forever, so how can you say, 'The Son of Man must be lifted up'? Who is this 'Son of Man'?"

The people believed the Messiah would be around forever, so they couldn't understand all this talk about Jesus' dying. What kind of a Messiah finds glory in dying? Old Testament passages such as Psalm 72:17, Isaiah 9:6-7, and Ezekiel 37:26-28 suggested the Messiah would be a warrior king who will destroy the enemies of Israel, lead the people into prosperity, and rule on the throne of David forever.

However, other Old Testament passages speak of the Messiah as a suffering servant who will die for his people:

- Isaiah 53:7—"He was led like a lamb to the slaughter."
- Daniel 9:26—"the Anointed One will be put to death and will have nothing."
- Zechariah 13:7—"Awake, sword, against my shepherd . . ."

Some Jews solved the puzzle of these two different depictions by concluding that the Messiah would appear as two individuals acting together. Yet we now know that these verses refer to the One who would die in the place of his people and then rise from the grave to become their everlasting king. Jesus comes first as the Lamb to die for the sake of all humanity. At the second coming, he will come as the Lion of Judah who will rule eternally.

They are mocking Jesus by asking, "Who is this 'Son of Man'?" (1:51). The crowd cannot understand the cross; in the words of 1 Corinthians 1:23, it is "a stumbling block to Jews and foolishness to Gentiles."

John 12:35-36

35 Then Jesus told them, "You are going to have the light just a little while longer. Walk while you have the light, before darkness overtakes you. Whoever walks in the dark does not know where they are going. 36 Believe in the light while you have the light, so that you may become children of light." When he had finished speaking, Jesus left and hid himself from them.

In this section Jesus gives his last public appeal to Israel. Tragically, most of his listerners reject it. In just a few days, Jesus will be crucified.

People traveled by foot in those days. Whatever journey one wanted to make had to be done in the daylight; traveling at night was unsafe. Jesus is telling the people to begin the journey of faith while the Light is still with them—before darkness falls and they begin stumbling around in the dark.

Jesus encourages us to become "children of light." This means we become lights ourselves—or maybe it's more correct to say we become reflectors of the Light. We are to reflect the light of God as the moon reflects the light of the sun. Belief in Christ causes us to become children of light.

What a tragic verse to end this section of Scripture: "Jesus left and hid himself from them." Luke tells us the crowd went to the temple to look for Jesus the next day, but he never showed.

READ BETWEEN THE LINES

- Who are these Greeks? Why are they there?
- Why did they go to Philip?
- What does Jesus mean by "the hour has come"?
- Who is the "Son of Man"? What does this term mean?
- How will Jesus be glorified?
- What does it mean "anyone who loves their life will lose it"?
- What troubled Jesus' soul?
- Why did the crowd respond the way it did to the Father's voice?
- Who is the "prince of this world"? How will he be driven out?
- What is Jesus referring to when he says, "when I am lifted up"?
- Who are children of light?
- What is the first step to becoming children of light?

WELCOME TO MY WORLD

- Does worship of Jesus transcend culture? Are all people welcome in my church today?
- How do I respond to this statement: "11:00 A.M. on Sunday is the most segregated hour of the week"?
- How are we to hate our lives today?
- How can I spend more time walking in the Light instead of in the darkness?
- How am I trying to make Jesus fit into my own idea of the Messiah?
- What are some things in my life that need to die so I can really live?

Belief and Unbelief Among the Jews

John 12:37-41

37 Even after Jesus had performed so many signs in their presence, they still would not believe in him. 38 This was to fulfill the word of Isaiah the prophet:

"Lord, who has believed our message and to whom has the arm of the Lord been revealed?"[h]

39 For this reason they could not believe, because, as Isaiah says elsewhere:

40 "He has blinded their eyes and hardened their hearts, so they can neither see with their eyes, nor understand with their hearts, nor turn—and I would heal them."[i]

41 Isaiah said this because he saw Jesus' glory and spoke about him.

This is one of those difficult theological passages. The Gospel writer explains that Israel would not believe in Jesus despite the many signs they'd seen. In verse 38, John quotes Isaiah 53:1, which asks who has believed God's message. Then, as if to answer the question, he cites Isaiah 6:10, which says: "Make the heart of this people calloused; make their ears dull and close their eyes. Otherwise they might see with their eyes, hear with their ears, understand with their hearts, and turn and be healed."

Even after all the miracles and amazing teachings of Jesus, many people still wouldn't believe. The Gospel of John is pointing out that the problem was not with Jesus, but with the callous hardness and insensitivity of the people. It was their own choice, their own fault. People may think they can come to Jesus anytime, but there are times when God seems

h John 12:38 See Isaiah 53:1
i John 12:40 See Isaiah 6:10

to stop drawing people. Augustine wrote, "For God thus blinds and hardens, simply by letting alone and withdrawing His aid" (*Confessions* 63:6). This may seem unfair to us at first reading. How can people be held accountable for not believing if they're prevented from believing?

The sobering truth is that when sinners persistently reject Him, God may ultimately remove His grace and judge them. Nehemiah records God's extraordinary patience with Israel: "You bore with them for many years, and admonished them by your Spirit through your prophets (9:30a). But when "they would not give ear . . . [God] gave them into the hand of the peoples of the lands" (9:30b; cf. Judg. 10:13; 2 Kings 17:13-18; 2 Chron. 15:2; 24:20). In Psalm 81:11-12 God lamented, "My people did not listen to my voice, and Israel did not obey Me. So I gave them over to the stubbornness of their heart, to walk in their own devices." Hosea records God's shocking statement, "Ephraim (a symbolic name for the northern kingdom [Israel]) is joined to idols; let him alone" (Hos. 4:17). Because of Israel's hardhearted rejection of Him, God abandoned the people to the consequences of their sin. When Israel "rebelled and grieved the Holy Spirit," God eventually "turned Himself to become their enemy. He fought against them" (Isa. 63:10). Three times in Romans 1:18-32, Paul spoke of God's wrathful judgment in abandoning sinners to the consequences of their sin (vv. 24, 26, 28). Hebrews 10:26-27 warns that for those who "go on sinning willfully [refusing to repent] after receiving the knowledge of the truth, there no longer remains a sacrifice for sins, but a terrifying expectation of judgment and the fury of a fire which will consume the adversaries."

Those who reject Jesus Christ, never embracing Him in saving faith, will inevitably face God's vengeance, wrath, and judgment in eternal punishment.

—John MacArthur, *The MacArthur New Testament Commentary John 12–21*, 51

Those who harden their hearts against the truths of God may eventually find that God will harden their hearts even more. Pharaoh is an example of this principle. Exodus tells us that when Moses appealed to Pharaoh to release the Israelites, Pharaoh first hardened his own heart (8:15, 32; 9:34), and then God further hardened Pharaoh's heart (9:12; 10:1, 20, 27; 11:10, 14:8). God is not intentionally preventing people from believing in him or following his plan. He is simply confirming the choices they've already made (Romans 1:24-28; 2 Thessalonians 2:9-12).

Over the years some of the Jews had interpreted the Old Testament prophesies regarding the Messiah in such a way that when Jesus came in 12:37, they either would not, or perhaps could not believe. That's why Isaiah urges us all: "Seek the LORD while he may be found; call on him while he is near" (55:6). Those who steadfastly refuse to believe may eventually reach a place where they *cannot* believe. What a tragedy!

When John describes the hardening of Jesus' audiences in 12:37-41, he is not saying that God has forced into unbelief men and women who otherwise would have believed. It is wrong to conclude from 12:37-41 that John supports an extreme determinism in which God assigns otherwise neutral people to faith and others to unbelief. John's comment here is that people who refuse to believe will experience judgment. . . . Those who refuse the light will find it extinguished and the darkness closing over them. . . . To refuse the medicine is to succumb to the disease. To refuse to have faith is to be swallowed by the darkness.

—Gary Burge, *The NIV Application Commentary: John*, 359–360

John 12:42-43

⁴² Yet at the same time many even among the leaders believed in him. But because of the Pharisees

they would not openly acknowledge their faith for fear they would be put out of the synagogue; [43] for they loved human praise more than praise from God.

The first sentence here sounds like good news. But before you get too excited that "many even among the leaders believed in him," check out the next two verses. These leaders may have believed in Jesus, but they refused to become true disciples (followers of Jesus). Sadly, these leaders weren't willing to let go of their leadership positions within the community or the human praise it brought them. James 4:4, "You adulterous people, don't you know that friendship with the world means enmity against God? Therefore, anyone who chooses to be a friend of the world becomes an enemy of God."

For more information on the phrase "put out of the synagogue," see the commentary on John 9:22 and 16:2.

Along with those who refused to believe, many believed but refused to admit it. This is just as bad, and Jesus had strong words for such people (see Matthew 10:32-33). Many people will not take a stand for Jesus because they fear rejection or ridicule. Many Jewish leaders wouldn't admit to faith in Jesus because they feared excommunication from the synagogue (which was their livelihood) and loss of their prestigious place in the community. But the praise of people is fickle and short-lived. We should be much more concerned about God's eternal acceptance than about the temporary approval of other people.

—*Life Application Bible Commentary: John*, 264

John 12:44-50

[44] Then Jesus cried out, "Whoever believes in me does not believe in me only, but in the one who

sent me. ⁴⁵ The one who looks at me is seeing the one who sent me. ⁴⁶ I have come into the world as a light, so that no one who believes in me should stay in darkness.

⁴⁷ "If anyone hears my words but does not keep them, I do not judge that person. For I did not come to judge the world, but to save the world. ⁴⁸ There is a judge for the one who rejects me and does not accept my words; the very words I have spoken will condemn them at the last day. ⁴⁹ For I did not speak on my own, but the Father who sent me commanded me to say all that I have spoken. ⁵⁰ I know that his command leads to eternal life. So whatever I say is just what the Father has told me to say."

The words of Jesus that John records here recall some of his previous statements. These verses provide a summary of what Jesus has been saying and doing.

The person who believes in the Son also believes in the Father. Jesus is God. If you want to know what God is like, then study the life and teachings of Jesus. A person who believes will live in the Light, not hidden like a bug under a rock.

Jesus came not as judge, but as Savior. But those who reject him and his words will be judged. The same sun that brings light also casts shadows.

A judge's job is to enforce the law. If someone commits murder and gets sent to jail, that person should not blame the judge. The judge is there to rule about whether or not the law has been violated and to dole out the judgment. But people who refuse Jesus now sentence themselves to judgment. They seal their own destinies.

The Jewish nation was God's chosen nation (Amos 3:2). They had received many blessings from God. The Messiah came from the Jewish people, yet some rejected and refused to believe in him. A generation later, Jerusalem and the temple would be destroyed, and the people would scatter. The good news for Israel is that because of God's great love for his people, through the work of Christ, God's mercy and salvation is available to all (Romans 11:25-32).

READ BETWEEN THE LINES

- What were some of the signs Jesus refers to in verse 37?
- Does "they could not believe" in verse 39 mean the people had no free will? Why or why not?
- If many of the leaders believed, why wouldn't they openly say so?
- Is there a point where God removes his grace?
- Why did Jesus come into the world?
- How is Jesus like a light?
- What condemns people on the last day?
- What leads to eternal life?
- How can Jesus' words judge one person while leading another person to life?

WELCOME TO MY WORLD

- Do my friends and I openly express our faith? Why or why not?
- Was I ever inflexible as a child? Describe a specific incident.
- Where is it most difficult for me to live out my faith?
- When am I most afraid to share my faith?

Jesus Washes His Disciples' Feet

John 13:1-2

¹ It was just before the Passover Festival. Jesus knew that the hour had come for him to leave this world and go to the Father. Having loved his own who were in the world, he loved them to the end.

² The evening meal was in progress, and the devil had already prompted Judas, the son of Simon Iscariot, to betray Jesus.

The first 12 chapters of the Gospel of John focus primarily on the relationship between the Son and the Father. Once you get past chapter 12, the incarnational terms (such as *light*, *life*, *to be in*, and *abide*) that have been used to describe the relationship between Jesus and the Father now expand to include the rest of us. This is referred to as the "extension of the incarnation." We see the further extension of the incarnation portrayed in the book of Acts where, after the resurrection of Jesus, the Holy Spirit comes to all believers on the day of Pentecost.

> The career of the Johannine Jesus has been compared to the arc of a pendulum, swinging from on high to a low point and then rising to the heights again. Certainly one can verify this in the hymn that we call the prologue. It begins in heaven: "The Word was in God's presence" (1:1); then comes the crisis of the ministry: "he was in the world . . . yet the world did not recognize him" (1:10) and "We have seen his glory, the glory of an only Son coming from the Father" (1:14); finally the view is lifted once more to heaven: "It is God the only Son, ever at the Father's side" (1:18).

> The same pendulum arc is found in the Gospel proper. The Son is the one who has come down from heaven (3:13), but he is rejected by many who prefer darkness to the light (3:19); and his career reaches its nadir when he is rejected by his own people: "Even though Jesus had performed so many of his signs before them, they refused to believe him" (12:37). The Book of Signs described is the first half of the arc of the pendulum, namely, the downswing; the Book of Glory is the description of the upswing. The "lifting up" of the Son of Man which will draw all men to him (predicted in 12:32) begins on the cross where Jesus is physically lifted up from the earth. For other men crucifixion would have been an abasement; but Jesus lays down his life with power to take it up again (10:18), there is a triumphant element in the Johannine concept of crucifixion. It is a death that achieves glorification and the crucified Jesus is proclaimed as king in the principal languages of the world (19:19-20). The elevation of Jesus continues in the resurrection which is interpreted as part of the ascension of Jesus to the Father (20:17).
>
> —Raymond Brown, *The Gospel According to John, XIII-XXI*, 541–542

It is important to understand that, in the theology of John's Gospel, the death of Jesus is not a tragedy. The cross is not a low point (as might be said of Mark's Gospel). It is the highest moment of Jesus' glory. John uses language that reinterprets Jesus' crucifixion as glory: The Son of Man will be "lifted up" (12:32), and in this moment he will draw everyone to himself (3:13-14; 8:28). The cross is where Jesus is "elevated" above all, hailed as glorious ruler. Through his resurrection, he is empowered to return to his place in heaven.

In chapter 13 Jesus is with his disciples in Jerusalem in an upper room (Luke 22:12). This would be a large, furnished guest room, perhaps on the second story of an unnamed person's house (Mark 14:13-15; Matthew 26:18).

They are preparing to celebrate the Passover, the annual Jewish festival commemorating God's deliverance of Israel from bondage in Egypt. The Passover for the Jews is much like the Fourth of July (Independence Day) to Americans. Both holidays are celebrations of freedom.

But this Passover will mark a transition for followers of Christ. The Passover Feast, which remembers the lambs' blood placed on the doorposts in Egypt, was now being given new meaning for the Christian as it became the Lord's Supper (also called the Eucharist, Last Supper, the breaking of bread, the Mass, or the Holy Communion), which remembers the blood of the Lamb of God poured out for many for the forgiveness of sins.

In Matthew, Mark, and Luke, the Last Supper is part of the Passover meal. John's Gospel has no account of the Last Supper. But John does include the story of the footwashing, a story not found in the Synoptic Gospels.

There are some apparent differences in the chronology between events as they're presented in the Synoptic Gospels and the presentation in John. Traditionally, the Passover went from sundown on Thursday to sundown on Friday, the fifteenth day of the month of *Nisan*. Matthew, Mark, and Luke seem to indicate that Jesus and his disciples celebrated the Passover and the Last Supper on Thursday evening the night prior to the crucifixion (Matthew 26:17; Mark 14:12; Luke 22:7-15). Several passages in the Gospel of John seem to indicate that when Jesus is arrested and tried, the Passover meal is still to come (18:28; 19:12-14).

In John's Gospel Jesus is presented as dying on the cross as the final sacrificial Passover lamb. Jesus' crucifixion occurs at the same time on Friday that the Passover lambs would have been slaughtered in the temple. In John's Gospel, it appears that the Jews eat the Passover meal on Friday evening. One possible explanation is that the phrase "day of Preparation" may not be referring to the day before the Passover meal but to the day preceding the Sabbath. John 19:31 tells us it "was to be a special Sabbath." Perhaps this is because the Sabbath was during the Passover and Feast of Unleavened bread. One other possible explanation is that "Passover" may refer not just to the day of the Passover meal, but to the entire Passover week (both the day of Passover and the weeklong Feast of Unleavened Bread), making all four Gospels agree that Jesus' Last Supper was a Passover meal eaten on Thursday evening.

In any case, Jesus' washing of the disciples' feet occurs shortly before the Passover meal is to begin. Jesus' death on the cross is about 15 to 18 hours away. He is like a mother lying on her deathbed who uses her last breath to express her love for her children. Jesus deeply loves this diverse team of ragtag rebels. He is well aware of their past wavering, their present imperfections, and their future blemishes—and yet he loves them. Jesus knows he will be betrayed by one disciple, denied by another, and deserted by most of the rest while he hangs on the cross; yet "he loved them to the end" (13:1).

It would be helpful for us to dismiss from our minds Leonardo da Vinci's familiar image of the Lord's Supper, in which everyone is seated on one side of a long table. First, the disciples would not be sitting in chairs. The Jewish custom at that time was to recline on cushions. Second, they wouldn't be sitting on one side of a long table; instead, they'd be gathered around the perimeter of a low, U-shaped table, with each disciple propping himself up on his left elbow and eating with his right hand. And their feet would extend away from the table. The interior of the U-shaped table would offer access to those serving the meal.

Judas has already gone to the religious officials to turn in Jesus for 30 pieces of silver (Mark 14:1-11). Jesus' love for his disciples draws the men closer to him, yet it only drives Judas further away.

John 13:3-5

³ Jesus knew that the Father had put all things under his power, and that he had come from God and was returning to God; ⁴ so he got up from the meal, took off his outer clothing, and wrapped a towel around his waist. ⁵ After that, he poured water into a basin and began to wash his disciples' feet, drying them with the towel that was wrapped around him.

Jesus knows his origin (coming from God) and his destiny (returning to God). In chapter 12 Mary washes the feet of Jesus with expensive perfume. Here in chapter 13, Jesus is about to wash the feet of his disciples.

In ancient times people usually wore sandals and traveled on foot. While the Romans built a few paved roads (primarily for military use), most streets were unpaved. People walked everywhere. In the Palestinian countryside, the ground was either mud or thick dust. By the end of a journey, the travelers' feet would be pretty gross—covered with dirt, food, calluses, and animal waste.

My sons were very young when I began taking them with us on our annual mission trips to Tijuana. One year we went down over Easter break to build homes with Amor Ministries. On the evening that we arrived in Tijuana, along with dozens of other U.S. youth groups, it was pouring rain. We were going to spend the week sleeping in tents. But the rain fell so hard that first night, it was impossible to set up the tents, let alone sleep in them.

The mud in Tijuana is similar in consistency to the mud in Israel. It was so muddy that first night that we spent the night in the van and got out only for emergencies. The outhouses were located about 50 yards from our van. When you stepped out of the van and into the mud, your foot sank in about 10 to 12 inches; and when you pulled your foot up to take your next step, you'd lose your shoe. It was ugly. After slogging over to the outhouses and then returning to the van, you couldn't help but drag huge globs of mud back into the vehicle. There were 12 of us packed into our 15-passenger van, along with all of our luggage, bedding, and food for the week. We were tired, sweaty, smelly, dirty, and now very muddy. We stayed in that van for 48 hours hoping the rain would stop. It didn't.

In the middle of the second night, my youngest son, who was eight years old, tried sleeping in the front passenger seat next to the driver. He started dreaming and began kicking the dashboard. And then he accidentally kicked the fire extinguisher and set it off, sending streams of white foam over all of us.

We weren't able to build any homes that week. And it took us several hours just to drive out of the thick, gluey mud.

—Les

Inside the entryways of typical first-century homes sat large pots of water, a pitcher, and a basin; and on the wall there hung a towel. When you entered the home, you'd remove your sandals at the door. A servant would then pour water over your feet and dry them off with a towel. This washing of dirty feet was considered the most menial of tasks and would be performed only by the lowest of servants. In fact, it was such a lowly job that Jewish servants were never required to perform this task, only Gentiles. The footwasher in this society was at the bottom of the social food chain. After your feet were washed, you'd remain barefoot during your time in the home.

In the upper room, the water and towel are there, but there is no servant. Usually if a servant wasn't present, then the first guests to arrive would take on the job of being the servant. Jesus waits a long time for one of the disciples to volunteer to wash the other men's feet. Perhaps Luke 22:24 indicates why none of them volunteered, telling us, "A dispute also arose among them as to which of them was considered to be greatest." Evidently, they had ignored Jesus' words in Matthew 23:11—"The greatest among you will be your servant."

They begin eating the evening meal with dirty feet. Then Jesus stands up, removes his outer garment, wraps a servant's cloth around his waist, and begins washing the disciples' feet like a common servant (Philippians 2:5-7). He must have knelt in front of each disciple, first unlacing the man's sandals and then gently lifting each foot and placing it in the basin.

Can you imagine the pain, regret, and embarrassment that must have shot through that room? This humble act was far more powerful than any lecture on humility. The disciples were willing to fight over the throne, but none of them were willing to fight over the basin and towel. Jesus is silently telling them that in order to be the greatest, one must humble oneself and serve others. If you want to be first, then be last. If you want to be highest, be lowest.

Of course, this is more than just one fisherman washing another fisherman's feet. This is the King of Kings washing the feet of a bunch of fisherman. How embarrassing it must have been for the disciples as Jesus took on the servant's role. From then on I imagine it was a race to see who could get to the towel and water basin first.

Not once does Jesus say, "I am now going to demonstrate humility." You cannot demonstrate humility by calling attention to it. As soon as you do this, you become proud. We cannot be humble with the hope of getting something out of it.

Humility is not the same as having low self-esteem. It is, rather, a proper reckoning of ourselves in comparison to God.

One by one Jesus washes each disciple's feet—including Judas's feet—until he comes to Peter.

John 13:6-9

6 He came to Simon Peter, who said to him, "Lord, are you going to wash my feet?"

7 Jesus replied, "You do not realize now what I am doing, but later you will understand."

8 "No," said Peter, "you shall never wash my feet."

Jesus answered, "Unless I wash you, you have no part with me."

9 "Then, Lord," Simon Peter replied, "not just my feet but my hands and my head as well!"

Peter may have pulled his feet back. Jesus tells Peter that he is protesting out of his own ignorance. Someday Peter will understand that Jesus came to be a servant, and that Jesus would be humbled further on the cross.

"No," Peter insists, "you shall never wash my feet." Here, Peter uses the strongest Greek word for "no." Greek scholar Kenneth Wuest translates Peter's statement as, "You shall by no means wash my feet, no, never." Peter assumes he should be washing his Master's feet. His words may seem to honor Jesus; but at the core, aren't they also honoring Peter? Perhaps Peter is unwilling to admit he has dirty feet that are in need of cleansing. This kind of pride can keep us from being vulnerable, being exposed. It's hard for many of us to admit we have a need, and that's especially true of Peter. Like all of us, Peter needs to understand that Jesus is the world's Redeemer. We are not the gospel. We bear witness to the gospel.

After Jesus makes it clear to Peter that it isn't just about getting his feet washed, but about being a disciple, impulsive Peter makes a big U-turn and goes to the opposite extreme, asking Jesus to give him a bath. How typical of Peter! Now he wants to be set apart from the others in a whole new way, asking Jesus to wash his head, arms, legs, and his whole body! But we know Peter eventually learns his lesson because he writes in 1 Peter 5:5 that we should all clothe ourselves in humility.

John 13:10-11

10 Jesus answered, "Those who have had a bath need only to wash their feet; their whole body is clean. And you are clean, though not every one of you." 11 For he knew who was going to betray him, and that was why he said not every one was clean.

Here, Jesus may be referring to the Jewish tradition of purification in the ritual baths in preparation for the Passover. The Judaism of Jesus' day gave great attention to ritual purity, carefully following elaborate rules based on passages like Leviticus 11–15 and Deuteronomy 23–24. The goal of these rules was to mark the Israelites as distinct from their heathen neighbors. Among the many things that would render a person unclean were contact with blood, sexual fluids, leprosy, or dead bodies. In addition to contact with any of these, contact with foreigners or anything that belonged to a foreigner would make a person unclean for up to a week. If somebody touched you while he or she was unclean, this would cause you to become unclean for up to a week. If you were unclean and your shadow fell across someone, that person would be unclean for a day.

To have these sins cleansed, people had to purify themselves by taking a ritual bath. They would go into the bath prayerfully and emerge in order to restore their relationship with God. Archeologists have found 150 ritual baths around the temple area. There was a charge to use these baths. Wealthy families often had private baths in or under their homes. These ritual baths were only for spiritual cleansing, not for hygiene purposes.

Jesus gives new spiritual meaning to all of this. When a person puts his faith in the power of Jesus, he or she becomes clean on the inside. There is no need for that person to be saved again. When you are cleansed by being born again and you get dirty later on (as every born-again person does), you don't need to be born again, again.

- John 15:3—"You are already clean because of the word I have spoken to you."
- 1 John 1:9—"If we confess our sins, he is faithful and just and will forgive us our sins and purify us from all unrighteousness."

As we walk through this world, our feet will be dirtied spiritually. But when we come to God in repentance, it's as if we're allowing Jesus to wash the dust off our feet. When we allow Jesus to wash our feet daily, we'll experience that constant cleansing. We need to commune with Jesus on a daily basis through prayer, meditation, and the reading of Scripture.

> It's not about losing salvation—it's about losing intimacy. In Exodus 30, we see the Old Testament illustration of this New Testament principle....
>
> *When a priest was first called, he was washed from head to toe in a ceremonial bathing equivalent to our baptism. From that point on, although he never again needed a head-to-toe cleansing, before entering the tabernacle, he would wash his hands and feet in the laver that stood in the tabernacle courtyard. Otherwise, although he would still be a priest, although he would still be a son of Aaron, he wouldn't be allowed access to the Tabernacle and would therefore be hindered in his ability to minister and receive blessing.*
>
> **—Jon Courson's Application Commentary: New Testament, 548**

As the priests needed to cleanse their hands and feet continually, we also need a continual cleansing of our hearts through confession (1 John 1:9). *Homologeo* is the Greek word for *confession*, and it means "to speak the same thing"—to agree that sin is sin and to ask God to have mercy on us.

Referring to Judas, John writes, "For [Jesus] knew who was going to betray him, and that was why he said not everyone was clean." This seems to be Jesus' last appeal to Judas, but Judas would not be deterred from his evil deed. Jesus wasn't surprised by Judas's act (John 6:70), and God used Judas as part of his saving work. But this does not excuse Judas of the responsibility for his wicked act.

John 13:12-17

12 When he had finished washing their feet, he put on his clothes and returned to his place. "Do you understand what I have done for you?" he asked them. 13 "You call me 'Teacher' and 'Lord,' and rightly so, for that is what I am. 14 Now that I, your Lord and Teacher, have washed your feet, you also should wash one another's feet. 15 I have set you an example that you should do as I have done for you. 16 Very truly I tell you, no servant is greater than his master, nor is a messenger greater than the one who sent him. 17 Now that you know these things, you will be blessed if you do them."

After washing their feet, Jesus tells the disciples they should wash one another's feet. This must have surprised the disciples; they probably expected Jesus to say, "I have washed your feet, now you should wash my feet." He doesn't. He throws them (and us) a curve ball. Most of us would stand in a long line to wash Jesus' feet. We'd consider it an honor. But Jesus commands us to wash other people's feet instead.

This is the lesson of humility that he is teaching. He wants his disciples (then and now) to love and serve one another, not to debate over who is the greatest among them. He is teaching the importance of humble, loving service.

Some churches and denominations believe footwashing is an ordinance instituted by Christ that should be practiced and perpetuated by the church today. On the Thursday before Easter each year (Maundy Thursday), some churches have a service where the pastors, following Jesus' example, wrap themselves in towels and wash the feet of 12 people. The washing of feet symbolizes a great spiritual truth, namely the cleansing of the daily walk of the believer by the application of the Word of God.

There are other congregations who see Jesus' footwashing not as an ordinance like Communion or baptism, but as a simple gesture that defines humility in terms of service to others. They note that verse 15 says, "you should do as I have done for you." The Greek word translated *as* here means "like" or "similar to." There is another Greek word that means "that which." If Jesus had used this other word instead, then his statement would clearly be an ordinance that should be done by all Christians on a regular basis.

These congregations would say that if we get hung up on the specific act of footwashing, then we're minimizing what Jesus is teaching here. While these churches wouldn't have a problem with having a footwashing service, they don't understand this passage as providing a mandate for ritual washings.

The word *blessed* in verse 17 could also be translated "happy." Blessings seem to come from obedience. The next time you feel depressed, distressed, discouraged, or despondent, don't "throw in the towel"; instead, grab a towel and find some dirty feet to wash. If you do, you'll experience happiness. Most of us are surrounded by opportunities for service that can include taking on a menial chore, not insisting on our own rights, meeting others' needs before our own, and looking for jobs that no one else will do and cheerfully doing them. More specifically, we can serve by calling, emailing, texting, or (even better) visiting someone who needs a word of encouragement; or by giving away something of ours that would help another person.

The footwashing also points to Jesus' death. When Jesus was crucified, he was most likely wearing just a towel, as he is here. Footwashing and the crucifixion are embarrassing acts that show Jesus being associated with the lowest of the low.

> If the footwashing points to Jesus' death and if disciples need to be "washed" in order to be a part of Jesus' following, is this washing also a symbol for baptism? This is a shorter step than we might expect. The Greek verb "to bathe" (*louo*, 13:10a) also appears in the New Testament for baptism. In Acts 22:16, for example, Ananias says to the converted Paul, "Get up, be baptized and wash [*apolouo*] your sins away" (see also 1 Cor. 6:11; Eph. 5:26; Titus 3:5; Heb. 10:22). Added to this is a strong patristic tradition that interpreted John 13:10 as a reference to baptism (e.g., Tertullian, Cyprian). "A person who has a bath needs only to wash feet; his whole body is clean" then may become a secondary exhortation underscoring the importance of baptismal washing for the believer.
>
> —Gary Burge, *The NIV Application Commentary: John*, 345–346

READ BETWEEN THE LINES

- How was the scene around the table in the upper room different from most artistic depictions?
- Who prompted Judas to do his shameful betrayal?

- Why didn't the disciples wash their own feet or each other's feet when they entered the room?
- Why did Jesus wash their feet?
- What do you think Jesus was thinking as he washed Judas's feet? How would Judas have felt?
- What was Jesus teaching his disciples?
- Why does Peter object to Jesus washing his feet?
- Is Jesus messing with Peter's theological understanding of the Messiah?
- Why does Jesus insist that Peter needs to have his feet washed but doesn't need a bath?
- Why did Peter change his mind?
- How does Jesus' footwashing relate to the crucifixion?

WELCOME TO MY WORLD

- Have I ever washed someone's feet or had my feet washed? If yes, how was that experience?
- What does footwashing mean for a Christian today?
- Is it easier to wash someone's feet or to have my feet washed? Why?
- How can a Christian be humble without being proud about it?
- What are the joys of serving others?
- Who washes my feet now? Whose feet do I wash?
- How willing am I to do little acts of service for others without drawing attention to them?

Jesus Predicts His Betrayal

John 13:18-20

¹⁸ "I am not referring to all of you; I know those I have chosen. But this is to fulfill this passage of Scripture: 'He who shared my bread has turned[a] against me.'[b]

¹⁹ "I am telling you now before it happens, so that when it does happen you will believe that I am who I am. ²⁰ Very truly I tell you, whoever accepts anyone I send accepts me; and whoever accepts me accepts the one who sent me."

This section deals with Judas. Judas has just allowed Jesus to wash his feet. What a hypocrite!

Before coming to the table that night, Judas decided to betray the Savior. He is a traitor—and in betraying Christ, he becomes Satan's puppet.

Traitor is a strong and ugly word. While Judas is perhaps the most notorious traitor in the Scriptures, he definitely isn't the only one. Absalom wanted the throne of his father King David. In his rebellion against David, Absalom was joined by Ahithophel, a man who was similar to Judas in many ways. Ahithophel was one of David's key advisors. (For more about this story, see 2 Samuel 15–17.) In Psalm 41:9 David writes, "Even my close friend, someone I trusted, one who shared my bread, has turned against me." Jesus was also betrayed by someone who ate bread with him. And, like Judas, Ahithophel eventually hanged himself because of his guilt (2 Samuel 17:23).

Jesus' statement, "I know those I have chosen," again indicates that Judas's actions were not a surprise to Jesus. The phrase "has turned against me" is sometimes translated

a John 13:18 Greek *has lifted up his heel*
b John 13:18 See Psalm 41:9

"has lifted up his heel," and it might refer to the brutal violence of crushing a person's neck when he is down. It could also refer to a horse preparing to kick.

There is a prophecy in Zechariah 11:12-13 that tells of Judas's betrayal: "I told them, 'If you think it best, give me my pay; but if not, keep it.' So they paid me thirty pieces of silver. And the LORD said to me, "Throw it to the potter"—the handsome price at which they valued me! So I took the thirty pieces of silver and threw them to the potter at the house of the LORD."

Judas seems to be out for wealth, power, and prestige. But Judas may have been fervently hoping that Jesus would overthrow the Romans and restore Israel's political strength. Perhaps Judas became disillusioned when he realized this wasn't Jesus' plan. Jesus showed no signs of becoming a political Messiah, and he rebuffed the people's desire to make him their king. The last straw for Judas may have occurred while he was at the dinner to honor Jesus in Bethany—when Mary poured that expensive perfume on Jesus' feet (John 12:1-6). Judas lost out on an opportunity to embezzle the year's wages that the perfume would have been worth on the open market. With his bitterness and disillusionment growing, he immediately went to the chief priests to betray Jesus.

God did not plan Judas's wretchedness. But Judas's wretchedness became part of God's plan. God knew what Judas would choose to do, and God used it for good. Genesis 50:20 reads, "You intended to harm me, but God intended it for good." John is letting us know that Judas has been playing around with the dark side. He wasn't some kind of android that God designed to betray Jesus involuntarily. His betrayal of Jesus wouldn't have happened unless Judas was a willing player.

Judas's betrayal may have been predetermined, but that doesn't contradict the truth that he acted of his own volition. Luke 22:22 affirms both truths when Jesus says, "The Son of Man will go as it has been decreed [God's sovereignty]. But woe to that man who betrays him!" In other words, it's still Judas's responsibility. Judas had every opportunity to turn from his sin. But Judas hardened his heart and refused to repent.

John 13:19—"I am telling you now before it happens, so that when it does happen you will believe that I am who I am"—is the first of four similar *proleptic* statements that Jesus makes in the book of John. Proleptic statements are those that anticipate or disclose a future reality that will take place. Each of these four statements refers to Jesus' prediction of what is to come. (The other three are found in John 14:29; 16:4; and 16:33.)

The phrase "I am who I am" has overtones of deity (Exodus 3:14).

John 13:21-22

21 After he had said this, Jesus was troubled in spirit and testified, "Very truly I tell you, one of you is going to betray me."
22 His disciples stared at one another, at a loss to know which of them he meant.

The word *troubled* is used here to speak of severe mental or spiritual turmoil. It is the same term (*tarasso*) Jesus used at Lazarus' tomb (11:33) and in describing Jesus' thoughts about the cross (12:27).

What troubled Jesus? Perhaps it was the ingratitude of Judas's heart. Maybe it was the fact that Jesus knew Judas's eternal destiny. With an omnipotent eye, Jesus must have seen Satan moving around Judas. Perhaps it was Jesus' deep hatred of sin, which Judas now embodied. Or perhaps it was the fact that Jesus had to go to the cross. Maybe it was the knowledge that he'd experience separation from the Father as he died on the cross (Matthew 27:46).

Jesus' statement—"one of you is going to betray me"—must have stopped the disciples in their tracks. Their hearts must have raced; their pulses must have been frantic. Matthew 26:22 says each disciple asked Jesus, "Surely you don't mean me, Lord?" Even Judas asked the question, maintaining his deceitful hypocrisy to the end. It appears the other disciples never suspected Judas. The fact that they didn't know Judas was the betrayer tells me that Jesus must have been just as gentle, loving, and kind to Judas as he was to the others—at least in public, while perhaps rebuking him privately.

John 13:23-26

23 One of them, the disciple whom Jesus loved, was reclining next to him. 24 Simon Peter motioned to this disciple and said, "Ask him which one he means."

25 Leaning back against Jesus, he asked him, "Lord, who is it?"

26 Jesus answered, "It is the one to whom I will give this piece of bread when I have dipped it in the dish." Then, dipping the piece of bread, he gave it to Judas, the son of Simon Iscariot.

This is the first time we've encountered John's use of the phrase "the disciple whom Jesus loved." It will appear several more times near the end of John's Gospel (19:26-27; 20:2-8; 21:7, 20). This phrase always gets to me. Usually, it's believed to be John's way of referring to himself. If so, then John's greatest claim to fame is that Jesus loved him, just as Jesus loves us.

Theologian Karl Barth was the father of neo-Orthodoxy, a prolific writer, and a man of great intellect. As he got older, his faith got simpler and deeper. Toward the end of his life, Barth was asked to share the most profound truth he knew. He replied by repeating the words of a well-known children's song: "Jesus loves me, this I know, for the Bible tells me so." John, who writes this Gospel as an old man, is still amazed that Jesus would love one like him.

Peter may have asked John to ask Jesus which disciple Jesus means because John seemed to have an intimate relationship with Jesus. But perhaps John was just the one in closest proximity to Jesus, sitting right next to him. It seems Jesus may have responded in a soft voice that only John could hear, saying the betrayer was the one to whom he would give a piece of bread. Jesus then dips the bread (the term used here could also mean "piece of meat" or "bitter herbs") into a common bowl with a sauce possibly made of dates, raisins, and sour wine, and he offers it to Judas. John doesn't seem to react to this; perhaps he didn't understand what Jesus was saying, or maybe he was just keeping it to himself.

Evidently Judas was also sitting close to Jesus, perhaps even in a seat of honor on Jesus' other side. Jesus goes even further by extending a special honor to Judas and offering Judas the morsel dipped in sauce. This was a sign of a special friendship. But Judas's heart remains hardened, and he spurns Jesus again, rejecting Christ's love for the final time.

Some note that John 13:26-30 is similar to 13:19-25 and suggest that this indicates that other writers may have contributed to the Gospel. But this may simply be John's writing style: John 6:35-50 is similar to 6:51-59, and John 13:31–14:31 is similar to 16:4-33.

John 13:27-30

27 As soon as Judas took the bread, Satan entered into him.

So Jesus told him, "What you are about to do, do quickly." 28 But no one at the meal understood why

Jesus said this to him. ²⁹ Since Judas had charge of the money, some thought Jesus was telling him to buy what was needed for the festival, or to give something to the poor. ³⁰ As soon as Judas had taken the bread, he went out. And it was night.

This is the only mention of Satan in the fourth Gospel. Judas had been duped by Satan, who first put thoughts into Judas's head and now enters Judas's body. At this point Jesus is through with Judas; Judas has crossed the line of grace. Jesus prods Judas to do what is already in his heart. This shows that Jesus is in charge and not merely a victim of events beyond his control.

Judas has flirted with darkness, and now he's being manipulated by those same dark forces. The same thing happens today when gifted, talented people mess around with stuff they shouldn't and find themselves unable to get out. There are even people who believe in Jesus who do this, but their appetite for the flesh is strong.

Satan may have believed that Jesus' death on earth would end Jesus' mission and put a stop to God's plan. Satan didn't realize that the cross was the most important part of God's plan.

Some disciples assumed that Judas was leaving to buy some needed items for the Passover Feast (which lasts seven days). Others thought Judas was departing to give money to the poor, which was a customary thing for pilgrims going to Jerusalem to do. But we know Judas leaves the upper room in order to finalize his deal with the Sanhedrin, informing them of the most opportune time and place to arrest Jesus.

John tells us it is night, which can be understood symbolically, as well as literally. "Night" may be referring to the darkness of Judas's soul. It isn't easy to know who is good and who is evil in this world. We all have some of each within us. However, it's always night when a person leaves Jesus' presence. John may again be contrasting light and darkness, as he's done throughout his Gospel.

The last image we have of Judas is a man filled with regret. From the accounts in Matthew and Acts, we know Judas tries to return the payment he received for the betrayal, but this gesture is refused. And Judas eventually commits suicide. While Judas's suicide is certainly the most well-known, his is not the only one recorded in the Bible. Others include Abimelech (Judges 9:52-54), Samson (Judges 16:29-30), Saul and his armor bearer (1 Samuel 31:4-6; 2 Samuel 1:2-16; 1 Chronicles 10:3-7), Ahithophel (2 Samuel 17:1-23), and Zimri (1 Kings 16:15-20).

Some (including Augustine and the Latin Vulgate) have sought to harmonize the details of the two differing accounts of the events surrounding Judas's death (Matthew 27:1-10; Acts 1:15-20). One inconsistency involves who purchased the land where Judas committed suicide. The common harmonization is that the Sanhedrin bought the property in Judas's name using the money he threw at them. The second discrepancy is how Judas died. The standard explanation is that the noose Judas used to hang himself broke (or someone cut it), resulting in a fatal fall on a sharp object (such as a stake or jagged stone), which then caused his body to burst open.

Judas teaches us many lessons:

- One can attend all of the religious meetings and still be far from Christ.
- In life there are lost opportunities.
- There will be hypocrites in the church.
- It is dangerous to put money above everything else.
- Satan is at work among the Lord's people.

Even when we fail him, Jesus remains patient, merciful, and loving.

READ BETWEEN THE LINES

- Did Jesus know what Judas was going to do?
- Why was Jesus troubled?
- How did the disciples respond to Jesus saying one of them would betray him?
- Why did no one think it was Judas?
- Why did Jesus reveal who the betrayer was only to John?
- Is John simply giving a time reference when he writes "it is night"? Or is there more to this?

WELCOME TO MY WORLD

- When have I been let down or betrayed by someone I cared about or admired?
- How did I feel or respond?
- What responsibility does Judas have for his actions?
- How would I have felt if I were sitting at the table as one of Jesus' disciples?
- How do I believe Jesus responds when I disappoint him?

Jesus Predicts Peter's Denial

John 13:31-33

[31] When he was gone, Jesus said, "Now the Son of Man is glorified and God is glorified in him. [32] If God is glorified in him,[c] God will glorify the Son in himself, and will glorify him at once.

[33] "My children, I will be with you only a little longer. You will look for me, and just as I told the Jews, so I tell you now: Where I am going, you cannot come."

Jesus' words here almost sound like a sigh of relief. Now that Judas is gone, Jesus begins speaking freely to his true disciples about his glory. This long speech at the end of Jesus' life (John 13–16) is similar in many ways to the Sermon on the Mount that began Jesus' ministry in Matthew 5–7. Each speech sums up the major teachings of its Gospel. However, this speech has a more intimate feel than the Sermon on the Mount because it's spoken only to Jesus' closest followers, and because the death of Jesus is looming. John 13:31 is the last time Jesus uses the phrase "Son of Man" in the Gospel of John.

The glory of the Lord is to be our purpose, our reason, our motive, and the theme for our lives. The Hebrew word for "glory" (*kavod*) is translated *doxa* in the Greek. It can be used as a noun (meaning both "glory" and "praise") or a verb (meaning "to glorify" or "to praise").

"My children" is an affectionate term Jesus uses for these 11 remaining disciples. This is the only time it appears in this Gospel. In this passage Jesus continues to explain to his disciples that he is going away and they cannot follow him just yet. His words here echo what Jesus told the Jews in John 7:34—"You will look for me, but you will not find me;

c John 13:32 Many early manuscripts do not have *If God is glorified in him.*

and where I am, you cannot come"—and in John 8:21—"I am going away, and you will look for me, and you will die in your sin. Where I go, you cannot come."

John 13:34-35

³⁴ "A new command I give you: Love one another. As I have loved you, so you must love one another. ³⁵ By this everyone will know that you are my disciples, if you love one another."

Loving one another isn't a totally new idea. Jesus noted that the whole of the Law and the Prophets could be summed up in two commandments: We are to love God and love our neighbor (Matthew 22:37-40). But what *is* unique in this passage is his addition of the phrase "as I have loved you." Jesus urges us to love one another in the same way he loves us—he willingly laid down his life for us.

Francis A. Schaeffer in his book *The Mark of a Christian* writes that with this commandment, Jesus gives the world the right to judge whether or not we are Christians on the basis of our observable love toward one another. Schaeffer also points out that Christians have historically displayed many different symbols as a way of showing they are believers. Today, these symbols may include:

- Pins on our lapels
- Chains around our necks (crosses)
- Special haircuts (the monk's *tonsure* or shaved crown of the head)
- Posters
- Screensavers
- Bumper stickers
- Wristbands
- T-shirts
- Christian symbols (e.g., the sign of the fish)

The only problem with these symbols is that they're totally external and superficial. But on the night before his death, Jesus gives a new way that believers are to be identified as belonging to the Christ.

> If you have a fish symbol on your car, that's fine. People will associate you with a movement. Do you display a cross? Nothing bad about that. People will link you to a religion. If you carry a Bible everywhere you go, people will assume you attend a particular church. If, however, you display love that is authentic to the core—observable love—then people will know you are a follower of Jesus Christ.
>
> —Chuck Swindoll, *Insights on John*, 218.

We are able to love others by Jesus loving through us. If we don't love as he loved, then we haven't fulfilled the new commandment. Loving one another will strengthen believers and bring us closer together, but it will also bring unbelievers to Jesus.

> The centrality of loving one another hit home for me in the third week of my junior year in high school. I'd become a Christian at a summer camp just two months earlier. Before that, I'd been part of a school club made up of guys who liked to work on customized Volkswagens. The guys in this club had done some crude things to other students at our school. For instance, there was a little person named Jimmy at my school. He was 3' 4" tall and a sophomore (a year younger than me). One afternoon during the first week of my junior year, some members of the club had locked him in a locker. He wasn't able to get out until the custodian heard him banging from inside the locker.
>
> A couple of weeks later, I was standing at the bus stop with a few other students, including Jimmy. I knew him; he lived just two blocks from my house, and I was friends with his

older brother. Jimmy turned to me and said he'd heard that I'd become a Christian. I looked down and shuffled my feet and said a weak "yes." Then he said something I've never forgotten. He said, "Well, Les, I just want you to know that your life doesn't show it."

I got on the bus and went to school as usual that day, but I couldn't shake Jimmy's words from my mind. He was right; my life didn't show it. I wasn't showing the love of Christ to anyone. That night I prayed that God would love others through me. Over a period of time, I became friends with Jimmy. And before the end of that school year, Jimmy came to know the love of Christ. This kind of love can come only from Jesus. "May the Lord make your love increase and overflow for each other and for everyone else" (1 Thessalonians 3:12).

—Les

John 13:36-38

[36] Simon Peter asked him, "Lord, where are you going?"

Jesus replied, "Where I am going, you cannot follow now, but you will follow later."

[37] Peter asked, "Lord, why can't I follow you now? I will lay down my life for you."

[38] Then Jesus answered, "Will you really lay down your life for me? Very truly I tell you, before the rooster crows, you will disown me three times!"

Jesus' statement that he would soon be leaving the disciples (13:33) really bothered Peter. It doesn't seem as though Peter heard a word Jesus said about loving one another. Peter was more concerned about his Master's imminent departure.

Peter's question reflects the disciples' continual inability and unwillingness to accept that Jesus must leave them.

They were unable to reconcile Jesus' repeated statements that he was going to die (Matthew 16:21; 17:22-23; 20:17-19; Mark 9:31-32; 10:32-34; Luke 18:31-34; 24:6-7, 26; John 7:33-34; 8:28; 10:15; 12:8; 12:23-24) with their preconceptions of a Messiah who would establish an earthly kingdom in fulfillment of the Old Testament covenants and promises.

Peter is being a braggart in this passage. In Matthew 26:33 his words are even more explicit: "Even if all fall away on account of you, I never will." Peter should have remembered 1 Kings 20:11 where the king of Israel says, "Tell him: 'One who puts on his armor should not boast like one who takes it off.'" As any athlete knows, you don't boast in the locker room *before* the game.

Jesus' statement—"Before the rooster crows, you will disown me three times!"—shocks Peter so much that he doesn't say another word throughout the rest of this scene. He couldn't imagine that he would ever deny his Lord.

Peter did, in fact, follow Jesus later on by being crucified—an event that Jesus predicts in John 21:18-19. Tradition says Peter was crucified upside down on an X-shaped cross because he didn't feel worthy to die as Christ had died.

READ BETWEEN THE LINES

- What were Jesus' first words after Judas leaves?
- Why did Jesus wait until Judas was gone to share these words?
- How will God be glorified by what is about to happen to Jesus?
- Where is Jesus going? Why can't the disciples go with him at this time?
- What is new about the commandment that Jesus gives to his disciples?
- How will people know we are followers of Jesus?

- Why did Peter respond the way he did?
- How does Peter's self-appraisal conflict with Jesus' appraisal of him?
- Which is worse—betrayal or denial? Why?

WELCOME TO MY WORLD

- If I knew I were going to die soon, how would I tell my friends?
- How am I similar to or different from Peter?
- What does it mean to deny Jesus?
- This week, how can I love someone as Jesus loves me?
- Why is loving one another the best way to reach the world for Christ?
- Do you think Christians today are mainly known for their self-sacrificing love? If not, what are Christians known for?
- How does my appraisal of myself compare with Jesus' appraisal of me?

Jesus Comforts His Disciples

This next text is one of the most familiar passages in the New Testament. Jesus is still speaking on the night before his death. Martin Luther once described John 14 as "the best and most comforting sermon that the Lord Christ delivered on earth." Jesus knows what he's facing on the cross, yet he's concerned about the needs of these 11 men who will be shocked, afraid, and disheartened when the crucifixion takes place.

> He expressed a wish that I should read to him, and when I asked from what book, he said—"Need you ask? There is but one." I chose the 14th chapter of St. John's Gospel; he listened with mild devotion, and said when I had done, "Well, this is a great comfort."
>
> —John Gibson Lockhart, *Memoirs of the Life of Sir Walter Scott, Volume 4*, 319

John 14:1

[1] "Do not let your hearts be troubled. You believe in God[a]; believe also in me."

Jesus is speaking words of comfort to the Eleven, urging them to keep the faith. The tense of the Greek word translated "believe" here conveys that Jesus is urging them to continue believing even after he is gone, even if things look bleak.

The disciples' hearts are perplexed. The last couple of days must have been an emotional roller coaster for them. A few days ago they were celebrating Jesus' triumphant arrival into Jerusalem. Now everything seems to be falling apart for them. They must be worried sick about what's going to happen to Jesus—and to them. They are just beginning to

---

a John 14:1 Or *Believe in God*

realize that Jesus really is going to leave—and they won't be going with him.

Just as Ancient Israel was challenged to believe in God before entering the Promised Land, Jesus encourages the disciples not to be troubled even when life seems to be coming apart at the seams. It's as if Jesus is saying, "Your ancestors believed in God then (before entering the Promised Land); you need to believe in me now." Jesus compares believing in God with believing in him, clearly putting himself on an equal basis with God.

John 14:2

2 "My Father's house has many rooms; if that were not so, would I have told you that I am going there to prepare a place for you?"

"My Father's house" can be understood as a reference to heaven. One reason we shouldn't remain distressed by the challenges we face on this earth is that we have a home in heaven. Many adults are familiar with the King James Version of this verse, which reads, "In my Father's house are many mansions." Yet the word *mansion* is actually misleading for modern readers. At the time of the King James translation, that word referred to a small dwelling—which is far different from how we understand the term today.

"My Father's house" can also refer to the kingdom of God. And the word translated as many "rooms" is *monai* (abiding places). "In my Father's kingdom there are many abiding places," Jesus says, "and I will prepare one of these for you." This passage refers to what a Jewish father would do each time one of his sons got married. He would add a new room onto his house for that son and his family. In the same way, our heavenly Father prepares a place for us in his house.

This is not just a future event. The primary message is that abundant life as a part of God's kingdom begins now for a believer. The secondary meaning of this passage is eternal life in heaven. And it's not just the place that's being prepared. There are two construction projects going on: God is preparing a place in heaven for you, and he's also preparing *you* for a place in heaven.

The only other time Jesus speaks of "my Father's house" is in John 2:16, where the phrase referred to the temple. The temple was understood to be the place where heaven and earth met. Jesus has now replaced the temple as the meeting place of earth and heaven.

This passage might also be a reference to the future messianic wedding events (3:27-30). In Jesus' day the groom would go away during the yearlong engagement period in order to build a home for his bride. He would then return for the wedding celebration and then take his bride to their new home. Here, we see Jesus as the groom who is going away to build a home for his bride (Israel/the church). At a future time, he will return to take his bride back to his home to be with him forever.

John 14:3

³ **"And if I go and prepare a place for you, I will come back and take you to be with me that you also may be where I am."**

This verse could refer to—

- the coming of the Holy Spirit;
- Christ's second coming; or
- human death when the soul goes to be with God.

Or it could mean all of the above. This is a verse of encouragement. Jesus knows that his leaving is necessary, but his return is certain. What makes heaven such a wonderful place is the fact that Jesus is there. Death won't interrupt the intimacy we have with Jesus.

READ BETWEEN THE LINES

- Why would the disciples' hearts be troubled?
- What does it mean to "trust in Jesus"?
- To what does "my Father's house" refer?
- How has Jesus replaced the temple (the place where heaven and earth meet)?
- What does "I will come back" refer to?

WELCOME TO MY WORLD

- How would Jesus' teaching about heaven comfort his disciples? How does thinking about heaven raise our spirits today?
- What do I think heaven will be like?
- How is God preparing us for heaven?
- When has my heart been troubled?
- Who do I go to or what do I do when I'm having troubles?
- What images come to mind when I think of my room in my Father's house? What does it have? How does it look?
- How do I feel about Jesus coming back? Am I excited or afraid?

Jesus, the Way to the Father

John 14:4-6

⁴ "You know the way to the place where I am going."

⁵ Thomas said to him, "Lord, we don't know where you are going, so how can we know the way?"

⁶ Jesus answered, "I am the way and the truth and the life. No one comes to the Father except through me."

"Doubting Thomas" is really honest Thomas. The disciples didn't know what to do after Jesus' death. They didn't know where they were going or the way to get there.

John 14:6 contains the sixth of the seven "I AM" statements in the Gospel of John (following John 6:35; 8:12; 10:7-9; 10:11-14; and 11:25; and the seventh appears in John 15:1-5). This statement has become one of the most controversial of all of Jesus' words. Jesus is saying, "You don't need a road map or an address to type into MapQuest. You need to trust me; I will take you there." Jesus is the only one who can lead the disciples (and us) to the place he is preparing.

In Matthew 7:13-14, Jesus states, "Enter through the narrow gate. For wide is the gate and broad is the road that leads to destruction, and many enter through it. But small is the gate and narrow the road that leads to life, and only a few find it." Jesus clarifies the concept even further here in John, when he states that he is:

- The Way (to the Father)
- The Truth (in this world and in the world to come)
- The Life (that is eternal, beginning now and going on forever)

Psalm 86:11 reads, "Teach me your way, LORD, that I may rely on your faithfulness." In Jesus, life and truth are connected. He is *the* way to the Father (not just *a* way to the Father). The only way to be connected to God is through Jesus (Matthew 7:13; Acts 4:12; 1 Corinthians 3:11; 1 Timothy 2:5). John is saying that the Christ, not the Law of Moses, is the means of entrance into the new covenant. It may not be a popular idea today, but John makes it clear that there is only one sure way to God and to all that God intends for us. It is Jesus.

I remember the question-and-answer session that was held at Princeton in 1963 during Karl Barth's Princeton lectures. . . . One student asked Dr. Barth, "Sir, don't you think God has revealed himself in other religions and not only in Christianity?" Barth's answer was like a shock of bright lightning in that packed lounge. He answered, "No, God has not revealed himself in any religion, including Christianity. He has revealed himself in his Son." That is it! "In Jesus Christ, God has spoken for himself, and we must hear that speech."

—Earl F. Palmer, *The Intimate Gospel*, 124

John 14:7-11

[7] "If you really know me, you will know[b] my Father as well. From now on, you do know him and have seen him."

[8] Philip said, "Lord, show us the Father and that will be enough for us."

[9] Jesus answered: "Don't you know me, Philip, even after I have been among you such a long time? Anyone who has seen me has seen the Father. How can you say, 'Show us the Father'? [10] Don't you believe that I am in the Father, and that the Father is in me? The words I say to you I do not speak on my own authority. Rather, it is

---

b John 14:7 Some manuscripts *If you really knew me, you would know*

**the Father, living in me, who is doing his work.
¹¹ Believe me when I say that I am in the Father
and the Father is in me; or at least believe on the
evidence of the works themselves."**

No one has seen God (1:18). Even Moses' request to see
God's face and glory on Mount Sinai was refused (Exodus
33:18-23). But in Jesus, the full personification of God has
been seen by humanity. Jesus isn't merely an agent of God.
He and the Father are one. The Father is in him, and he is in
the Father.

Philip makes a request most of us can relate to. He
asks for proof of God's presence: "Show us the Father,"
he says, "and that will be enough." We all yearn for God to
make a clear physical manifestation in front of our eyes or
to whisper unmistakable words of assurance in our ears.
Yet Philip's statement shows that he didn't get it. So Jesus
repeats it again, assuring Philip that the Father cannot be
any more physical or audible than what the disciples have
already seen in Jesus. As others have noted, Jesus may
have made this statement with a tinge of sadness. It's amazing how much patience Jesus has with us.

Jesus urges them to check out the evidence of his miracles and to look at his words. Even the crowds and authorities
agree that what Jesus said could have come only from God:

- Matthew 7:28-29—"When Jesus had finished saying
  these things, the crowds were amazed at his teaching, because he taught as one who had authority, and
  not as their teachers of the law."

- John 7:16—"Jesus answered, 'My teaching is not my
  own. It comes from the one who sent me.'"

- John 7:46—the temple guards said to the chief priests
  and Pharisees, "No one ever spoke the way this man
  does."

John 14:12

12 "Very truly I tell you, whoever believes in me will do the works I have been doing, and they will do even greater things than these, because I am going to the Father."

Jesus says that those who believe in him will do "even greater things" than he has done. The greater things (compared to what Jesus did in his humble human body) that Jesus' disciples will go on to do (quantitatively speaking, not qualitatively) include:

- They will have a worldwide ministry. Jesus never preached outside of Palestine.

- They will see even greater numbers of people getting healed. Acts 5:16 says, "Crowds gathered also from the towns around Jerusalem, bringing their sick and those tormented by impure spirits, and all of them were healed."

- They will see many more come to faith. When Peter preached the first time, 3,000 people came forward. That never happened to Jesus.

- They will reach more people outside the Jewish community. Many Gentiles will come to know Jesus through the disciples' preaching.

- They will write down the Word of God, guided by the Holy Spirit.

The disciples are to pick up where Jesus left off. This verse is primarily for the 11 disciples, but the secondary meaning of this passage applies to the millions of Christians today who are teaching God's Word, loving people, and serving others in Jesus' name all around the world. Jesus will carry out greater endeavors in and through his followers. What an honor to continue the work of Jesus!

John 14:13-14

¹³ "And I will do whatever you ask in my name, so that the Father may be glorified in the Son. ¹⁴ You may ask me for anything in my name, and I will do it."

Some people think of prayer as some kind of Aladdin's lamp. You rub it and say the magic words, and then Jesus comes out like a genie, ready to do whatever you ask. Others think Jesus has given them a "blank check." In order to cash it in for whatever they want, all they have to do is pray. That's not the way it works. "In my name" is no "abracadabra" or magical incantation. Prayer is not about *having* power but about giving up power.

Praying in Jesus' name doesn't mean we merely tack on the name of Jesus at the end of a prayer and then whatever we ask for is ours. It means we pray in his person; we pray as if Jesus were doing the asking. We are to ask in harmony with his spirit and nature. We are saying, "Dear Father, for Jesus I am asking . . . ." This approach eliminates the "gimme prayers." We pray for things that will bring glory to God. We pray for things that fit with God's character. Prayer doesn't always change our circumstances, but it often changes our attitudes and lifestyles. We are transformed through prayer.

Many years ago when I was in my early twenties, I served at a church where one of the women in the congregation was convinced I should marry her daughter. This mother would invite me to dinner at their home and try to get me to spend time with her daughter. She told me she'd been praying that God would bring the two of us together. I'm sure she meant well, but I was pretty certain this was *not* the girl I was intended to marry. I'm thankful that many prayers go unanswered!

—Les

READ BETWEEN THE LINES

- Why should the disciples have known the way to the place where Jesus was going?
- Why did Thomas ask this question? How did Jesus respond?
- What does it means to believe that Jesus is "the way and the truth and the life"? The way to where? The truth about what? What kind of life?
- Why did Philip ask to see the Father?
- How does Philip's request compare to Thomas's question?
- How are Jesus and the Father connected?
- What evidence does Jesus offer to support this assertion?
- What is different about Jesus' words?
- What "greater things" will the disciples do?
- What does it mean to ask for something in Jesus' name?

WELCOME TO MY WORLD

- How do people in my world describe how to get to heaven?
- How do I come to the Father?
- Is Jesus being narrow-minded here or truthful?
- What do I think about Karl Barth's statement?
- How patient is Jesus?
- What are some of the requests my friends ask of God?
- What questions would I want to ask Jesus?
- Do I know the way?

- What would I say to someone who suggests there are many ways to God?

- What kinds of things do I ask for in Jesus' name?

Jesus Promises the Holy Spirit

John 14:15-17

[15] "If you love me, keep my commands. [16] And I will ask the Father, and he will give you another advocate to help you and be with you forever— [17] the Spirit of truth. The world cannot accept him, because it neither sees him nor knows him. But you know him, for he lives with you and will be[c] in you."

Jesus says the test of our love for him is our obedience. In 1 John 5:3 we read, "In fact, this is love for God: to keep his commands. And his commands are not burdensome." Love is a great motivator. Love is birthed in the trust and assurance that God loves us. "We love because he first loved us," declares 1 John 4:19. And Romans 5:8 affirms, "But God demonstrates his own love for us in this: While we were still sinners, Christ died for us."

Jesus says the Father will send "another advocate." There are two different Greek words that might be translated "another." One word means "another of any kind." For example, if I asked you for another pair of glasses, you could hand me any kind you wanted—wire-framed, brightly colored, sunglasses, spectacles, reading glasses, etc. But the "another" that Jesus uses here means the exact same kind. The second would be identical, with no variations or differences from the first. Jesus is saying he will send another who is of the exact same essence as Jesus. Jesus is the first Comforter, Helper, and Counselor.

As Jesus speaks these words, the Spirit is with the disciples through Jesus himself; we can see this in the

---

c John 14:17 Some early manuscripts *and is*

often-overlooked phrase, "for he lives with you." A careful reading of the verb tenses reveals an astonishing truth. Jesus has the Spirit inside of him, so the Spirit is with the disciples now (because Jesus is with them); but after Jesus returns to the Father, the Spirit will dwell *inside* the disciples. This is the fulfillment of passages such as Ezekiel 36:26-27, where God promises not only to remove our hearts of stone and give us hearts of flesh, but also to put his Spirit *in* us.

John's Gospel is filled with truths about the Holy Spirit:

- The Spirit will be with us forever (14:16).
- The world at large cannot accept the Spirit (14:17).
- The Spirit lives with us and in us (14:17).
- The Spirit teaches us (14:26).
- The Spirit reminds us of Jesus' words (14:26; 15:26).
- The Spirit convicts us of sin, shows us God's righteousness, and announces God's judgment on evil (16:8).
- The Spirit guides us into truth and gives insights into future events (16:13).
- The Spirit brings glory to Christ (16:14).

We find additional attributes of the Holy Spirit described in other sections of the Bible. Scripture tells us that the Holy Spirit—

- has a mind and understanding (Acts 15:28);
- is a channel of God's love (Romans 5:5);
- helps us in our prayers (Romans 8:26; Jude 1:20-21);
- has power (Romans 15:13);
- knows the deep things of God (1 Corinthians 2:10-11);
- can be grieved (Ephesians 4:30); and
- inspired the prophets (2 Peter 1:21).

Jesus knows he must leave the disciples, but the Holy Spirit will not. The Holy Spirit will be with them—and with us—forever.

The King James Version uses the term "Holy Ghost." I believe this is an unfortunate translation that is misleading to many people today. For years, people have thought of the Holy Spirit as like Casper the Friendly Ghost. But the Holy Spirit is not some kind of a floating fog.

Jesus uses a curious term for the Holy Spirit: the Greek word *parakletos*. This word is translated "advocate," which literally means "called to one's side." And the word is exclusive to the writings of John. Those who work for the courts might think of an advocate as being a lawyer who defends a client in court. The earlier version of the NIV (1984) translated the word as "counselor." When high school and college students hear the word *counselor*, they may think of a person who helps them choose their courses for the school year, gives them advice about colleges, and helps them make plans for the future. There are also marriage counselors, camp counselors, and psychological counselors. Both *advocate* and *counselor* describe someone who comes alongside another person. The counselor or advocate is there to help, to point out certain things, and to guide his or her client to see the truth.

Muslims claim this verse is a reference to Muhammad, whom they see as Jesus' successor. The problem is that Muhammad came along five centuries later; therefore, he wasn't able to be inside these early disciples. Also, Muhammad was a man who eventually died—while the Holy Spirit remains.

Jesus says the world won't accept the Holy Spirit—whom they can't see—because the world didn't recognize him, Jesus the Messiah, the first Advocate whom they *could* see. Christ is warning the disciples in this verse that many people in the world won't respond—despite all that he has left for them.

The disciples know the Holy Spirit because this Spirit descended on Jesus at his baptism. The Holy Spirit in the Old Testament would come to individuals for a brief period of time, empowering men and women to accomplish God's work. But this passage tells us that the Holy Spirit now lives inside believers and remains with them forever. Ephesians 2:22 affirms, "And in him you too are being built together to become a dwelling in which God lives by his Spirit."

John 14:18-19

18 "I will not leave you as orphans; I will come to you. 19 Before long, the world will not see me anymore, but you will see me. Because I live, you also will live."

There are at least three different understandings of this verse:

1. Some say Jesus is talking about the rapture, a moment near the end of time when believers will be gathered together in the air to meet Christ. But others argue that if this were a reference to the rapture, it would read, "I will come *for* you," not "*to* you."
2. Some believe Jesus is referring to his resurrection, but he will walk on the earth for only 40 more days.
3. Others understand this as a reference to the mystery of the Trinity. When the Holy Spirit comes into our lives as Christians, Jesus also comes in. In fact, in Romans 8:9 the Holy Spirit is called the "Spirit of Christ." God the Father, God the Son, and God the Holy Spirit are all in there. Consider these Scriptures:

   • 1 John 4:12—"If we love one another, God lives in us and his love is made complete in us" (the Father).

- Colossians 1:27—"Christ in you, the hope of glory" (the Son).
- 1 Corinthians 6:19—"Do you not know that your bodies are temples of the Holy Spirit, who is in you, whom you have received from God?" (the Spirit).

John 14:20-24

20 "On that day you will realize that I am in my Father, and you are in me, and I am in you. 21 Whoever has my commands and keeps them is the one who loves me. The one who loves me will be loved by my Father, and I too will love them and show myself to them."

22 Then Judas (not Judas Iscariot) said, "But, Lord, why do you intend to show yourself to us and not to the world?"

23 Jesus replied, "Anyone who loves me will obey my teaching. My Father will love them, and we will come to them and make our home with them. 24 Anyone who does not love me will not obey my teaching. These words you hear are not my own; they belong to the Father who sent me."

"On that day" may refer to the resurrection or to the day of Pentecost when the Holy Spirit comes into the church (Acts 2). After Pentecost, Jesus—through the Holy Spirit—will dwell in his people permanently and will empower them to demonstrate their love through obedience to his commands.

Judas in verse 22 is not the one who betrayed Christ. If you were this man, you would definitely want this to be made clear (bummer of a name). This disciple is probably "Judas son of James," who is referenced in Luke 6:16 and Acts 1:13, not Judas the half-brother of Jesus (Matthew 13:55; Mark 6:3). He may also be referred to as either Libbias or Thaddeus.

"We will come to them and make our home with them" (14:23) is the only place in the New Testament where it directly states that both the Father and the Son will dwell in believers. Scripture also makes two things clear about our relationship with Christ.

As Christians, we are in Christ:

- "Therefore, there is now no condemnation for those who **are in Christ** Jesus" (Romans 8:1).
- "It is because of him that you are **in Christ** Jesus" (1 Corinthians 1:30).
- "Therefore, if anyone is **in Christ**, the new creation has come. The old has gone, the new is here!" (2 Corinthians 5:17).

And, Christ is also in us:

- "I have been crucified with Christ and I no longer live, but **Christ lives in me**" (Galatians 2:20).
- "To them God has chosen to make known among the Gentiles the glorious riches of this mystery, which is **Christ in you**, the hope of glory" (Colossians 1:27).

As parents, we tend to love people who love our kids. When I was a student at Trinity Evangelical Divinity School, Warren Benson was the academic dean. He was a terrific man of God—caring, bright, and sensitive. I had befriended his son years before I began attending the school. His son was also a terrific guy. Warren had to make a decision about whether the school would allow me to transfer two classes from my previous work into the Doctor of Ministry program. It was his call. He told me the transfer I'd proposed would be acceptable (as he did for many students). But he also added that he appreciated the time I'd spent with his son. I believe God responds to our love for his Son in a similar way.

—Les

John 14:25-26

25 "All this I have spoken while still with you. 26 But the Advocate, the Holy Spirit, whom the Father will send in my name, will teach you all things and will remind you of everything I have said to you."

Jesus says the Holy Spirit will take his place. The Spirit will teach as Christ taught. The Spirit desires what Christ desires. The Holy Spirit is not in the world to bring glory to himself. "He will glorify me because it is from me that he will receive what he will make known to you" (John 16:14). The Spirit of Truth goes out from the Father and will testify about Jesus. The Holy Spirit points to the Christ, not to himself. There are many people and groups today who seem to glorify the Holy Spirit more than Jesus. (I believe this grieves the Spirit.) There are others who limit the Holy Spirit.

Different understandings of this passage were among the disagreements that led to the split between the Eastern (Greek) Orthodox Church and the Western Roman (Latin) Catholic Church in 1054. The issue was whether the Spirit comes from the Father alone (Eastern), or from the Father and the Son together (Western). The East preferred to view the Spirit as an independent person sent from the Father. The West prefers not to separate the Spirit from the Son.

We see this verse being partially fulfilled in the disciples when the Holy Spirit inspires them in writing the Bible. For example, Acts 11:16 records Peter saying, "Then I remembered what the Lord had said . . ."

The Holy Spirit "will remind you of everything I have said to you" also happens to us today, in a way. When we face temptation, the Holy Spirit brings to our minds verses from the Bible that we've read or heard.

John 14:27

²⁷ "Peace I leave with you; my peace I give you. I do not give to you as the world gives. Do not let your hearts be troubled and do not be afraid."

In our pre-Christian days, we were at war with God. But when we became Christians, we had peace with God. And when we have peace with God, we have peace with one another. The world's peace is determined by circumstances. It is a counterfeit peace. Jesus is offering the real deal. Peace is not just the absence of war and tension. True peace devours fear and trouble and turns it into joy. It's a peace that passes all understanding; in other words, it may not seem "reasonable" in the middle of the circumstances we face.

> If you look at the world, you'll be distressed. If you look within, you'll be depressed. If you look at God you'll be at rest."
> — **Corrie ten Boom**

But before you can have the peace *of* God, you must have peace *with* God. Remember the bumper sticker: "No God, No Peace. Know God, Know Peace." Scripture affirms that peace is central to God's nature:

- "peace through Jesus Christ" (Acts 10:36)
- "For God is not a God of disorder but of peace" (1 Corinthians 14:33)
- "But the fruit of the Spirit is . . . peace . . ." (Galatians 5:22)
- "And the God of peace will be with you" (Philippians 4:9)
- "the God of peace" (1 Thessalonians 5:23; Hebrews 13:20)
- "king of peace" (Hebrews 7:2)

Jesus Christ is the Lord of Peace. The Holy Spirit is the Messenger of peace. And prayer is the vehicle of peace. As the old hymn goes: "O what peace we often forfeit, O what needless pain we bear; all because we do not carry, everything to God in prayer" ("What a Friend We Have in Jesus," Joseph M. Scriven).

An Aussie private . . . had been caught outside the fence while trying to obtain medicine from the Thais for his sick friends. He was summarily tried and sentenced to death [by the Japanese prison authorities].

On the morning set for his execution he marched cheerfully between his guards to the parade-ground. The Japanese were out in full force to observe the scene. The Aussie was permitted to have his commanding officer and a chaplain in attendance as witnesses. The party came to a halt. The CO and the chaplain were waved to one side, and the Aussie was left standing alone.

Calmly, he surveyed his executioners. He knelt down and drew a small copy of the New Testament from the pocket of his ragged shorts. Unhurriedly, his lips moving but no sound coming from them, he read a passage to himself.

What that passage was, no one will ever know. I cannot help wondering, however, if it was not those words addressed by Jesus to his disciples in the Upper Room . . .

He finished reading, returned his New Testament to his pocket, looked up, and saw the distressed face of his chaplain. He smiled, waved to him and called out, "Cheer up, Padre, it isn't as bad as all that. I'll be all right."

He nodded to his executioner as a sign that he was ready. He knelt down, and bent his head forward to expose his neck. The Samurai sword flashed in the sunlight.

—Ernest Gordon, *To End All Wars*

The Greek word *tarasso* is translated as "trouble" here; it's the same word used in John 13:21, "Jesus was troubled in spirit." Just as Jesus was able to quiet his own heart, he gives his disciples the tools and resources to quiet theirs.

John 14:28

28 "You heard me say, 'I am going away and I am coming back to you.' If you loved me, you would be glad that I am going to the Father, for the Father is greater than I."

Jesus is going back to his Father, and he tells the disciples they should be glad. He knows that when he returns to his Father, he will be restored to full glory again. The 33 years of humiliation that Jesus experienced on this earth are finishing; he looks forward to getting back to where he was before the world began. The disciples should also be glad because Jesus is coming back in the form of the Holy Spirit.

> Over the last 40 years, I've had the privilege of speaking all over the United States and in several foreign countries. As such, I've been on way too many airplanes. At this point in my life, the best part about these trips is coming home. As I travel, I often have a deep longing to be back in my own home and with my own family, sleeping in my own bed. When seasoned airline travelers are heading home, they'll often sit in an aisle seat close to the front of the plane. They can't wait for the final "ding" after the plane stops at the gate, the sound that lets you know it's okay to get out of your seat. Veteran flyers will get up quickly, grab their carry-on bags, and head for the exit. In this passage Jesus longs to be home with his Father. He is homesick "for the joy set before him" (Hebrews 12:2).
>
> **—Les**

The phrase "the Father is greater than I" has stirred up quite a controversy. We've already encountered several passages in John where Jesus is depicted as being equal to God or one with God (1:1-18; 5:16-18; 10:30; 20:28). This seemingly contradictory statement indicates that only at this point in time, Jesus has taken on the subordinate role as a necessary part of the incarnation. This time of temporary subordination would soon be ending, as Jesus would return to the glory he once had with the Father.

Augustine and others have explained this passage by saying the Son is subordinate in person but not in essence. Many of Christ's early followers who were raised as Jews were unsettled by the idea of placing Jesus on par with God; to them, this seemed to compromise their monotheistic faith. John answers that criticism by emphasizing more than any other Gospel that Jesus is God's Son, subordinate to the Father only while on earth. This truth is underscored by Philippians 2:5–11—

> In your relationships with one another, have the same mindset as Christ Jesus: Who, being in very nature God, did not consider equality with God something to be used to his own advantage; rather, he made himself nothing by taking the very nature of a servant, being made in human likeness. And being found in appearance as a man, he humbled himself by becoming obedient to death—even death on a cross! Therefore God exalted him to the highest place and gave him the name that is above every name, that at the name of Jesus every knee should bow, in heaven and on earth and under the earth, and every tongue acknowledge that Jesus Christ is Lord, to the glory of God the Father.

God sent Jesus to join the human experience, which means to make a lot of mistakes. Jesus didn't arrive here knowing how to walk. He had fingers and toes, confusion, sexual feelings, crazy human internal processes. He had the same prejudices as the rest of his tribe: he had to learn that the Canaanite woman was a person. He had to suffer the hardships and tedium and

> setbacks of being a regular person. If he hadn't, the incarnation would mean nothing.
>
> — **Anne Lamott, *Grace (Eventually): Thoughts on Faith***

John 14:29-31

[29] "I have told you now before it happens, so that when it does happen you will believe. [30] I will not say much more to you, for the prince of this world is coming. He has no hold over me, [31] but he comes so that the world may learn that I love the Father and do exactly what my Father has commanded me.

"Come now; let us leave."

The "prince of this world" is Satan (12:30-33). Jesus could sense Satan's coming. He may have seen Satan enter Judas. This would be Jesus' final conflict and struggle with Satan during his earthly ministry.

Jesus had conflicts with Satan throughout his life:

- Satan had Herod decree that all male babies born around the time of Jesus' birth be killed.
- Satan tempted Jesus in the wilderness for 40 days.
- Satan led both people and demons to confront Jesus with extreme hatred.

Satan has a hold on people because of their fallen state. Since Jesus was sinless throughout his life, Satan had no hold on him. Satan had nothing on Jesus with which to condemn him. There was no vulnerable spot on Jesus. He was tested in every way, yet he never sinned. If we love and obey Jesus and align ourselves closely with God's purposes, Satan will have no power over us.

Some say, "But isn't Satan still running around?" Yes, but he has been rendered powerless. The only time Satan can affect our lives is when we let him. Satan has already been defeated. He may be the prince of this world, but there is One more powerful than him. Revelation 1:5 says, "Jesus Christ, who is the faithful witness, the firstborn from the dead, and the ruler of the kings of the earth." Clearly, Jesus is greater than any earthly ruler—and that includes Satan.

Satan is a "lame duck" whose limited power will soon end. In the United States, presidential elections occur in early November, but the person elected does not take office until January. During the interim months, the seated president is referred to as a lame duck, because this president still has the title, but his or her real power and influence has been diminished. In the same way, Satan's power has been diminished. Satan exists and influences the powers of this world only because God allows this. Jesus stresses the importance of his followers being obedient, and here he sets the example by his obedience to the Father.

During an appearance on the *Focus on the Family* radio show, Frank Peretti told the story of a vacationing family that was driving along in their car, windows rolled down, enjoying the warm summer breeze of the sunny day. All of a sudden a big black bee darted in the window and started buzzing around inside the car. A little girl, highly allergic to bee stings, cringes in the back seat. If she is stung, she could die within an hour. "Oh, Daddy," she squeals in terror. "It's a bee! It's going to sting me!"

The father pulls the car over to a stop, and reaches back to try to catch the bee. Buzzing around towards him, the bee bumps against the front windshield where the father traps it in his fist. Holding it in his closed hand, the father waits for the inevitable sting. The bee stings the father's hand and in pain, the father lets go of the bee.

> The bee is loose in the car again. The little girl again panics. "Daddy, it's going to sting me!"
>
> The father gently says, "No honey, he's not going to sting you now. Look at my hand." She sees the bee's stinger in his hand.
>
> Likewise, Jesus says to us, "Look at my hands." He has Satan's sting, the sting of death, the sting of sin, the sting of deceit. Jesus has all of those stingers in his hands. When you see that nail-scarred hand, realize that, on your behalf, Jesus took all the pain that Satan could throw at him. Jesus has reduced Satan to a big black bee that's lost its stinger—all Satan can do now is buzz. That's the victory that Jesus won for you!

In the final sentence of chapter 14, Jesus says, "Come now; let us leave." Some find this to be a problem because Jesus continues to instruct the disciples for three more chapters (15–17). There is no clear indication that they leave the room until John 18:1 where it says, "When he had finished praying, Jesus left with his disciples and crossed the Kidron Valley."

John doesn't say whether Jesus and the disciples leave the room at this point. Some believe that they remain in the upper room, and that by saying it was time to "leave," Jesus was suggesting not a change of location, but a change of topics. Still others think the group may have left the room at this point and continued the conversations found in the next three chapters as they slowly walk across the Kidron Valley.

READ BETWEEN THE LINES

- If you love Jesus, what will you do?
- What does Jesus mean by saying the Father will send the Advocate? Who is the first Advocate?
- Where does the Spirit of Truth live?

- What does Jesus mean when he says, "I will come to you"?
- What is the difference between the world's peace and the peace of Christ?
- Why should the disciples be glad that Jesus is going to the Father?
- What does Jesus mean when he says "the Father is greater than I"?
- Describe the relationship between love and obedience.
- Who is the Prince of this world? Why is he a "lame duck"?

WELCOME TO MY WORLD

- How are we to show love to one another (13:36)?
- How are we to show love to Jesus (14:15)?
- What do I know about the Holy Spirit?
- What image comes to mind when I think of the Holy Spirit?
- What makes someone a good counselor?
- If I can't see the Holy Spirit, how do I know the Spirit is there?
- What is the difference between "Jesus shows us the way" and "Jesus is the way"?
- How many of my friends who say they love Jesus actually obey his commands?
- Am I at peace? What does that mean?
- Who lives in me and in whom do I live? What does that mean in my life?
- Are the Father, Son, and Holy Spirit occasional guests in my life, or are they residents and owners?

- What does it feel like to experience God's presence and God's peace?
- How has the Holy Spirit spoken to me personally through God's Word?
- Does the prince of this world have a hold on me? If yes, how? If no, how do I keep it that way?

The Vine and the Branches

Jesus is speaking with his disciples on the night before the crucifixion. It's not clear whether they have left the upper room or not (14:31). If they've left the room, they would likely be walking quietly through the city of Jerusalem and down into the Kidron Valley, which would have brought them to the garden of Gethsemane on the Mount of Olives.

John 15:1-3

1 "I am the true vine, and my Father is the gardener. 2 He cuts off every branch in me that bears no fruit, while every branch that does bear fruit he prunes[a] so that it will be even more fruitful. 3 You are already clean because of the word I have spoken to you."

The first eight verses of chapter 15 command the disciples to remain in Jesus. The nine verses that follow command the disciples to love one another. The sequence is significant; they will be able to love one another only if they remain in Jesus.

If Jesus and the disciples are already walking, they may have passed a vine with branches. Or they may have seen the magnificent temple structure with its enormous grapevine made of pure gold around the entrance to the Holy Place.

Grapes are the most widely grown fruit in the world. There is archeological evidence from Egyptian tombs showing that grapes were being cultivated 2,500 years before Christ. Jewish coins from Jesus' day also contained the stamped image of a vine with branches.

In the Old Testament, the vine or vineyard is a symbol for Israel. "What more could have been done for my vineyard than I have done for it?" says the Lord through the prophet Isaiah. "When I looked for good grapes, why did it yield only bad? . . . The vineyard of the LORD Almighty is the nation of

a John 15:2 The Greek for *he prunes* also means *he cleans.*

Israel" (Isaiah 5:4, 7). We see a similar reference to Israel again in Jeremiah 2:21—"I had planted you like a choice vine of sound and reliable stock. How then did you turn against me into a corrupt, wild vine?" The symbol of the vine would have been as familiar to a first-century Jew as the Stars and Stripes or the bald eagle are to Americans today.

The vine (Israel) refused to give God love and obedience. So Jesus now says that *he* is the vine who will take the place of Israel. In order to be connected to the Gardener (God), we must remain a part of the vine and stay connected to Jesus.

By saying that he is the true vine—and also the true tabernacle (Hebrews 8:1-2), true light (1:9), and true bread (6:32-33)—Jesus makes it clear that there are false vines. The many false vines that people cling to today include bank accounts, educational degrees, popularity, personality, fame, possessions, and false religious systems.

Here, Jesus is showing how the Father (the Gardener) cares for the Son (the true vine) and those who belong to the Son, his disciples (the branches). As Gardener, the Father has two specific duties.

First, the gardener cuts off branches that have borne no fruit because these tend to sap energy from the fruit-bearing branches. Dead branches may also have diseases and insects that could spread to the healthy branches. This may refer to people like those described in 1 John 2:19, "They went out from us, but they did not really belong to us. For if they had belonged to us, they would have remained with us; but their going showed that none of them belonged to us." Such people may attend every religious meeting, but their commitment is superficial; and they never make Jesus their Lord. Judas would be the ultimate example of such a dead branch.

Second, the gardener constantly prunes those branches that do bear fruit so they will bear even *more* fruit. Little shoots must be removed because they can rob energy from the main branches, limiting their fruit production. In the first three to five years of life, vines are purposely pruned back quite dramatically in order to "train" them and prevent them from bearing fruit. This is done so the plant can develop strength and energy for the time when it will produce fruit.

The Greek word *kathairo* which is translated as "to prune" can also be translated as "to cleanse." And we see in verse 3 that God cleanses us through his Word. Just as a knife is used in pruning the branches, the knife used here is the Word of God, which is "sharper than any double-edged sword" (Hebrews 4:12). It leaps off the pages of the Bible. Our initial salvation came through the Word (Romans 10:17) and our continual pruning also comes through the Word.

God doesn't stand far away from us with his whip and yell down from heaven: "BEAR FRUIT!" The fruit of our lives grows naturally out of an intimacy with God. God is working alongside us, helping us to bear fruit. "For we are God's handiwork, created in Christ Jesus to do good works, which God prepared in advance for us to do" (Ephesians 2:10). Our works and the fruit we bear do not save us, but the evidence that we are saved can be seen in our lives. As Matthew 7:16-17 notes, "By their fruit you will recognize them. Do people pick grapes from thornbushes, or figs from thistles? Likewise, every good tree bears good fruit, but a bad tree bears bad fruit."

John 15:4-5

⁴ "Remain in me, as I also remain in you. No branch can bear fruit by itself; it must remain in the vine. Neither can you bear fruit unless you remain in me.

⁵ "I am the vine; you are the branches. If you remain in me and I in you, you will bear much fruit; apart from me you can do nothing."

We cannot produce fruit on our own. To remain in Christ means to depend on the Lord moment by moment, day by day, month by month, and year by year.

God wants us to have lives that are productive. In the Old Testament, there are more than 100 references to fruit. And in the New Testament, fruit is mentioned 70 times. But apart from God, there is no fruit at all. We can see the progression of healthy growth from verses 2 to 5: "no fruit" (15:2); "does bear fruit" (15:2); "even more fruitful" (15:2); and "bear much fruit" (15:5).

A unique paraphrase of what Jesus is saying in this passage puts it this way: "I am the true generator, and you are the power lines. A power line can't produce electricity by itself." The fruit that our lives bear is a byproduct of our being connected to Jesus. Faithfulness seems to be the key—simply hanging in there and staying close to Jesus.

John 15:6

⁶ "If you do not remain in me, you are like a branch that is thrown away and withers; such branches are picked up, thrown into the fire and burned."

If we do not have a living connection with Jesus, we will wither away, like seeds planted on rocky ground (Matthew 13:1-9). But what does Jesus mean when he says those who do not remain in him will be "picked up, thrown into the fire and burned"? This passage has been interpreted in several different ways.

Some suggest John is talking about physical death. While the person's salvation may be intact, God doesn't want his reputation to be ruined by an unproductive branch—so these unproductive people are removed from the earth.

Another view of this passage draws on 1 Corinthians 3:11-15—

For no one can lay any foundation other than the one already laid, which is Jesus Christ. If anyone builds on this foundation using gold, silver, costly stones, wood, hay or straw, their work will be shown for what it is, because the Day will bring it to light. It will be revealed with fire, and the fire will test the quality of each person's work. If what has been built survives, the builder will receive a reward. If it is burned up, the builder will suffer loss but yet will be saved—even though only as one escaping through the flames.

In other words, the *works* are tossed into the fire and tested—not the person.

Others view this passage as referring to those who aren't saved because they've never genuinely given their lives to the Lord. James 2:19, "You believe that there is one God. Good! Even the demons believe that—and shudder."

Finally, there are others who suggest this verse refers to true believers who have lost their salvation. Romans 11:20-22 says—

But they were broken off because of unbelief, and you stand by faith. Do not be arrogant, but tremble. For if God did not spare the natural branches, he will not spare you either. Consider therefore the kindness and sternness of God: sternness to those who fell, but kindness to you, provided that you continue in his kindness. Otherwise, you also will be cut off.

It may also be helpful to look at Hebrews 6:8—"But land that produces thorns and thistles is worthless and is in danger of being cursed. In the end it will be burned."

It is unwise to build a theological doctrine on a parable or allegory. Jesus was teaching one main truth—the fruitful life of the believer—and we must not press the details too much.

—Warren W. Wiersbe, *The Bible Exposition Commentary: New Testament, Volume 1,* 356

John 15:7-11

7 "If you remain in me and my words remain in you, ask whatever you wish, and it will be done for you. **8** This is to my Father's glory, that you bear much fruit, showing yourselves to be my disciples.

9 "As the Father has loved me, so have I loved you. Now remain in my love. **10** If you keep my commands, you will remain in my love, just as I have kept my Father's commands and remain in his love. **11** I have told you this so that my joy may be in you and that your joy may be complete."

If we remain in Jesus, whatever we wish will be done (see 14:13-14). Jesus lays out four blessings that come to those who remain (abide) in him:

1. The first blessing is that we'll produce much fruit (15:5).
2. The second blessing is that God will answer our prayers (15:7).
3. The third blessing is that our lives will bring glory to God (15:8).
4. The fourth blessing is that we'll be filled with joy (15:11).

After David sinned with Bathsheba, he experienced the loss of joy that comes when our relationship with God is distorted by sin. He prayed, "Restore to me the joy of your salvation and grant me a willing spirit, to sustain me" (Psalm 51:12). Joy is deeper than a happiness that is contingent on circumstances. True joy rises above the rolling waves of circumstances. True joy goes beyond contentment. It means being at peace with God and self, even in the midst of insecurity and turmoil.

John 15:12-13

¹² "My command is this: Love each other as I have loved you. ¹³ Greater love has no one than this: to lay down one's life for one's friends."

We are to love one another as Jesus has loved us. But how do we do this? How do we love as Jesus loved? The answer is that we do it by allowing Jesus to come into every part of our lives and love others *through* us.

Here's one way to think of it: What if when Michelangelo was halfway finished sculpting his statue *David*, he gave you his chisel and told you to go ahead and finish chipping away at it? You'd probably say, "No way." But if Michelangelo could get inside your body, under your skin, and into your hands, then you could do it.

Or what if Beethoven asked you to sit down at the piano and perform a concert featuring his latest work? Again, you'd probably say there's no way you could do it. But if Beethoven could somehow get into your body, under your skin, and into your hands, then you could do it.

What if Leonardo da Vinci went on vacation and handed you his paintbrushes to finish painting *The Last Supper*? You might ask, "Where are the numbers?" Or you might say, "The only things I can draw are flies." But if da Vinci could get into your body, under your skin, and into your hands, then you could do it. (Plus, think of the fun you could have if you signed up for Art 101 at the local community college. You could explain that you'd never had any art training whatsoever. But then when you began to paint, the entire class would be blown away by your talent!)

In the same way, we are capable of loving people as Jesus loved only because we have Jesus inside of us. Romans 5:5 declares, "God's love has been poured out into our hearts through the Holy Spirit." Jesus loves through us.

And seeing the way we love one another, the world is drawn to Christ.

In the first five centuries of the Christian faith, two of the catalysts in drawing people to Christ were the martyrs (those who died for their faith) and the unfaltering commitment of Christians to the well-being of others. Roman Emperor Julian the Apostate wrote in exasperation, "These impious Galileans not only feed their own poor, but ours also; welcoming them into their agapae [love feasts], they attract them, as children are attracted, with cakes." When a plague hit, it was the Christians who stayed and cared for others. And by doing so, they impacted the world.

In Charles Dickens's book *A Tale of Two Cities*, Charles Darnay and Sydney Carton become friends in the midst of the insanity of the French Revolution. Darnay, a young Frenchman, gets thrown into a dungeon having been wrongly sentenced to death for supposedly betraying the people. He is scheduled to go to the guillotine the next day. Sydney Carton receives word of Darnay's imprisonment. Carton is a loose-living English lawyer who is in love with Darnay's wife. Through a chain of events, Carton gets into the dungeon and changes garments with Darnay, allowing the Frenchman to escape. And the next morning, Carton takes the place of the husband of the woman he adores. He makes his way up the steps to the guillotine, repeating the words from John's Gospel, "I am the Resurrection and the Life, saith the Lord: he that believeth in me, though he were dead, yet shall he live: and whosoever liveth and believeth in me shall never die." At the end of the book, Dickens includes this moving last line of Sydney Carton: "It is a far, far better thing that I do, than I have ever done; it is a far, far better rest that I go to, than I have ever known." These words echo Jesus' statement in John 15:13—"Greater love has no one than this: to lay down one's life for one's friends."

—Les

Some have taken John 15:13 out of context and tried using Jesus' words about laying down one's life to justify wars and settle disputes. But Jesus laid down his life to make us more human, not less.

John 15:14-15

14 "You are my friends if you do what I command. 15 I no longer call you servants, because a servant does not know his master's business. Instead, I have called you friends, for everything that I learned from my Father I have made known to you."

Jesus calls his followers "friends." Many people have lots of acquaintances but very few friends. What an honor that we—and all who do what Christ commands—would be called his friends. That places us in good company, along with two heroes of the Old Testament whom the Scriptures refer to as friends of God: Abraham (2 Chronicles 20:7) and Moses (Exodus 33:11).

A servant is simply told what to do. He or she is never told why; the servant is expected to do as requested. Servants just work to get their pay (and avoid punishment). Friends are expected to understand the will of the master. Servants are not. We are more than servants; we are friends of Jesus.

The Greek word *philos* is translated as "friend" in this passage, and it refers to the inner circle of people around a king or emperor. Friends of the king would be close to him and know his secrets, but they would still be subject to him and would obey his commands.

John 15:16

16 "You did not choose me, but I chose you and appointed you so that you might go and bear fruit—fruit that will last—and so that whatever you ask in my name the Father will give you."

Jesus calls every human being to come to him, and then he sends each of us back out into the world to bear long-lasting fruit. We aren't supposed to just sit around holding hands and singing songs until Jesus comes again.

We already know that *fruit* can be understood here to mean "good works" in general; but more specifically, fruit seems to be relational. Here are five actions that the Bible refers to as *fruit*:

1. **Having a life patterned after Jesus' life.** "But the fruit of the Spirit is love, joy, peace, forbearance, kindness, goodness, faithfulness, gentleness and self-control" (Galatians 5:22-23). The fruit of the Spirit is concerned not so much with service as it is with personal character.

2. **Praising God.** "Through Jesus, therefore, let us continually offer to God a sacrifice of praise—the fruit of lips that openly profess his name" (Hebrews 13:15).

3. **Contributing to those in need (when done in love).** "Not that I desire your gifts; what I desire is that more be credited to your account" (Philippians 4:17). Here the apostle Paul is saying he doesn't want people to give him gifts for his sake, but because giving to others produces fruit in the lives of the givers.

4. **Pleasing God.** "For this reason, since the day we heard about you, we have not stopped praying for you. We continually ask God to fill you with the knowledge of his will through all the wisdom and understanding that the Spirit gives, so that you may live a life worthy of the Lord and please him in every way: bearing fruit in every good work, growing in the knowledge of God" (Colossians 1:9-10; see also 2 Peter 1:5-8).

5. **Bringing people to Jesus.** "Don't you have a saying, 'It's still four months until harvest'? I tell you,

open your eyes and look at the fields! They are ripe for harvest. Even now the one who reaps draws a wage and harvests a crop for eternal life, so that the sower and the reaper may be glad together" (John 4:35-36). Both the person who sows and the person who reaps are considered fruit-bearers.

John 15:17

¹⁷ "**This is my command: Love each other.**"

The passage closes with a summary command: "Love each other." Jesus knows that the disciples, then and now, will need to love one another and stay close to each other as he warns in Mark 13:9—"You must be on your guard. You will be handed over to the local councils and flogged in the synagogues."

READ BETWEEN THE LINES

- Why would Jesus use the vine as an illustration?
- Who is the true vine? What does this mean?
- What does a gardener do?
- What is the key to bearing fruit?
- How does the Word of God cleanse?
- What does it mean to remain in Jesus?
- What does Jesus mean when he says, "apart from me you can do nothing" (v. 5)?
- How can we remain in God's love?
- How do obedience and love go together?
- How does Jesus' command in John 15:12-13 compare with John 13:34-35?

WELCOME TO MY WORLD

- How have I been pruned in my life?
- What kinds of false vines do I see people clinging to?
- What is the connection between obedience and prayer?
- How is joy evident in my life?
- If Jesus is our friend, what can we give to him?
- What would the Gardener want to do in my life right now?
- How can I stay connected to Jesus? What makes it difficult to remain in the vine?
- Do I consider myself a friend of God?

The World Hates the Disciples

John 15:18-19

18 "If the world hates you, keep in mind that it hated me first. 19 If you belonged to the world, it would love you as its own. As it is, you do not belong to the world, but I have chosen you out of the world. That is why the world hates you."

In this section Jesus wants the disciples to know that just because they are blessed to be his friends, this doesn't mean their lives will be easy. In fact, just the opposite. Jesus moves from talking about love to talking about hatred. He is giving them a realistic view of life.

The "world" being referred to here is the part of the human system that opposes God's purposes and has fallen under Satan's influence. Jesus came to save the world (3:16), but the world rejected him (12:48); so he began separating his own people from the world. Jesus is letting his disciples know that if they are faithful to him, they will go through the same kind of persecution that he'll soon experience.

And the question becomes . . . If we love God and we love them, why in the world would they declare war on us? And I think Jesus has told us, very simply, that because he has come into this world, others have become cognizant of their sin. It's very simple, that as people are living in darkness, light comes, and people run from the light. And if you love God to any degree, you will find that there are certain people that dislike you. Not because you have done anything to them, but just your existence is a condemnation on their conduct. Just the way you are is an assault upon their person. What I mean by that is this: if you are walking with God uprightly, you are pointing out all the crookedness in their life.

—Mark Driscoll, Sermon notes

The world loves crummy people because they make the world feel better. But the church is, in some sense, a conscience to the world. Jesus is saying that the world is going to despise you, persecute you, and kill you—and they'll think they're doing it all for God. This isn't new. In Genesis 4:1-8 we learn that Cain was jealous of his brother Abel—apparently because Abel was worshiping the Lord—and so Cain killed him.

The early Christians were hated and accused of many things:

- They were maligned for not worshiping Caesar or calling him "Lord." This accusation was true; they claimed Jesus as Lord.

- They were called cannibals because non-Christians misunderstood the Communion service.

- They were accused of immoral behavior because non-Christians misunderstood the "love feasts" (Jude 1:12) and the practice of "greeting one another with a holy kiss" (Romans 16:16).

- They were charged with breaking up families when one spouse became a Christian and the other spouse did not.

- They were called incendiaries because of their talk about hell and fire. Emperor Nero falsely blamed Christians for the burning of Rome.

Nero was known for his persecution of Christians. Ancient historians tell us that Nero would throw large political and civic events on the grounds of his home, and he'd need light to illuminate the evening parties. So Christians would be covered in wax or wrapped in pitch and resin, impaled on a pole, and then their bodies would be set on fire to serve as torches to illuminate his parties.

Nero was also known for "drawing and quartering" his enemies. A rope was tied to each of the four limbs of a prisoner, and the ropes were then tied to four horses facing different directions. Nero would whip the horses to send them running, and the young men would be dismembered while they were still very much alive. In the large Roman amphitheaters, the primary entertainment included the murdering of Christians by feeding them to wild animals, running them through with swords, or having gladiators chase them around for sport.

Many Christians were killed for simply being a Christian. The Roman historian Tacitus wrote, "Covered with the skins of beasts, [the Christians] were torn by dogs and perished, or were nailed to crosses, or were doomed to the flames and burnt, to serve as nightly illumination, when the daylight had expired." According to ancient Christian tradition, all of the disciples except John were killed for being Christians. Peter, Andrew, and James son of Alphaeus were all crucified. Both James son of Zebedee and the apostle Paul were beheaded. Bartholomew was whipped to death. Thomas was stabbed with spears. Mark was dragged to death through the streets of Alexandria. Stephen, the first martyr, was murdered by stoning (Acts 7:54-60), as was Philip. Matthew, the author of the Gospel bearing his name, was said to have been executed by being bludgeoned with a long-handled axe and then run through with a sword. Tradition says that Matthias, who replaced Judas Iscariot as the twelfth disciple (Acts 1:23-26), was also stoned and beheaded.

It was common in that day for the government to behead its opponents and display the heads on posts in a public area as basically a testimony to all who walked by. When Christians were executed, the message was clear: Do not mess with the government, and do not continue worshipping Jesus Christ.

John 15:18-19

Women were also persecuted for their faith. Agatha was a Christian woman who refused to have sexual relations with a Roman ruler who propositioned her multiple times. The Roman official gave her one more chance to sleep with him. When she refused and tried to share her faith with him, he had her scourged and burned with irons. Hooks were put into her flesh, and she was laid naked upon a bed of hot coals and glass. Although she was near death, she still did not die. So he imprisoned her, leaving her to deteriorate and die a slow, painful death.

To strike terror in the hearts of the Christian families, authorities arrested a woman named Perpetua, a godly woman who loved the Lord. Church history tells us she was very pregnant and near her due date. They put her in the coliseum where she and her unborn child were attacked and killed by wild boars.

While persecution wasn't constant, there is no doubt that many early Christians faced torture, cruelty, and violence. Even today, there are many places in the world where Christians face hostility and violence because of their faith.

John was about to be exiled to the isle of Patmos. He'd already seen most of his good friends killed by the sword or the lion because of their faith in Christ. So he wanted to equip those who remained—and us, for the days ahead.

John 15:20-25

20 "Remember what I told you: 'A servant is not greater than his master.'[b] If they persecuted me, they will persecute you also. If they obeyed my teaching, they will obey yours also. **21** They will treat you this way because of my name, for they do not know the one who sent me. **22** If I had not come and spoken to them, they would not be guilty of sin; but now they have no excuse for their sin.

b John 15:20 See John 13:16

23 Whoever hates me hates my Father as well. 24 If I had not done among them the works no one else did, they would not be guilty of sin. As it is, they have seen, and yet they have hated both me and my Father. 25 But this is to fulfill what is written in their Law: 'They hated me without reason.'"c

Just as some loved Christ while others hated him, some will love you while others hate you as you share your faith. When you confront the world, you get a reaction. If you aren't getting a reaction, then you aren't confronting the world.

Jesus says the world will persecute his followers "because of my name." This happens because Christians claim that Jesus is Lord, and that means no one and nothing else can claim that title. Roman emperors claimed the title of "Lord" for themselves. Roman Emperor Domitian, who probably reigned at the time John wrote his Gospel, insisted on being called "Lord and God" when addressed.

We need to insert a disclaimer here: There's a big difference between enduring persecution and picking a fight. Some Christians are so obnoxious and lacking of all social skills that they cause a lot of problems for themselves. They think they're suffering for Jesus, when they're really suffering from problems they've created through their own behavior. These Christians are an embarrassment to the rest of us; unfortunately, they tend to be the ones who proudly display bumper stickers to let everyone know they are Christians—even though their lives don't show it. They're also the ones who tend to be featured in magazines and on television shows, giving the church a bad name.

Verse 22 refers to those who have sinned by willfully rejecting Jesus despite having total revelation. The leaders of Jesus' day had the advantage of having the Son of God walking among them. When they rejected Jesus, they were

c John 15:25 See Psalms 35:19; 69:4

guilty—and they have no excuse because they saw Jesus and his good works.

Some Christians have come to the conclusion that Christians should escape the world by moving to some isolated area. However, I believe the Lord's plan is not to take us out of the world, but to give us protection as we live in the world for him (17:15). The answer is not to lead a survival group to some isolated place in Oregon where we can all eat canary mix and sing hymns. The answer is to live in this world and love it as Christ did.

READ BETWEEN THE LINES

- What does it mean to "belong to the world"?
- What does it mean to be "out of the world"?
- Why did the world hate believers in the first century?
- Why were believers treated this way?
- Why does the world hate both Jesus and the Father?
- What do you see in these verses about the relationship of the Father, the Son, and the disciples?
- How did Jesus prepare his disciples for the persecution to come?

WELCOME TO MY WORLD

- How does my world respond to Christians?
- How have I experienced people not liking me or my friends because of our faith?
- How do and should Christians react to the world?
- How do I respond to disapproval from the world?

The Work of the Holy Spirit

John 15:26-27

26 "When the Advocate comes, whom I will send to you from the Father—the Spirit of truth who goes out from the Father—he will testify about me. 27 And you also must testify, for you have been with me from the beginning."

The Holy Spirit is the third part of the Trinity (1:1-2). There is one God who exists as God the Father, God the Son, and God the Holy Spirit. The Holy Spirit is mentioned numerous times in John (3:1-8; 3:34; 4:23-24; 7:37-29; 14:15-17, 25-26; 15:26-27; 16:7-11, 12-15; 20:21-22), beginning in the very first chapter with the account of Jesus' baptism:

> Then John [the Baptist] gave this testimony: "I saw the Spirit come down from heaven as a dove and remain on him. And I myself did not know him, but the one who sent me to baptize with water told me, 'The man on whom you see the Spirit come down and remain is the one who will baptize with the Holy Spirit.' I have seen and I testify that this is God's Chosen One." (John 1:32-34)

As we noted in Volume 1, we see all three members of the Trinity at Jesus' baptism. God the Father speaks from heaven and says, "This is my Son, whom I love; with him I am well pleased" (Matthew 3:17). And then the Spirit of God descends like a dove and rests upon the Son as he comes up out of the water.

Here in John 15, Jesus may be referring to when the Advocate (Holy Spirit) comes on the day of Pentecost. The Holy Spirit's ministries include taking the promises of Christ and making them happen in the lives of Christians:

- Jesus promises to go away and come back in John 14:1-6; the Holy Spirit makes it happen in 2 Corinthians 5:1-5.

- Jesus promises power in John 14:12; the Holy Spirit makes it happen in Acts 1:8 and Ephesians 3:20.

- Jesus promises to hear and answer prayer in John 14:13-14; the Holy Spirit makes it happen in Romans 8:26.

- Jesus promises to abide in them in John 14:18-23; the Holy Spirit makes it happen in Acts 2.

- Jesus promises peace, love, and joy in John 13–15; the Holy Spirit makes it happen in Galatians 5:22-23.

The Holy Spirit energizes and brings to life these promises of Jesus. The expression "And you also must testify" is imperative. We are called to testify boldly about our faith in Christ. But this doesn't mean cramming our beliefs down other people's throats. Jesus tells us the world may reject us, but that rejection should occur only because we represent Jesus, not because we are rude, obnoxious, or unlawful.

> In the Old Testament prophetic literature (especially Isaiah), God's end-time people are called God's "witnesses" to the nations (e.g., Isaiah 43:10-12; 44:8). In the New Testament, believers are frequently promised the Spirit's help in times of persecution (Matthew 10:20; Mark 13:11; Luke 12:12). Particularly in Luke's writings, the Spirit is presented as vitally engaged in missionary outreach (Acts 1:8; cf. Luke 24:48; Acts 5:32; 6:10).
>
> —Andreas J. Köstenberger in *Zondervan Illustrated Bible Backgrounds Commentary: New Testament, Volume 2,* 148

When giving testimony, witnessing, or sharing our faith, the focus should always be on Jesus. Here's a simple three-step method for sharing your faith if someone should ask why you believe and live as you do:

1. Briefly talk about your old life before you became a Christian.
2. Share how you became a Christian.
3. Describe what your new life is like now.

The center of your testimony needs to be Jesus Christ. After hearing your testimony, people should be thinking not about what a great person you are, but about what a great God you have.

John 16:1-4a

[1] "All this I have told you so that you will not fall away. [2] They will put you out of the synagogue; in fact, the time is coming when anyone who kills you will think they are offering a service to God. [3] They will do such things because they have not known the Father or me. [4] I have told you this, so that when their time comes you will remember that I warned you about them."

This is an unfortunate chapter break. "All this" is logically tied with John 15. The Bible in its original languages had no chapter or verse designations. The chapter divisions were inserted in the early 1200s; the verses were inserted in the 1500s.

Jesus has been the primary target of hostility, but so far he's been able to protect his disciples. That is about to change. There will be people who think they are doing God's will by killing Jesus—and those who follow him.

The term *fall away* is the Greek word *skandalizo*—which has the same root as our word *scandalize*. Some translations use *stumble*, which means to be caught off balance. Stumbling is an interruption in your walk. All of these words are effective in helping us understand what Jesus is saying in this passage.

Jesus is warning the disciples, again, that they will be persecuted as they testify about him. Jesus alludes to this in the Sermon on the Mount in Matthew 5:11-12—

> "Blessed are you when people insult you, perse-cute you, and falsely say all kinds of evil against you because of me. Rejoice and be glad, because great is your reward in heaven, for in the same way they persecuted the prophets who were before you."

Other Scriptures echo the same theme. Second Timo-thy 3:12 says, "In fact, everyone who wants to live a godly life in Christ Jesus will be persecuted"; and Philippians 1:29 says, "For it has been granted to you on behalf of Christ not only to believe in him, but also to suffer for him."

While Jesus has already discussed persecution in John 15:18-25, here he specifies two types of persecution: excom-munication (see also 9:19-23; 12:42) and murder (Acts 7:54-60). The other startling difference in this passage is that the persecution Jesus describes here is not coming from the secular world, but from those who are religious. Some of the cruelest acts in history have been committed in the very name of God. Jesus announces that these religious people who will persecute his followers do not know the Father, nor do they know him.

It is commonly suggested that John, perhaps writing in as late as the nineties, was influenced by a decision made by the reconstituted Sanhedrin a few years earlier. In the period after the destruction of the temple in AD 70, the San-hedrin was reconstituted with Roman permission. During this period the Sanhedrin was made up exclusively of doc-tors of the law. One of these, Samuel the Less (Small), and others later on, reworded the *Birkat ha-Minim*—one of the blessings (benedictions) recited daily in the synagogues—so as to make it impossible for "Nazarenes" to take part in synagogue worship. This blessing, which traditionally had included a curse on the enemies of God ("let all wickedness perish as in a moment"), was now to read: "let Nazarenes and heretics perish as in a moment; let them be blotted out of the Book of Life and not be enrolled with the righteous."

While some scholars believe this rewording was intended to reference a broader group of Jewish heretics, others believe it was intended to specifically target Jewish followers of Christ. The revision was approved by the Sanhedrin and adopted in synagogues. Nazarenes would keep silent when these new words were recited by the congregation, thereby giving themselves away. John may have been alluding to this situation when he chose to include this passage in the Gospel.

The persecution of Christians continued under the Roman emperors for the next three centuries. The persecution was sporadic, although it could be locally intense. Later, during the Reformation period, both the persecutors and the persecuted were Christians.

> John Huss (1369–1415) died defending his faith in front of a mocking crowd. When the wood had been piled around Huss, the duke of Bavaria begged the doomed man, for the last time, to recant. "No," firmly replied the martyr, "I have never preached any false doctrine; and that which I have taught with my lips, I now seal with my blood" He died singing a hymn as the flames engulfed his body.
>
> —John Foxe, *Foxe's Christian Martyrs of the World*, 270

Jesus offers not a way of ease but the way of glory. He wants men and women whose eyes are open to the challenges they will face, yet still remain eager to venture forth in his name.

John 16:1-4a

John 16:4b-7

4b "I did not tell you this from the beginning because I was with you, 5 but now I am going to him who sent me. None of you asks me, 'Where are you going?' 6 Rather, you are filled with grief because I have said these things. 7 But very truly I tell you, it is for your good that I am going away. Unless I go away, the Advocate will not come to you; but if I go, I will send him to you."

Some have noted that John 16:4b-33 is very similar to John 13:31–14:31, which might suggest that more than one author contributed to this Gospel. But again, this may simply be John's writing style. (John 6:35-50 is similar to 6:51-59; and John 13:19-25 is similar to 13:26-30).

Jesus notes here that the disciples have stopped asking where he is going. "Where are you going?" was the question Peter asked in 13:36 and Thomas asked in 14:5. Thomas also added, "How can we know the way?" These earlier questions may have revealed more of a concern for what would happen to them than an actual interest in where Jesus was going. But at this point the disciples are confused and sad that Jesus continues to insist that he will leave them. Again he reminds them that the Holy Spirit will come to take his place. Jesus doesn't indicate why the Holy Spirit won't come until he departs. But he does clearly talk about his work on the cross as being necessary before sending the Spirit.

John 16:8-11

8 "When he comes, he will prove the world to be in the wrong about sin and righteousness and judgment: 9 about sin, because people do not believe in me; 10 about righteousness, because I am going to the Father, where you can see me no longer;

¹¹ and about judgment, because the prince of this world now stands condemned."

The Holy Spirit is active not just in the lives of Christians. The Spirit also ministers to nonbelievers. "The world" in this passage refers not only to the nonbelieving nations, but also to Israel insofar as it hasn't believed in Jesus. The word *prove* could also be translated "reprove." Reproving someone involves correcting an error or undoing a previous wrong, while *prove* would suggest convincing someone of a previously unknown idea.

Jesus says the Holy Spirit will show that the world is wrong in three areas: First, the world is wrong about sin. The world is guilty of the sin of not believing in Jesus and failing to realize the true nature of the One they are about to crucify. Peter addresses this in his sermon at Pentecost, the day the Spirit came to the gathered believers (Acts 2:36-37).

Second, the Holy Spirit convicts the world that it's been wrong about righteousness. Some believed Jesus could not be righteous because he didn't follow the human interpretations of Sabbath law. However, God has already decided in favor of the righteousness of Jesus. All those who follow Jesus share God's favor. This may also mean exposing those who are self-righteous, those who trust in their proper performance of ceremony and rituals to save them.

Third, the Holy Spirit convinces the world they've been wrong about judgment. The world thinks it can pass judgment on Jesus, when in fact it is Jesus who will judge all. Jesus is partially speaking of the defeat of Satan, which was a form of judgment. Satan continues to seek to harden, coerce, and deceive those in this world (1 Peter 5:8). The good news is that, in the resurrection of Jesus, the power of the evil one has been broken.

This third point also means that our job as Jesus-followers is not to go around trying to prove to our neighbors that they're sinners. As Christians we often fall into the trap of believing we have to convict others of their sinfulness. That is the task of the Holy Spirit. The Spirit will expose the sin, hurt, and emptiness of so many in this world. Our job is to affirm the truth in Jesus. God has prepared the way for us to have a positive impact on the world.

The Lion, the Witch, and the Wardrobe is C. S. Lewis's first novel in the Chronicles of Narnia. When the four British children are told that they were brought to Narnia to meet Aslan, the son of the Emperor beyond the Sea, they are at first delighted at the honor. (Aslan is the Christ figure throughout the Chronicles.) But then in further discussion it comes out that Aslan is a great lion. Now they are not so sure they are up to meeting him. Lucy is uneasy and nervous. "Is he quite safe?" she asks one of the family of talking beavers they are staying with. Mr. Beaver answers, "Safe? . . .'Course he isn't safe. But he's good" (p. 64).

Jesus has already created a great uneasiness by his ministry. He has shown the world its sins. He is not safe; he is the Lord and he exposes who we are. He threatens the status quo.

—Earl F. Palmer, *The Intimate Gospel*, 138

John 16:12-13

¹² "I have much more to say to you, more than you can now bear. ¹³ But when he, the Spirit of truth, comes, he will guide you into all the truth. He will not speak on his own; he will speak only what he hears, and he will tell you what is yet to come."

Jesus has a lot more he wants to tell them, but the disciples are not yet ready. Their background and expectations about the Messiah makes it difficult for them to understand what he is saying, especially the thought of the cross. Deuteronomy 21:23 tells us, "anyone who is hung on a pole is under God's curse." At this point the disciples couldn't comprehend a crucified Messiah who came to conquer sin and death rather than the Romans. Jesus is sensitive and doesn't rebuke his disciples because they are incapable of understanding all this. Just as a parent who knows his child has eaten enough will take the food away from him, so Jesus holds back in revealing all that will occur.

The Holy Spirit will pick up where Jesus left off and guide them into all truth. This is called the "ministry of illumination." The Holy Spirit communicates the Truth of God to you and me. The Spirit doesn't reveal to us all the truth in the universe, but all the truth necessary to make us complete. The Spirit will not speak on his own authority, just as Jesus does not speak on his own authority.

The Spirit will direct the disciples into writing the New Testament, just as the Spirit guided the writing of the Old Testament. Second Peter 1:21 says, "For prophecy never had its origin in the human will, but prophets, though human, spoke from God as they were carried along by the Holy Spirit." Jesus is telling the disciples that this same thing will happen to them as they write the New Testament. Paul affirms in 1 Corinthians 2:10, "These are the things God has revealed to us by his Spirit."

John 16:14-15

14 "He will glorify me because it is from me that he will receive what he will make known to you. 15 All that belongs to the Father is mine. That is why I said the Spirit will receive from me what he will make known to you."

The Spirit draws no attention to itself. Jesus is assuring the disciples that what the Holy Spirit makes known to them will come from Jesus and the Father. For this reason, we should be very skeptical whenever someone says the Spirit is leading them toward actions that seem to violate the teachings of Jesus. I get so ticked off when I hear people say the Holy Spirit (God) told them to—

- disobey their parents;
- have an affair;
- abuse drugs;
- get a divorce;
- marry a non-Christian;
- destroy someone else's property;
- steal something;
- set something on fire;
- kill someone;
- gamble on a sports team; or
- commit an act of violence.

Since October 9, 1936, much of the electricity that powers homes in the Los Angeles basin has come from the Hoover Dam. Through the genius and innovation of engineers, the Colorado River was dammed in a way that provides hundreds of thousands of volts of electricity to meet the needs of millions of people in the Los Angeles area.

If you were to start at the dam and follow the 266 miles of power lines that lead away from it to the homes in Los Angeles, you would come across various transmission plants along the way that are marked with signs that say DANGER, HIGH VOLTAGE, and NO TRESPASSING. The amount of energy generated at the dam could easily destroy the homes along these lines. But the engineers and electricians have built into the system these transformers, which break down the energy into meaningful units that meet the precise energy needs of various homes and businesses. And the appliances in our homes contain smaller transformers that break down the 110 volts coming in from the outlet to an even smaller amount that's just right for each particular appliance.

The Holy Spirit does the same with God's Word. The Spirit will dispense the message of God to you in the level you need it. Having the mind of God, the Spirit never makes a mistake. He gives you just what you can handle.

—Les

READ BETWEEN THE LINES

- Who is the Advocate?
- What does it mean to testify?
- What does it mean to go astray? Why would someone do this?
- How are the Father and Son connected?
- What does it mean to be put out of the synagogue? What would they have done to cause this?
- Why is it good that Jesus goes away?
- What is the work of the Holy Spirit?
- How does the Spirit convict unbelievers today?

WELCOME TO MY WORLD

- When friends must separate, is it harder to be the one who leaves or the one who remains behind?
- How have I felt when someone I loved has left me?
- Does the Holy Spirit lead each generation to apply the truths of Jesus in new ways? Why or why not?
- For which function of the Holy Spirit (mentioned in this passage) am I the most grateful? Why?
- How does reading about the deaths of the early Christians make me feel?

- Do I think the people in my community are aware that they're sinners? What should I say to them?

- Have I ever experienced how it feels to not be able to tell someone everything I know because that person couldn't handle it at the time?

- When have I sensed the Holy Spirit being active in my life?

The Disciples' Grief Will Turn to Joy

John 16:16-19

16 Jesus went on to say, "In a little while you will see me no more, and then after a little while you will see me."

17 At this, some of his disciples said to one another, "What does he mean by saying, 'In a little while you will see me no more, and then after a little while you will see me,' and 'Because I am going to the Father'?" 18 They kept asking, "What does he mean by 'a little while'? We don't understand what he is saying."

19 Jesus saw that they wanted to ask him about this, so he said to them, "Are you asking one another what I meant when I said, 'In a little while you will see me no more, and then after a little while you will see me'?"

"In a little while" can mean hours (John 13:33; 16:16), days (John 12:35), or weeks (John 7:33). The first "In a little while you will see me no more" could refer to the interval between Jesus' arrest and crucifixion, or the time between the crucifixion and the resurrection, or the period after his ascension.

The second "after a little while you will see me" is also debated. Some think this could refer to just before the crucifixion or after the resurrection or at the second coming. Others think this means the time when the Holy Spirit comes on the day of Pentecost after Jesus was raised (although we don't physically *see* the Holy Spirit). And perhaps these words include all of those options.

John 16:20-22

20 "Very truly I tell you, you will weep and mourn while the world rejoices. You will grieve, but your grief will turn to joy. 21 A woman giving birth to a child has pain because her time has come; but when her baby is born she forgets the anguish because of her joy that a child is born into the world. 22 So with you: Now is your time of grief, but I will see you again and you will rejoice, and no one will take away your joy."

The world will rejoice to see Christ on the cross, and his followers will be brokenhearted. Yet this same event that causes them grief (loud wailing) in the moment will be turned to joy. As Romans 8:28 affirms, "And we know that in all things God works for the good of those who love him, who have been called according to his purpose."

> There's a lovely Hasidic story of a rabbi who always told his people that if they studied the Torah, it would put Scripture on their hearts. One of them asked, "Why *on* our hearts, and not *in* them?" The rabbi answered, "Only God can put Scripture inside. But reading sacred text can put it on your hearts, and then when your hearts break, the holy words will fall inside."
>
> —Anne Lamott, *Plan B: Further Thoughts on Faith*, 73

A woman has intense pain during childbirth; in fact, her agony increases as the child is about to be born. Labor brings great distress, but that pain gives way to great joy as the child appears. An event that starts in struggle and sorrow ends in celebration. Jesus also uses this terminology in Matthew 24:8, where he says, "All these are the beginning of birth pains" to describe events in the end times. Once we are on the other side, the pain will begin to dissipate, and there will be understanding and joy. Psalm 30:5 declares, "weeping may stay for the night, but rejoicing comes in the morning."

John 16:23-27

23 "In that day you will no longer ask me anything. Very truly I tell you, my Father will give you whatever you ask in my name. 24 Until now you have not asked for anything in my name. Ask and you will receive, and your joy will be complete.

25 "Though I have been speaking figuratively, a time is coming when I will no longer use this kind of language but will tell you plainly about my Father. 26 In that day you will ask in my name. I am not saying that I will ask the Father on your behalf. 27 No, the Father himself loves you because you have loved me and have believed that I came from God."

"In that day" may refer to the time after Jesus' resurrection and ascension, and perhaps after Act 2:1-6 when the disciples were filled with the Holy Spirit. The phrase "you will no longer ask me anything" seems to be in relation to their asking for information about this particular topic (Jesus' crucifixion), which won't be necessary after the resurrection. Another possibility is that Jesus may be saying that instead of asking him questions, the disciples will go directly to God with their requests, asking in Jesus' name.

A figurative statement is also referred to as a "veiled, pointed statement." Some have asked why Jesus spoke with veiled statements. It seems that Jesus communicated in this way during his sojourn on earth so people would be forced to wrestle mentally with all he was saying. If he said it all super-plain, then they would have just let it drift by them. As the events in the next few hours and weeks unfold, what Jesus was saying will become much clearer.

> I'm not a great fan of Christian T-shirts that are real cutesy, nor those that are in-your-face and basically say, "I'm going to heaven and you're not." I like Christian T-shirts that have twists and turns to them, the kind that get me thinking. For a similar reason, I appreciate the way Jesus sometimes used language and images that forced people to think. Although he often used very familiar images (shepherd and sheep, vine and branches), he spoke in ways that challenged his listeners to dig deep.
>
> —Les

"A time is coming" refers to the period after the resurrection and perhaps more specifically to the day of Pentecost. Peter, Paul, James, and the rest of the disciples don't speak in parables as Jesus often did; they speak very plainly. The closest thing to figurative language is found in Revelation. One reason Revelation is among the most difficult Scriptures to understand is because we're still on this side of the last days and the events the book describes—just as the disciples were confused as they listened to Jesus speaking in this passage because they hadn't yet experienced the resurrection.

> In John 16:16, Jesus announced that in a little while, they would not see Him; then, in a little while, they would see Him. It was a deliberately puzzling statement (John 16:25, He spoke in proverbs ["dark sayings"]), and the disciples did not understand. This also encourages me as I study my Bible and find statements that I cannot understand. Even the disciples had their hours of spiritual ignorance!
>
> —Warren Wiersbe, *Be Transformed*, 79

Jesus is also saying that when that day comes, they will pray in his name. Until the Holy Spirit comes to dwell within them, the disciples cannot clearly discern God's will and purpose, and so they cannot ask according to that will and purpose (which is what "ask in my name" means). When the Spirit comes to dwell in them, they will have the capacity to discern God's will to the degree that they will learn to listen to the voice of the Spirit.

Starting on the day of Pentecost, the disciples will have direct and immediate access to the Father in the name of Jesus. Jesus doesn't have to ask for us. When we go to the Father in prayer, we are to go saying, "Father, I am coming to you because Jesus sent me to ask this for him . . ." (14:13-14). We don't have to pray through priests, angels, or saints.

How reassuring it is to hear Jesus say, "the Father himself loves you." Do you grasp the fact that the Father loves you? Outside of the Trinity, you are the hottest commodity in the universe, someone who is loved deeply by the God who created it all. When was the last time you reminded yourself, *I am loved by the Creator of the universe*?

The central theme of [John 16:23–28] is prayer. "Ask, and ye shall receive, that your joy may be full" (John 16:24). It is important to note that the text uses two different words for "ask," although they can be used interchangeably. The word used in John 16:19, 23a, and 26 means "to ask a question" or "to ask a request." It is used when someone makes a request of someone equal. The word translated "ask" in John 16:23b, 24, and 26b means "to request something of a superior." This latter word was never used by Jesus in His prayer life because He is equal to the Father. We come as inferiors to God, asking for His blessing, but He came as the very Son of God, equal with the Father.

—Warren Wiersbe, *Be Transformed*, 80–81

John 16:28-30

28 "I came from the Father and entered the world; now I am leaving the world and going back to the Father."

29 Then Jesus' disciples said, "Now you are speaking clearly and without figures of speech. 30 Now we can see that you know all things and that you do not even need to have anyone ask you questions. This makes us believe that you came from God."

Jesus' entering our world is known as the *incarnation*. He came down to be our Savior, to pay the penalty for our sins. He is like a judge who passes a guilty sentence on his son or daughter, but then gets off the bench and pays the penalty. "Leaving the world and going back to the Father" might refer to Jesus' death on the cross, or to his ascending to God after the resurrection.

The disciples believe Jesus has the ability to anticipate their questions without their even needing to ask them. In Matthew's Gospel, Jesus affirms, "your Father knows what you need before you ask him" (Matthew 6:8b).

John 16:31-33

31 "Do you now believe?" Jesus replied. 32 "A time is coming and in fact has come when you will be scattered, each to your own home. You will leave me all alone. Yet I am not alone, for my Father is with me.

33 "I have told you these things, so that in me you may have peace. In this world you will have trouble. But take heart! I have overcome the world."

Jesus knows that even though his disciples really do believe in him, their faith is still immature. When Jesus goes to the cross, the disciples will scatter like sheep without a shepherd. "Strike the shepherd, and the sheep will be scattered," says Zechariah 13:7. But Jesus won't be left alone. He knows he will have the Father's presence.

Notice the contrast between "in me you may have peace" and "in this world you will have trouble." While the disciples will experience struggles in this world, they need not lose heart because Christ is more powerful than the world.

This is a wonderful ending to this long discourse (chapters 13–16). We can have peace because Jesus has overcome the world. The cross and the resurrection represent Jesus' triumph over sin and death. Jesus has defeated Satan (John 12:31; 14:30; Colossians 2:15; Revelation 12:10-11) and has done away with the penalty of sin once and for all (Hebrews 9:15, 26, 28; 10:10, 12-14).

Our lives may not be easy, but we can go forward with the peace and strength of Christ. In spite of unavoidable struggles, we will not be alone.

> Jesus offers us genuinely good news, "Have courage! I have faced your enemy and vanquished him. I have fought your battle on the battleground of human experience where you might fight. I have routed the foe. You can never do it; but I have done it and I can do it again in you. Abide in me and my victory is yours."
>
> **—Donald Miller, former president of Pittsburgh Theological Seminary**

READ BETWEEN THE LINES

- How is Jesus' leaving like a mother giving birth?
- Why does Jesus speak figuratively?
- Why will the disciples scatter?
- How do you think the disciples feel during these conversations with Jesus?
- When will Jesus be left alone?

- What does it mean to have peace?
- How does childbirth illustrate what is happening to the disciples?

WELCOME TO MY WORLD

- How would I feel if Jesus said, "You will see me no more"?
- Have I ever suffered pain to get something I wanted?
- Have I ever read a passage of Scripture and didn't understand it, but then returned to it later to find it seemed clear?
- How would I have reacted to Jesus' answers?
- What kind of a student do I think Jesus was in school?
- How can I be at peace in the midst of trouble?
- Have I had teachers who made me think? How did they do that?
- How does it make me feel to read, "I have overcome the world"?
- When has something in my life that seemed dreadful turned out to be an excellent thing?
- How have I grown through pain and struggle?
- Am I at peace in my life? Why or why not?

Jesus Prays to Be Glorified

John 17:1a

¹After Jesus said this, he looked toward heaven and prayed:

The "this" refers to Jesus' farewell discourse that has spanned chapters 14–16. Chapter 17 has been called the "High-Priestly Prayer" or the "Farewell Prayer" or the "Parting Prayer." Don't let the loftiness of those titles turn you off. This is a heartfelt, loving, and passionate prayer.

Jesus may have prayed this in the upper room or en route to the garden of Gethsemane. It's the longest prayer of Jesus recorded in the Bible, an intimate prayer from Jesus to his heavenly Father. It's as if we are eavesdropping on a conversation within the Trinity. In this prayer we have an opportunity to explore Jesus' inner thoughts, including his concerns and hopes. We also get another glimpse of his relationship with his Father.

Have you ever thought about "public prayers"? In the first century on the Sabbath and during the festivals, there would be a reading from the Torah and some type of message in the synagogues, but there does not appear to be any communal prayer. Prayer seems to be a private matter, or perhaps something shared among friends and family within a home. In Matthew 6:5-6, Jesus tells us, "And when you pray, do not be like the hypocrites, for they love to pray standing in the synagogues and on the street corners to be seen by others. Truly I tell you, they have received their reward in full. But when you pray, go into your room, close the door and pray to your Father, who is unseen. Then your Father, who sees what is done in secret, will reward you."

Jesus makes a similar point in the parable found in Luke 18:9-14, where he contrasts a Pharisee and a tax collector who go up the temple to pray. The Pharisee stood up for all to see and prayed an arrogant prayer. The tax collector stood at a distance and lowered his head to pray a humble prayer, asking God for mercy. Jesus said, "I tell you that this man, rather than the other, went home justified before God" (v. 14).

—Les

Jesus begins his prayer by lifting his eyes toward heaven, which was a common Jewish posture for prayer (Psalm 123:1; Mark 7:34; John 11:41). "Looked toward heaven" may also be John's way of letting the reader know that something particularly significant is about to happen.

The theme of vision is particularly important in John's Gospel. When a crowd sees Jesus perform a miracle, some people see God at work, while others see a blasphemer.

Often, we spend our days looking around, but we fail to see the significance of what is happening right before us. In November 2011, I was changing planes at Denver International Airport. As I was leaving one plane to catch another, I realized that the man who'd been seated across the aisle from me had left his laptop in the seatback in front of him. So I took the laptop to the flight attendant. After I exited the plane, I began looking around the concourse to find the man, so he could return to the plane and retrieve the computer. I remembered he was wearing a large cowboy hat. Do you know how many people in the B Concourse of the Denver Airport on a Monday morning wear cowboy hats? 27! It never occurred to me that so many people wear cowboy hats.

Once I began focusing on cowboy hats, I saw them everywhere. John is reminding us that God is always at work all around us. We simply need to be alert and ready to see God at work.

—Les

Unlike Jesus' prayer in Matthew 6:9-13 (The Lord's Prayer), the prayer in John 17 isn't specifically meant as an example for Christians to recite. Instead, this prayer gives us a glimpse at the concerns on Jesus' heart as he faces the cross.

The prayer divides easily into three parts:

1. Jesus' prayer for himself (17:1-5)
2. Jesus' prayer for his disciples (17:6-19)
3. Jesus' prayer for all believers (17:20-26)

> What wings are to a bird, and sails to a ship, so is prayer to the soul.
>
> —Corrie ten Boom

John 17:1b-2

"Father, the hour has come. Glorify your Son, that your Son may glorify you. ² For you granted him authority over all people that he might give eternal life to all those you have given him."

Jesus begins by praying for himself, but even here he is also praying for us. Dr. R. A. Torrey (1856–1928), an American evangelist and educator, once noted, "A prayer for self is not by any means necessarily a selfish prayer."

Notice that Jesus addresses God as "Father." John's Gospel uses this word 133 times.

Earlier in the Gospel, John noted that Jesus' hour or time had "not yet come" (2:4; 7:30; 8:20). But now, for the third time, John makes it clear that the time "has come" (12:23; 13:1). This is the hour that was fixed before creation, before time even existed. This is the focal point of all history.

Some have said that John 17:1 marks the middle of the Bible. You may be doubtful of this bit of trivia—and rightly so. How would we calculate the middle of the Bible? Some suggest a page count—take the total number of pages and divide it in half. That would put you in the Old Testament somewhere around Psalm 130. Others suggest a verse count. The Bible contains 31,173 verses, which means the verse at the halfway point would be Psalm 118:8. Others say the middle is the space between the end of the Old Testament (the last verse of Malachi) and the first verse of Matthew, which begins the New Testament.

But what if there is another way to calculate the midpoint? The entire Old Testament looks forward to the Messiah's work of salvation. The theme begins in Genesis 3 when God mentions a time when evil would be conquered. Anticipation of the Messiah is woven throughout the Old Testament like a tapestry. Even the Gospel accounts of Jesus' life and ministry build toward the decisive moment when sin is defeated on the cross. And the rest of the New Testament looks back at the cross and forward to Christ' return.

So perhaps the true middle of the Bible is the moment when the work of Christ on the cross begins. When you think about it that way, Jesus' statement that "the hour has come" in John 17:1 marks that true middle of the biblical story.

Glory is a frequent theme in John. "We have seen his glory," the prologue tells us (1:14), and then John elaborates on the subject throughout the book. It's the Son who glorifies the Father (14:13), and the Father also glorifies the Son (8:54); they glory in each other (13:31-32). And then, remarkably, the Son shares his glory—the glory he received from his Father—with those who love him. And we, in turn, can glorify God through what we say and do (15:8; 21:19). But what exactly is glory? It seems it can only be described, not defined. God's glory includes his splendor, honor, majesty, brilliance, and goodness.

—*A Walk Thru the Book of John*, 62

Isaiah declares that God the Father will not give his glory to another (42:8; 48:11). The fact that Jesus shares the Father's glory means that he is God.

I can still remember the first time I heard Tony Campolo speak. He delivered a message at a Youth Specialties event in 1979 that helped catapult his career. He told the story of the annual Good Friday service at the church he attends. Each year they have a "preach-off" where several preachers speak one after the other in a daylong meeting. Tony was one of the speakers. He said he preached well, but his pastor's message that day was spellbinding. And the whole sermon was built around a single line: "It's Friday, but Sunday's coming." Tony told us how his pastor kept repeating that one line over and over and over again with slight variations for more than an hour: "It's Friday, and Jesus was dead on the cross, but that was Friday . . . Sunday's coming. It's Friday, and it looks like evil will always rule and injustice will prevail. But, that's Friday . . . Sunday's a-coming . . ."

The Gospel writers Mark and Luke would probably agree with Tony and his pastor: Things looked bad on Friday, but Sunday's resurrection turned it all around. But I think John would add that Friday is where the glory is. Friday is where our salvation is secured, as Jesus dies on the cross for our sins. Friday is where Jesus is in complete unity with the Father. Friday is where Jesus is lifted up and brings glory to the Father.

—Les

The cross for Jesus is not a place of shame, especially in John's Gospel. Instead, the cross is a place where the Father is honored because of the Son's obedience. Jesus did not have a self-centered mission but stressed the superior place of the Father. That's his ministry. That's the reason for his existence. That's his purpose, to glorify the Father.

We should share that same purpose in our lives. Novelist Martha Ostenso once described one of her characters in this way: "Edith was a little country bounded on the north, south, east, and west by Edith." This should never be said about us. Our lives and everything we do and say should not be focused on us, but on bringing glory to God. Matthew 5:16 says, "In the same way, let your light shine before others, that they may see your good deeds and glorify your Father in heaven." People should not be saying, "What a great person you are!" They should be saying, "What a great God you have!" All the glory goes to God.

> [Humpty Dumpty said,] . . . "There's glory for you!"
>
> "I don't know what you mean by 'glory,'" Alice said.
>
> Humpty Dumpty smiled contemptuously. "Of course you don't—till I tell you. I meant 'there's a nice knock-down argument for you!'"
>
> "But 'glory' doesn't mean 'a nice knock-down argument,'" Alice objected.
>
> "When I use a word," Humpty Dumpty said in rather a scornful tone, "it means just what I choose it to mean—neither more nor less."
>
> "The question is," said Alice, "whether you CAN make words mean so many different things."
>
> "The question is," said Humpty Dumpty, "which is to be master—that's all."
>
> —Lewis Carroll, *Through the Looking-Glass*

Verse 2—"For you granted him authority over all people that he might give eternal life to all those you have given him"—also reminds us that Jesus has "authority" to do all that he does. Some translations use the word *power*, which is not the preferred meaning of the word.

John 17:3-5

³ "Now this is eternal life: that they know you, the only true God, and Jesus Christ, whom you have sent. ⁴ I have brought you glory on earth by finishing the work you gave me to do. ⁵ And now, Father, glorify me in your presence with the glory I had with you before the world began."

The first step in receiving eternal life is to understand that we don't already have eternal life. To receive eternal life, we must believe in Jesus Christ and enter into a relationship with God. Then the Holy Spirit takes up residence in our lives. In the Gospel of John, eternal life is not appropriated in the age to come, but it happens in the here and now.

Jesus prays to the Father "that they know you." This does not mean a simple awareness of the existence of God. Believing that God exists does not constitute salvation. This "know" refers to the type of relationship that close friends would have. Just as there is only one true God, there is only one way to God the Father—and that is through Jesus. Jesus is God's one and only sanctioned agent.

Here, Jesus refers to himself as "Jesus Christ." This phrase is used only twice in John's Gospel, here and in John 1:17. Note that "Christ" is not Jesus' last name! *Christ* is the Greek equivalent of the Hebrew word *Messiah*. Jesus is saying, quite plainly, "I, Jesus, am the Messiah."

Jesus asks the Father to "glorify me in your presence with the glory I had with you before the world began." This refers to Jesus' existence before the incarnation, indicating that Jesus has always been. This passage also makes it clear that Jesus is asking for further glory beyond what he has already displayed. The glory is the love relationship and unity of purpose between the Father and the Son. Jesus wants to again take his place alongside the Father. In Daniel 7:13-14 we read about Daniel's vision of "one like a son of man" who is led into the presence of the Ancient of Days (God) and given authority, glory, and sovereign power.

How can Jesus have been in glory even before the world began? The Jewish commentary on Genesis 1:1 notes that when a builder starts a project, he consults a blueprint; he doesn't just start banging away. John is saying that God's purpose, God's plan for humanity existed long before creation. While Jesus has been on earth, he's been following that plan. So the glory the Father and Son shared before the world began was this purpose, this plan, which is about to come to fruition. In the crucifixion and resurrection, that plan reaches its climax. Jesus is subservient to the Father, but sometimes the Father listens to the Son. They are both working out of a common purpose. God's desire and plan has always been to live in connection with human beings, just as was the case in the garden of Eden before the fall.

It's interesting that even as Jesus faces death on a cross, only one-fifth of his prayer is focused on himself. This may be a lesson for all of us in our prayers.

READ BETWEEN THE LINES

- How does this prayer compare with the agony of Gethsemane (Matthew 26:36-44; Mark 14:32-42; Luke 22:41-45)?
- How does this prayer compare with the "Song of Moses," his farewell address in Deuteronomy 32?
- Why does Jesus look to heaven? Which direction is that?
- How do we get eternal life?
- What does it mean to "glorify" someone?
- How have Jesus and the Father done that?
- What is eternal life?
- What work did Jesus complete?

- What does it mean to know God?
- What was it like for Jesus before the world began?

WELCOME TO MY WORLD

- Where did I learn to pray?
- When friends pray with me, what do their prayers indicate about their hearts?
- How am I glorifying God?
- Who receives the glory from the things I say and do?
- What work has God given me to do?
- Have I finished the work God has given me to do?

Jesus Prays for His Disciples

John 17:6-8

6 "I have revealed you[a] to those whom you gave me out of the world. They were yours; you gave them to me and they have obeyed your word. 7 Now they know that everything you have given me comes from you. 8 For I gave them the words you gave me and they accepted them. They knew with certainty that I came from you, and they believed that you sent me."

After spending three years with Jesus, the disciples' faith in him has been strengthened. Throughout those years, Jesus has been talking about his Father to his disciples. Now in this prayer, Jesus talks about his disciples to his Father. Jesus is saying everything he is comes from God.

As Jesus obeyed the Father, so have the disciples obeyed Jesus' words that come from the Father. They believe the Father sent Jesus. Their faith in Jesus grew over time until finally Simon Peter could say, "You are the Messiah, the Son of the living God" (Matthew 16:16).

John 17:9-11

9 "I pray for them. I am not praying for the world, but for those you have given me, for they are yours. 10 All I have is yours, and all you have is mine. And glory has come to me through them. 11 I will remain in the world no longer, but they are still in the world, and I am coming to you. Holy Father, protect them by the power of[b] your name, the name you gave me, so that they may be one as we are one."

---

a John 17:6 Greek *your name*

b John 17:11 Or *Father, keep them faithful to*

"The world" in this passage refers to the powers and principalities of this earth, a spiritual atmosphere of darkness and unbelief. Here, Jesus isn't praying for transformation of the world system; he is praying for believers who are in the world—that his disciples would be protected from evil.

John 17:11 is the only place in the entire Bible where God is referred to as "Holy Father." Jesus asks his Father to protect the disciples by the power of his name, knowing that God's name will be a refuge for them. Proverbs 18:10 tells us, "The name of the LORD is a fortified tower; the righteous run to it and are safe." Psalm 124:8 affirms, "Our help is in the name of the LORD, the Maker of heaven and earth." Jesus is also praying for unity among the disciples in their mission.

Jesus was given the task of taking care of the disciples. If you've ever taken care of someone else's property, you know this can be a daunting task. When I was a college student and part-time youth minister in Garden Grove, California, one of the families in our church asked me to "house sit" for them while they were on vacation for a week. I thought it might be fun to get out of my small dorm room for a while, so I agreed.

I knew they had a dog that I'd need to take care of; and after agreeing to house sit, I discovered they also had a pregnant cat. Three days after they left on vacation, their dog was poisoned and died. (Suspicions pointed toward their next-door neighbor.) That same day the cat had her kittens in a drawer in the kitchen cabinet. I almost freaked out.

When the family called to find out how things were going, I had to tell them. I felt terrible. The parents decided to tell their three young children about the dog after they got home. And I learned that week that taking care of someone else's property can be quite stressful!

—Les

John 17:12

12 "While I was with them, I protected them and kept them safe by[c] that name you gave me. None has been lost except the one doomed to destruction so that Scripture would be fulfilled."

While he was with them, Jesus kept the disciples safe—except for Judas, whom Jesus says was "doomed to destruction so the Scripture would be fulfilled." The Scripture Jesus refers to here may be Psalm 41:9—"Even my close friend, someone I trusted, one who shared my bread, has turned against me." Judas followed Satan's lead in betraying Jesus (13:27).

There's no indication that Judas actually believed in and received Jesus. He seems to have stood with the true disciples but wasn't a true disciple himself. God used Judas's evilness to bring about God's own intention. But Judas was no puppet on a string. The temptation of Satan was not stronger than Jesus' ability to protect Judas.

John 17:13-19

13 "I am coming to you now, but I say these things while I am still in the world, so that they may have the full measure of my joy within them. 14 I have given them your word and the world has hated them, for they are not of the world any more than I am of the world. 15 My prayer is not that you take them out of the world but that you protect them from the evil one. 16 They are not of the world, even as I am not of it. 17 Sanctify them by[d] the truth; your word is truth. 18 As you sent me into the world, I have sent them into the world. 19 For them I sanctify myself, that they too may be truly sanctified.

---

c John 17:12 Or *kept them faithful to*

d John 17:17 Or *them to live in accordance with*

Jesus doesn't pray that the Father will remove or insulate true believers from the world around them. God doesn't intend that all believers live secluded from the world like monks or hermits. Instead, we are to shine like bright lights in a dark world (Matthew 5:13-16). Jesus doesn't pray that his disciples will be removed from the persecution to come, but that they will be protected through those difficult times. In Romans 12:2 we read, "Do not conform to the pattern of this world, but be transformed by the renewing of your mind." We are to be in the world but not of the world.

In these seven verses, Jesus gives four characteristics that should identify the church. The first characteristic is "joy." He's talking about the kind of joy that overcomes circumstances. "But the angel said to them, 'Do not be afraid. I bring you good news that will cause great joy for all the people'" (Luke 2:10). James 1:2 states, "Consider it pure joy, my brothers and sisters, whenever you face trials of many kinds." As Christians, we won't avoid all trouble. But Jesus prays we'll have abundant joy in the midst of this trouble.

The second characteristic is "sanctification." The word *sanctify* means to be "set apart" for a purpose. The chair you're sitting on now was set apart—designed for a purpose. So are you.

"Of course not," said the Mock Turtle. "Why, if a fish came to ME, and told me he was going on a journey, I should say, 'With what porpoise?'"

"Don't you mean 'purpose'?" said Alice.

"I mean what I say," the Mock Turtle replied in an offended tone.

—**Lewis Carroll,** *Alice in Wonderland*

The phrase "I sanctify myself" is interesting. In the Septuagint (the Greek translation of the Old Testament), the same verb is used to describe the consecrating of priests (Exodus 28:41) and sacrifices (Exodus 28:38; Numbers 18:9). The high priest had to go through special ceremonies of consecration so he would be "set apart" in order to enter into the presence of the holy God and pray in the Holy of Holies for his people. Jesus is declaring that he has been set apart to do God's will.

The term *sanctified* can also mean to "make clean" or to "be holy." We are to seek to be holy not just as individuals, but together as the whole church. Jesus is asking the Father to preserve his people from evil, from the tricks and traps of "the world." The people of God are to be holy while still living in the world. Moses (Numbers 11:15), Elijah (1 Kings 19:4), and Jonah (Jonah 4:3) all asked to be taken out of this world, but none of their prayers were granted. (Elijah was taken up to heaven, but at a later time.)

The third characteristic is "truth." We are to continually check our individual lives (everything we say and do) and the life of the church by and with the Truth of God's Word.

The fourth characteristic, "mission," is summed up by Jesus' words in verse 18: "As you have sent me into the world, I have sent them into the world." Heaven certainly will be a wonderful place, but we are on this earth to bring others with us to heaven. The task God gave to Jesus has now been passed on to us. We are to be God's agents reaching out to people with the Good News.

READ BETWEEN THE LINES

- What does "obey your word" include?
- Why doesn't Jesus pray for the world?
- What is the "world"?
- Who was doomed to destruction?
- Describe joy.

- What does Jesus mean by "your word is truth"?
- What does "sanctify" mean?
- Why is it essential that the disciples stay in the world?
- What is the disciples' mission?

WELCOME TO MY WORLD

- What is my purpose in life?
- What do I specifically pray for when I think of my friends?
- How is someone sanctified?
- Why do some groups choose to separate themselves from society in order to practice their pursuit of God?
- Do I pray mostly for immediate needs or long-term needs? Why?
- How does having Jesus in my life set me apart?
- What does it mean for me to be in the world but not of the world?

Jesus Prays for All Believers

John 17:20-23

20 "My prayer is not for them alone. I pray also for those who will believe in me through their message, 21 that all of them may be one, Father, just as you are in me and I am in you. May they also be in us so that the world may believe that you have sent me. 22 I have given them the glory that you gave me, that they may be one as we are one— 23 I in them and you in me—so that they may be brought to complete unity. Then the world will know that you sent me and have loved them even as you have loved me."

In the third section of his prayer, Jesus is praying for all those who will believe through his disciples' message. In other words, Jesus is praying for us—you and me! Wow! Think about it: 2,000 years ago, Jesus was thinking about and praying for you. How amazing is that!

Verse 20 also underlines the importance of passing the faith on to others. An old youth ministry motto says that the church is always only one generation away from extinction. Now, let's be clear: Jesus doesn't *need* anyone's help. But it seems that he invites us to be a part of the process of reaching the world with his message. Jesus welcomes our involvement, but he doesn't *need* it.

Jesus also prays that all believers will be one, just as the Father and Son are one. As a result of the crucifixion and resurrection, we can also enjoy an intimate relationship with God because of the Spirit living within us. In that way we are invited into that love relationship and unity of purpose between Father, Son, and Spirit.

As I've traveled around the world to speak, I've met delight-ful Christians from all walks of life and almost every conceiv-able denomination. When I was first getting started in ministry, the leadership of one school told me that if I attended a certain theological graduate school, I would never be invited back to speak at their school. I went to that school anyway—and the school that said they'd never invite me back asked me to not only speak, but teach an entire semester course that next year! Seems they were either bluffing, or they came to their senses.

I don't believe Jesus is half as concerned about all of the denominations and distinctions as we are. I am hopeful that, as Christians, we will continue to grow in grace and knowledge, as well as in unity.

I'm a Beatles fan (hey, I'm a Liverpudlian or a Scouser), and I tend to believe that John Lennon got it right in the opening line of "I Am the Walrus"—"I am he as you are he as you are me and we are all together."

—Les

The church needs to express a unity in Christ. This doesn't mean Christians have to agree on everything, espe-cially matters of opinion. It also doesn't mean that we all need to be a part of the same denomination or organization. Nor does it mean total conformity—where everyone is alike. That's dull—and I believe God likes diversity and multiplicity.

Unity means loving all of our brothers and sisters in Christ, being committed to one another, and sharing our thoughts and lives together. Psalm 133:1 says, "How good and pleasant it is when God's people live together in unity!" The Christian life is not one of rugged individualism. E. Stanley Jones expresses the point of this final part of Jesus' prayer very well in his three-part sentence: "You belong to Christ; I belong to Christ; we belong to each other." This is the crucial thread of the entire tapestry, the one strand that is woven in and around all of us.

The phrase "I in them and you in me" indicates two indwellings—the Son in the believer, and the Father in the Son. We are to hold up Jesus' unity with the Father as our model and the source of our unity with one another. When we lift up and display such unity, the world will be attracted to Jesus.

Unity is based upon telling the truth in love—not always easy, but absolutely necessary.

Such a powerful evangelist was George Whitefield that thirty thousand people would regularly attend his open-air meetings. So anointed and eloquent was he, history records many orators and actors would come just to watch him. Charles Wesley, a contemporary of Whitefield's, was also preaching to multitudes. Yet so diverse were the views of these two men on certain doctrines, they took out advertisements in the newspapers explaining why they believed what they did—and why the other was amiss. People thought these men hated each other—until one reporter asked Whitefield, "Tell me, Mr. Whitefield, do you expect to see Charles Wesley in heaven?"

"No," answered Whitefield. "He's going to be so close to the throne, and I'm going to be so far back, I'll never see him."

I like that! Here these guys had very different views doctrinally, and very different flavors in ministry, but they had unity through love in their diversity.

—*Jon Courson's Application Commentary, New Testament*, 575–576

The Father loves us just as he loves the Son! Think of how the Father loves Jesus: Infinite love. Eternal love. Perfect love. That's how the Father loves us. In 1 John 4:10 we read, "This is love: not that we loved God, but that he loved us and sent his Son as an atoning sacrifice for our sins."

Love and unity are the central themes of Jesus' prayer. Believers should be characterized by love for and unity with one another. Unbelievers who see these two qualities would be attracted to Jesus. Unfortunately, the church so far has failed to live out Jesus' prayer—and our witness to the world has been compromised. Rather than love and unity, Christian groups around the world often display excruciating separatism, aggressive partisanism, and vindictive attitudes toward one another. We must change our ways.

John 17:24-26

24 "Father, I want those you have given me to be with me where I am, and to see my glory, the glory you have given me because you loved me before the creation of the world.

25 "Righteous Father, though the world does not know you, I know you, and they know that you have sent me. 26 I have made you[e] known to them, and will continue to make you known in order that the love you have for me may be in them and that I myself may be in them."

Jesus longs for his disciples to see his full glory, his eternal majesty. On earth, his glory is cloaked in a human body. But in heaven we will see his full glory. In the presence of God there is no darkness. Perhaps it is only in the life to come that we will have a full appreciation of Jesus' lowly service here.

Verse 25 is the only place in the New Testament where God is referred to as "Righteous Father." However, God's righteousness is celebrated throughout the Old Testament. The psalmist declares: "For the LORD is righteous, he loves justice; the upright will see his face (Psalm 11:7).

The training of the Twelve has been the centerpiece of Jesus' three-year mission. Now, his death and resurrection will give them the message to be proclaimed in love to the entire world.

---

e John 17:26 Greek *your name*

> It doesn't matter how you pray—with your head bowed in silence, or crying out in grief, or dancing. Churches are good for prayer, but so are garages and cars and mountains and showers and dance floors. Years ago I wrote an essay that began, "Some people think that God is in the details, but I have come to believe that God is in the bathroom."
>
> — Anne Lamott, *Plan B: Further Thoughts on Faith*, 37.

READ BETWEEN THE LINES

- For whom is Jesus praying in this passage?
- What is the basis for Christian unity?
- What does unity in the church look like?
- Why is unity important to Jesus?
- How has Jesus made the Righteous Father known?

WELCOME TO MY WORLD

- Whom do I call in times of need?
- What would Jesus pray for my friends and me?
- How does unity among Christians attract people to Jesus?
- Does my church reflect this kind of unity?
- What turns people off from the church?
- What part of this entire prayer relates to me the most?
- How am I doing at loving others?
- How can I overcome discouragement when my prayers seem to go unanswered?
- Read this prayer again but insert your name, as appropriate, in place of the words *they*, *them*, or *those*. Then ask yourself: *How do I feel knowing that Jesus was praying for me?*

Jesus Is Arrested

Some would have us think that Jesus did not plan on going to the cross. In the 1971 rock opera *Jesus Christ Superstar*, we hear these words addressed to Jesus, "You'd have managed better if you'd had it planned."

We've seen in the Gospel of John that Jesus always planned on going to the cross. He wasn't trapped, tricked, or surprised by the cross. There has never been a day when Jesus shook his head and said, "Wow, I never saw that one coming!" He knew what was ahead. He was born for that very purpose. Jesus makes this clear in John 12:27—"Now my soul is troubled, and what shall I say? 'Father, save me from this hour?' No, it was for this very reason I came to this hour."

John 18:1

¹ When he had finished praying, Jesus left with his disciples and crossed the Kidron Valley. On the other side there was a garden, and he and his disciples went into it.

As we have mentioned, some commentators believe the words at the end of John 14:31—"Come now; let us leave"—indicate that Jesus and the disciples departed the upper room at that time and that Jesus continued talking (15:1–17:27) as they walked through the Kidron Valley. Others feel the group left the upper room after Jesus' prayer in chapter 17. Either way, as chapter 18 begins, Jesus and the disciples have made their way to a garden on the other side of the Kidron Valley.

The gardens on the Mount of Olives (Matthew 26:30) belonged to rich people from Jerusalem who'd go there to escape the heat of the city. Jesus must have known one of these people. This one may have been a walled garden because they "went into it" and later Jesus "went out" (18:4). There are still gardens in that area today. However, John writes, "there was a garden," which may indicate that this particular garden had been destroyed and no longer existed at the time he wrote his Gospel.

Some of the olive trees on the Mount of Olives are said to be up to 2,000 years old. Olives are crushed to produce oil. Soon Jesus would be crushed as he obeyed the Father, and he would sweat drops of blood as he prayed (Luke 22:44). We know from the other Gospels (Matthew 26:36; Mark 14:32) that this place was called Gethsemane (meaning "oil press").

Jewish custom required all Jews to stay within the city limits during Passover. The city limits extended out to include the Mount of Olives, but Bethany (where Jesus normally stayed) would have been outside the city.

The garden of Gethsemane echoes in some ways the garden of Eden, where the first Adam rebelled against the Father's will (Genesis 1–3). In this garden Jesus, the "last Adam" (1 Corinthians 15:45), submits to the Father's will. In the first garden a sword was revealed (Genesis 3:24). In this garden a sword is put away (18:11). In the first garden, the first Adam sinned and humanity fell away from God. Now, in the garden of Gethsemane, the last Adam is beginning the process of bringing humanity back into right relationship with the Father. What was lost in the first garden is redeemed in this second garden.

Again, this was the Passover season. Historians tell us that hundreds of thousands of lambs were slain each year at the one temple altar during Passover. There was a ravine or channel that began near the temple grounds at the top of the Valley of Kidron. The blood of the slain lambs would then run down the channel and into the Brook Kidron (meaning "murky" or "darkness") and out of the city. As Jesus crossed this brook, he may have seen the blood and thought about his own impending death.

John 18:2

² Now Judas, who betrayed him, knew the place, because Jesus had often met there with his disciples.

Jesus could have left town and escaped into the wilderness. But he willingly gave himself up; it was God's plan.

Why did Jesus choose this particular place to be betrayed? Jesus knew Judas was familiar with it since Jesus had been there many times before with his disciples (Luke 21:37; 22:39). This was a spot where they would go to pray. Jesus knew this garden was a private place where he could pour out his heart to his Father (Matthew 26:36-46; Mark 14:32-42; Luke 22:39-46).

But Jesus may have had other reasons for choosing this isolated place instead of the city. Jesus knew the Pharisees feared the crowds who followed Jesus. In this secluded garden, few people would be present. But if he'd been in the city, the Pharisees might have been too afraid to act. And if they'd attempted to arrest him in the city, the crowds might have rioted, and his disciples could have been hurt. Even as he faces the cross, Jesus continues to take care of his disciples.

Jesus' agony in the garden, which is so movingly described in the other Gospels, is absent from John's account—even though John was one of the three (with Peter and James) who went with Jesus into the garden. It was there that Jesus put his face to the ground and prayed, "My Father, if it is possible, may this cup be taken from me. Yet not as I will, but as you will" (Matthew 26:39). Perhaps John leaves out the specifics of Jesus' prayer in the garden because he's already described Jesus' deeply troubled heart (11:33; 12:27; 13:21). After praying, Jesus was prepared for the events at hand: "Rise! Let us go! Here comes my betrayer" (Mark 14:42).

By passing through the Kidron Valley on his way to the garden to pray, Jesus was fulfilling prophecy on the very site of an earlier biblical betrayal. In 2 Samuel 15, we find a story out of the life of King David, the greatest king in the history of Israel. It was said that a son of David would sit on his throne forever. Jesus was a son of David both through the bloodline of his mother Mary, and through Joseph who later married Mary.

In 2 Samuel 15:23, we read how David passed through that same valley, aware that his son Absalom was conspiring against him: "The whole countryside wept aloud as all the people passed by. The king also crossed the Kidron Valley, and all the people moved on toward the wilderness." King David crossed over the same brook that Jesus now crosses. Then, in 15:30-31, we read: "But David continued up the Mount of Olives, weeping as he went; his head was covered and he was barefoot. All the people with him covered their heads too and were weeping as they went up. Now David had been told, 'Ahithophel is among the conspirators with Absalom.'" Ahithophel was one of David's trusted advisors.

Jesus, the son of David, went up to the Mount of Olives and wept tears of blood. Then, like David, Jesus was betrayed by a friend.

John 18:3

3 So Judas came to the garden, guiding a detachment of soldiers and some officials from the chief priests and the Pharisees. They were carrying torches, lanterns and weapons.

The religious leaders have tried to have Jesus arrested on other occasions, but he'd always vanished before their eyes (7:32-34, 44-46; Luke 4:28-30). This time, Judas and a group of officials from the chief priests and Pharises, along with perhaps 200 Roman soldiers fully armed with swords and clubs, were walking toward Jesus. We know it was a large number of soldiers because the Greek word *speira*, which the NIV translates as "detachment," can refer to as few as 200 or as many as 1,000 soldiers.

John is the only one to mention these soldiers. They could be Roman auxiliaries, but more likely they are what we might call private soldiers under the employ of the temple hierarchy—after all, Jesus is taken to the temple authorities first, not to the Romans. That's quite a compliment to Jesus that they would send so many soldiers to arrest one Galilean carpenter accompanied by his 11 friends with only two weapons between them (Luke 22:38). The number of soldiers may be due to the volatile environment that existed because of the large crowds gathering for Passover. The combination of temple officials and soldiers shows that both Jews and Gentiles were intertwined in this deadly deed. John wants to make it clear that it's not any particular group but the entire world that is responsible for what happens next.

The torches and lanterns attest to the fact that Jesus was arrested at night. Why did these soldiers bring the torches and lanterns when the Passover was celebrated during a full moon? The soldiers likely assumed Jesus would attempt to flee and hide in the nooks and crannies of the hillside or in the shadows of the olive trees.

John doesn't record that Judas greets Jesus with a kiss. The Greek wording indicates that Judas kisses Jesus repeatedly (Matthew 26:49; Mark 14:45; Luke 22:47-48). Judas doesn't merely point out Jesus to the soldiers; he betrays Jesus with a gesture that's usually used as an expression of love. With that kiss, Judas seals his own fate. This is one of the greatest acts of betrayal in history.

John 18:4-9

⁴ Jesus, knowing all that was going to happen to him, went out and asked them, "Who is it you want?"

⁵ "Jesus of Nazareth," they replied.

"I am he," Jesus said. (And Judas the traitor was standing there with them.) ⁶ When Jesus said, "I am he," they drew back and fell to the ground.

⁷ Again he asked them, "Who is it you want?"

"Jesus of Nazareth," they said.

⁸ Jesus answered, "I told you that I am he. If you are looking for me, then let these men go." ⁹ This happened so that the words he had spoken would be fulfilled: "I have not lost one of those you gave me."[a]

Jesus goes out to meet them and asks, "Who is it you want?"—words that recall the very first words of Jesus in this Gospel (1:38). This must have taken supreme courage. Jesus initiates the whole arrest; he is in control. This must have surprised the soldiers. Jesus saw the group coming before they ever got to the garden (Mark 14:42), and yet he did not hide.

Their reply, "Jesus of Nazareth," is found in only two other places in John's Gospel—in Philip's words to Nathanael at the very beginning of Jesus' ministry (1:45), and as part of the title placed on the cross (19:19).

The NIV translates Jesus' response as, "I am he." But the word *he* is not there in the Greek text; Jesus simply said, *ego eimi*—"I AM" (4:26; 8:24, 28, 58; 13:19; also Exodus 3:14). By answering in this way, Jesus is claiming to be God—and these guys all fall to the ground, including Judas. This is a fulfillment of prophecy. Psalm 27:2 states, "When the wicked advance against me to devour me, it is my enemies and my foes who will stumble and fall." Another possible explanation for why the soldiers "drew back and fell to the ground" is that they expected a counter-offensive, so they were taking a self-protective position.

Jesus could have walked away, but he waits for them to get up. A second time Jesus has these soldiers repeat who

---

a John 18:9 See John 6:39

they are looking for. And once more he confirms his identity and encourages the soldiers to take him and let his disciples go. Here, we again see Jesus as the Good Shepherd who protects his sheep (10:11, 15, 17-18, 28). John notes that by protecting his disciples here, Jesus fulfills the words he spoke in his prayer in 17:12—"While I was with them, I protected them and kept them safe by that name you gave me. None has been lost except the one doomed to destruction so that Scripture would be fulfilled."

Jesus knows these same disciples will eventually face persecution. But if any of them had been taken into custody at this time and tortured, what little faith they had might have vanished. Jesus protects them until their faith grows and they are ready for the struggles that lie ahead. Jesus does not allow anything (disasters, adversity, failures, and tragedies) to come into our lives that would be more than our faith can handle

John 18:10-11

10 Then Simon Peter, who had a sword, drew it and struck the high priest's servant, cutting off his right ear. (The servant's name was Malchus.)

11 Jesus commanded Peter, "Put your sword away! Shall I not drink the cup the Father has given me?"

Peter whips out his sword and chops off the ear of a servant named Malchus (whose name may mean "kingly one"—interesting choice for a servant). Peter may have been intending to slice the man in half, but perhaps he is such a lousy swordsman that he cuts off only the servant's right ear. Other commentators have suggested that Peter struck only the ear in order to insult and humiliate Malchus. Luke 22:49-51 tells us that Jesus rebukes Peter and then heals the ear of this insignificant (but not to Jesus) servant.

John is the only Gospel who reveals who had the sword and the servant's name. We don't know where Peter got the *machaira* (long knife or short sword). It would have been unusual for Peter, a fisherman, to have such a sword. But, in Luke 22:36 Jesus had said to the disciples, "But now if you have a purse, take it, and also a bag; and if you don't have a sword, sell your cloak and buy one." Perhaps Peter took Jesus seriously. In a moment of impulsive desperation Peter pulls out the sword in the midst of this large group of armed professional soldiers. This took courage but it also created a more dangerous situation.

But there is a deeper theological reality present here. Jesus and he alone is to be the world's Savior. The disciples are not able nor are they permitted by Jesus to intervene. Their moral courage and their moral purity is no match for the power of sin and death.

—Earl F. Palmer, *The Intimate Gospel: Studies in John*, 151

Why didn't Peter understand that Jesus had to drink of this cup? Maybe he would have understood if he'd stayed awake as Jesus prayed to his Father (Matthew 26:40; Mark 14:37). Jesus didn't need Peter to defend him. The Father could have sent down thousands of angels to Jesus' side (Matthew 26:53).

The cup Jesus must drink is the cross (Matthew 20:22; 26:29; Mark 14:36; Luke 22:42). Jeremiah 25:15 speaks of a "cup filled with the wine of my wrath." On the cross Jesus is taking the cup of wrath that should have gone to us. We read in 2 Corinthians 5:21, "God made him who had no sin to be sin for us, so that in him we might become the righteousness of God."

John 18:12-14

12 Then the detachment of soldiers with its commander and the Jewish officials arrested Jesus.

They bound him ¹³ and brought him first to Annas, who was the father-in-law of Caiaphas, the high priest that year. ¹⁴ Caiaphas was the one who had advised the Jewish leaders that it would be good if one man died for the people.

John tells us the soldiers bound Jesus after arresting him. It was common for criminals to be bound when arrested, but it also fulfills Scripture describing what was done to the lamb that was to be sacrificed at the Passover: "Bind the festal sacrifice with ropes and take it up to the horns of the altar" (Psalm 118:27).

The binding of the Son of God also recalls the Old Testament story of Abraham and his son Isaac. Genesis 22:9 says, "When they reached the place God had told him about; Abraham built an altar there and arranged the wood on it. He bound his son Isaac and laid him on the altar, on top of the wood."

> **They came forward and arrested Jesus. The proper manner taught by the academy of soldiery in Rome, was to take the victim by the right wrist, twist his arm behind him so that his knuckles touched between his shoulder blades and, at the same time, jam the heel down on his right instep. This was the beginning of the pain Jesus would feel this day.**
>
> **Some of the temple guards, not wishing to be shamed in the presence of the Gentiles, grabbed the other arm and put it behind his back and brought out rope and tied his hands. A long noose was placed about his neck.**
>
> **—Jim Bishop, *The Day Christ Died*, 174**

Jesus was bound and taken to Annas, the father-in-law of the current high priest, Caiaphas. Annas himself had been the high priest from AD 6 to AD 15, until he was deposed by Pilate's predecessor, Valerius Gratus. (All high priests retain the title as a courtesy.) Even as an old man, Annas still had enough power and influence to get his five sons and his son-in-law, Caiaphas, all appointed to serve as high priest at different times. Originally, the high priest was to serve in that position for life (Numbers 35:25), but the Roman government didn't want one person to gain too much power. So Roman politicians used their authority to change the high priest periodically. Caiaphas was the one technically in office from AD 18 to AD 36, but make no mistake about it—Annas was running the show.

There were some among the Sanhedrin who seemed overly interested in power and money. Annas and his family appear to have been among them. Even the Jewish Talmud presents this family in an unfavorable light: "Woe to the house of Annas! Woe to their serpent's hiss! They are High Priests; their sons are keepers of the treasury, their sons-in-law are guardians of the temple, and their servants beat people with staves" (*Pesachim*, 57a). It is likely that Annas had used his position to become wealthy; many of his fellow Jews likely viewed him as too cozy with the Romans.

Jesus had become a bit of a problem for Annas and the Sanhedrin, due to his overturning of the tables of Annas' moneychangers in the temple (2:13-15), and his frequent criticism of the Jewish leadership. But Jesus' popularity and his criticism of their authority was more than just an inconvenience. The large crowds following Jesus might have caused the Romans to doubt the religious leaders' ability to maintain order in Judea. The members of the Sanhedrin may have feared that their own power could be in jeopardy if they did not eliminate Jesus.

Perhaps Annas was hoping Jesus would confess to a crime so there'd be no need for a trial. According to the four Gospels, Jesus didn't have just one trial but six different meetings with various ruling authorities—a combination of preliminary hearings, investigations, interrogations, and trials. There are a variety of opinions about the specific function of each one. For simplicity's sake, we'll refer to each of Jesus' six appearances before a ruling authority as a "trial," even though, technically speaking, they aren't all trials.

Israel could decide that Jesus should die, but because Israel was under Roman rule, only Rome could execute him. For that reason Jesus is brought before both Jewish religious leaders and Roman civil authorities. Jesus has three Jewish religious trials:

- Before Annas, former High Priest (John 18:12-14, 19-23);
- Before Caiaphas, current High Priest, and the Sanhedrin (John 18:24; Matthew 26:57, 59-68; Mark 14:53, 55-65; Luke 22:54, 63-65);
- Before the Sanhedrin (Matthew 27:1-2; Mark 15:1; Luke 22:66-71).

He also had three Roman civil trials:

- Before Pilate, governor of Judea (Matthew 27:2, 11-14; Luke 23:1-7; John 18:28-38);
- Before Herod Antipas, governor of Galilee (Luke 23:6-12);
- Before Pilate (Matthew 27:15-26; Mark 15:6-15; Luke 23:13-25; John 18:39-19:16);

To the Romans, Palestine was a small insignificant finger of land in a massive piece of real estate known as the Roman Empire. The Romans were ruled by Caesar, whom they considered to be a god on earth. The Caesar in Jesus' day was Tiberius. Tiberius ruled with an iron fist. He was a sadistic, anti-Semitic Gentile.

The religious leaders were in a hurry, eager to have Jesus executed before the Sabbath so they could move on with their Passover celebration. If the Jewish leaders could have, they would have stoned Jesus because that was their method of capital punishment. But since they were under Roman authority, Jesus had to be executed by the Roman method of crucifixion. The Jewish authorities could try a man, but they could bring him only so far—namely to their ruling council, a body of 71 men called the "greater Sanhedrin." (There was also a "lesser Sanhedrin" of 23 men, but they couldn't pass judgment on capital crimes.) Once the greater Sanhedrin came to the decision that Jesus must die, he had to be brought to the Roman authority, which was Pilate. Only after Pilate gave the orders could Jesus be executed.

The Jewish leaders tried Jesus for blasphemy, but then they altered the charge and accused Jesus of treason when they brought him before the Romans. This was because in Rome, those guilty of treason were immediately executed. That's why Jesus was crucified for treason instead of being stoned for blasphemy.

Caiaphas had advised the Jewish leaders back in John 11:49-53 that it would be better if one man died for the good of all people. Caiaphas was saying this in ignorance, but God made it come out as a prophecy. The words of Caiaphas became true in a way he never imagined. John may have wanted to remind his readers of Caiaphas's earlier statement, as a way of showing that the trial in front of Caiaphas would not be unbiased.

READ BETWEEN THE LINES

- Did Jesus leave for the Mount of Olives in 14:31 or in 18:1?
- What do you know about gardens on the Mount of Olives?

- Why would Jesus pick this location?
- Why would the religious leaders want to arrest Jesus at night?
- What was Jesus most concerned about?
- Why would Jesus ask, "Who is it you want?"—twice?
- What made the soldiers fall down?
- Why does Simon Peter have a sword?
- How did Peter feel when Jesus rebuked him?
- What "cup" is Jesus referring to?
- What does it mean by "they bound him"?
- How are the disciples feeling as these events unfold?
- Who are Annas and Caiaphas? Which one is the High Priest?

WELCOME TO MY WORLD

- Where would my friends probably look for me if I were going through difficult times?
- Do I have a spot where I can go to slow down, read Scripture, and pray?
- How do I respond to unfairness?
- Have there ever been times when I've taken things into my own hands instead of allowing God's plan to unfold?
- Have I ever stood before a judge? How did that go?
- When I got in trouble as a child, who was the person I least wanted to see? Why?

Peter's First Denial

John 18:15-16

¹⁵ Simon Peter and another disciple were following Jesus. Because this disciple was known to the high priest, he went with Jesus into the high priest's courtyard, ¹⁶ but Peter had to wait outside at the door. The other disciple, who was known to the high priest, came back, spoke to the servant girl on duty there and brought Peter in.

After Jesus was arrested, the disciples scattered (Matthew 26:56). The other Gospel writers emphasize that Peter and another unnamed disciple returned and followed Jesus far behind, "at a distance" (Matthew 26:58; Luke 22:54). When you follow Jesus but keep some distance from him, you get in trouble.

When I was in the fifth grade, my family went to Knott's Berry Farm, which was 90 minutes from our West Los Angeles home. Back then, Knott's Berry Farm was just a small farm with a restaurant that served chicken dinners. They also had a few small shops that made it look like an Old West ghost town. Among those shops was a chapel. We went in the chapel, heard some music, and saw a life-sized painting of Jesus, then walked out the back door into a conveniently located gift shop. After my dad purchased a couple of items, we went home.

That evening my dad wanted to show me something he'd bought at the gift shop. He held something small in his fist. But before he would show it to me, he insisted that we find the darkest place in our small home, which turned out to be a closet. As we stood in the darkened closet, my dad opened his fist, and I saw that he was holding a small glowing cross. You've probably seen lots of these, but back then it was a brand-new product I'd never seen. I thought it was so cool. Then he put it in my hand

and said it was for me. I was delighted. I was surprised by how thin it was. I thought it had to be powered by a battery or an electric cord, but there was nothing.

I put it in my pocket and then went to find my sister, who is four years younger than me. I finally found her playing outside. Because of all the tricks I'd played on her in the past, it took me a while to convince her to go into that same closet with me. But finally she agreed. I pulled the cross out of my pocket, held it inside my fist, and said, "Watch this!" But when I opened my hand expecting to wow her, we saw nothing. No glow, nothing. I hit it a couple of times, but still we saw no glow. My sister said, "This is stupid," and went back outside.

I found my dad and told him that Knott's had ripped him off because the cross was busted already. He patiently took me over to the floor lamp in our living room and held the cross close to the light bulb for a minute. Then we went back into the closet, and it glowed like crazy. I learned that in order for it to glow, it had to be close to the light. The longer it was away from the light, the less it glowed.

Peter "followed at a distance" (far from the light of Jesus, both physically and spiritually), and it caused him problems for the rest of the evening. When we aren't in close proximity to Jesus, we lose the glow, the joy, and the ability to share his light with others.

—Les

Many scholars think the "other disciple" may be the same person referred to elsewhere as the "beloved disciple"—which many believe to be John's way of speaking about himself in the Gospel. Peter and this unnamed disciple appear together several times (13:23-26; 20:2-10; 21:7, 20-23).

John was a fisherman but that doesn't mean he was poor or uneducated. The fact that his father Zebedee had servants (Mark 1:19-20) would indicate that he had a flourishing fishing business. Perhaps Zebedee and his sons had a contract to sell fish to the high priest's household—that might explain how the disciple was able to get into the high priest's courtyard.

Other suggestions about the identity of this "other disciple" include Judas, Joseph of Arimathea (19:38), Nicodemus, and Lazarus.

The fact that it's a servant girl who questions the disciples indicates that this courtyard was outside the temple area, because only men were allowed to serve inside the temple. The high priest's house may have been in the Hasmonean Palace that faced the temple. Annas and Caiaphas may have lived in separate wings of the same palace, sharing a common courtyard.

John 18:17-18

17 "You aren't one of this man's disciples too, are you?" she asked Peter.

He replied, "I am not."

18 It was cold, and the servants and officials stood around a fire they had made to keep warm. Peter also was standing with them, warming himself.

The palace was probably more like a compound surrounded by thick walls, with a small hallway leading into the courtyard. In the darkness of the hallway, a servant girl thinks she recognizes Peter and asks him the first of three questions (13:38). Gary Burge believes her question indicates that she knows Jesus has many followers. Burge suggests we might paraphrase her question to read, "What is this? Not another of this man's disciples, is it?"

Peter wasn't expecting to be questioned by this inconsequential servant girl. Unfortunately, he folds by quickly responding with an abrupt, "I am not." Perhaps he responded this way because he felt suddenly on the defensive, or maybe it was the unfamiliar setting. Many of us find it much easier to plan for and face temptations that we know are coming in two weeks; it's the surprise attacks that throw us. I think after Peter blurted out, "I am not," he was probably stunned by his response to the question.

In Jerusalem it can get chilly at night during the spring. Peter warmed himself around "a charcoal fire" according to the NASB and ESV translations. The Greek word *anthrakia* found in many original Biblical manuscripts can be translated "charcoal." For some reason, the NIV translation left out this word, which is unfortunate. You may think this is a seemingly inconsequential detail, and I would generally agree (although it does indicate an eyewitness account). But it's worth noting that this word is used only twice in the New Testament. And in that second reference (John 21:9), it takes on more significance. (You can jump ahead now and look at that passage, or wait till we get there.)

The saddest part of this passage is where it says, "Peter also was standing with them." Andreas J. Köstenberger has pointed out, "Like Judas earlier (18:5), Peter here 'stands' with Jesus' enemies." Those with whom we spend the most time end up shaping our character. We should all heed the words of 1 Corinthians 15:33 "Do not be misled: 'Bad company corrupts good character.'"

> Just outside Anchorage, Alaska, there's a place called the Turnagain Arm. This particular area has one of the fastest tide rates in the world. The tide rushes in and out at up to 10 feet per minute. And the water is so cold that if you got caught in it, you'd die within a few minutes. When the tide is out, there is a huge flat area of mud. It looks like it might be a great place to ride off-road vehicles. But this area—called the mud flats—is made up of not just mud, but also glacial silt. When the tide

rushes out, the water that's left settles quickly. When it settles, it leaves air pockets; and those air pockets form vacuums. You never know where they are, and they're never in the same place twice. If you step in one of them, it will suck you in, making it impossible to get out. It's not exactly like quicksand, but more like superglue as it locks you in.

In the summer of 1991, a newlywed couple decided to spend their honeymoon in this part of Alaska. They went out riding ATVs and decided to ride around on one of these mud flats. The bride's vehicle stalled, and she jumped off to see what the problem was. But she jumped into one of these areas of glacial silt and immediately sank in up to her knees. As she struggled to get out, she soon sunk to her thighs. When her husband rode up on his ATV, she warned him not to get off his vehicle. People on the road above saw what was happening and called for help, yelling at the man not to get off his vehicle.

Within moments the fire department arrived. The bride was now up to her waist in glacial silt. They tried blasting her out of the mud flat using water hoses. It didn't work. Then they brought in a helicopter from the nearby Air Force base. They tried to pull her out with a rope and harness attached around her waist. As the helicopter pulled her up, her legs dislocated. They knew that if they'd pulled any more, they would have ripped her legs from her body. They tried to put a wetsuit around her, hoping to keep her warm when the tides came in. But she could only get the wetsuit around part of her body. When the tides came in, she died as her new husband watched helplessly. Today, there are numerous signs posted in the area warning people of the danger.

Sin works the same way as this glacial silt: It sucks you in. When you participate in a sin the first time, you may feel remorse. But if you continue doing it, it becomes easier to do it again and again until soon it becomes a habit you can't shake loose. It clings to you like this mud, and ultimately it ends up taking your life. We see this happening to Peter in this passage.

—Les

READ BETWEEN THE LINES

- Who was the "other disciple"?
- How might this person have known the high priest?
- Why did the servant girl ask her question?
- After being so bold with his sword moments earlier, why did Peter respond to her question the way he did?
- Why does Peter stand with the enemies of Jesus? How is he feeling?

WELCOME TO MY WORLD

- What happened the last time I put my foot in my mouth?
- When have I found it difficult to admit I am a Christian?
- Have I ever been embarrassed by my relationship with Jesus? What could I have done differently?
- With whom am I "standing" today?

The High Priest Questions Jesus

John 18:19-21

¹⁹ Meanwhile, the high priest questioned Jesus about his disciples and his teaching.

²⁰ "I have spoken openly to the world," Jesus replied. "I always taught in synagogues or at the temple, where all the Jews come together. I said nothing in secret. ²¹ Why question me? Ask those who heard me. Surely they know what I said."

In 18:12-27, Jesus' trials and Peter's denials are intertwined. The Jewish leaders and the Roman authorities agreed on very little, but here we see them working together to get rid of Jesus. The fact that Jesus has just miraculously healed a servant's severed ear does nothing to faze them.

The case against Jesus would be thrown out of any court today. The interrogations are a mockery of justice. These religious leaders have already decided what they will do with Jesus (11:47-53).

These trials also break several Jewish laws:

1. A prisoner could not be compelled to testify against himself.
2. A person is innocent until proven guilty.
3. A criminal cannot be tried on a feast day.
4. A trial cannot take place in the high priest's house; it can be held only in the council chamber.
5. Witnesses had to be brought in and cross-examined.
6. Burden of proof was to be on the court.
7. Specific charges had to be made.
8. There was to be no striking of the prisoner and no showing of emotion.

9. Between the hearing of the case and the delivery of the verdict, there had to be a minimum of one day. During this time the court members were to meet in pairs, eat light food, drink light wines, and sleep well so they could render a decision the next day.
10. No trial is to be held secretly or at night because members of the court may not be alert during darkness.

Annas (who still has considerable power) is referred to again as the high priest, and he questions Jesus directly. Annas may have been hoping to get an incriminating confession. Jesus responds calmly to those who are indicting him—and his words indict *them*. Annas is trying to get Jesus to admit that he is a false prophet who deceives the people and does things in secret (Matthew 24:11, 24; Mark 13:5, 22; Luke 21:8). The penalty for being a false prophet was death (Deuteronomy 13:1-11).

Jesus makes it clear that he "said nothing in secret" (7:26). He has always taught in public places. He tells them that what he's said during the quiet, private talks with his disciples are the same things he's said in public. He is an open book. Jesus points out that there are plenty of eyewitnesses available who could verify what he did and said. His self-confidence and assertiveness must have surprised those in attendance.

John 18:22-24

22 **When Jesus said this, one of the officials nearby slapped him in the face. "Is this the way you answer the high priest?" he demanded.**
23 **"If I said something wrong," Jesus replied, "testify as to what is wrong. But if I spoke the truth, why did you strike me?" 24 Then Annas sent him bound to Caiaphas the high priest.**

This official, probably one of the temple guards, slaps Jesus on the face sharply. Later, others will spit on him and hit him with their fists (Matthew 26:67). Such treatment was both immoral and illegal. Brutality was never allowed in the courts. This abusive treatment fulfills Scripture: "They will strike Israel's ruler on the cheek with a rod" (Micah 5:1). Yet Jesus remains in control.

It's interesting to compare Jesus' reaction here to the apostle Paul's behavior in a similar situation. Check out Acts 23:1-5, where Paul is struck in the mouth by a guard while appearing before the high priest. Paul responds in a very human way, using the biblical equivalent of cursing by saying, "God will strike you, you whitewashed wall!"

Annas is getting nowhere with Jesus, so he sends him to Caiaphas, the current high priest (Matthew 26:57-68; Mark 14:53-65). This involved a move to another courtroom, possibly in the same building. Annas knows that in order to bring this case to Pilate, it had to come via the reigning high priest and the Sanhedrin.

John doesn't give us any details about Jesus' appearance before Caiaphas. According to Mark 14:53-65, Caiaphas gathered whatever members of the Sanhedrin he could find at that late hour for a second (mock) trial. Witnesses brought false and conflicting testimony. Jesus confessed openly and clearly that he was the Christ (Son of Man). Then some began to spit on him; others blindfolded him and struck him with their fists, saying "Prophesy!" Then the guards took him and beat him.

This group may have dismissed and then reconvened early the next morning under the directions of Caiaphas, the high priest. This meeting would have been held in the official place of judgment, a semicircular hall at the east end of the Royal Portico of the temple. This would be the third part of the religious trial. Mark 15:1 tells us, "Very early in

the morning, the chief priests, with the elders, the teachers of the law and the whole Sanhedrin, made their plans.
So they bound Jesus, led him away and handed him over to
Pilate." Matthew's account is similar: "Early in the morning,
all the chief priests and the elders of the people made their
plans how to have Jesus executed" (27:1). They twisted the
charges against Jesus before bringing him to Pontius Pilate,
now accusing Jesus of treason against Rome.

By now, Jesus' face would have been swollen from the
soldiers' beatings during these trials. The swelling around
his eyes would have become so puffed up that it would have
been difficult for him to open them. Some believe Jesus'
beard was torn off, in keeping with the words of Isaiah 50:6,
"I offered my back to those who beat me, my cheeks to those
who pulled out my beard; I did not hide my face from mocking and spitting."

> The true high priest will be sent to death by the false one, so
> that through his death God will rescue his people. The true
> Adam will be sent to his death by the false ones, so that the
> garden may be restored, and instead of bloodshed there may be
> healing and forgiveness.
>
> —Tom Wright, *John for Everyone, Part Two, Chapters 11–21*, 104

READ BETWEEN THE LINES

- What was illegal about the high priest's questioning
  of Jesus?
- What does Jesus mean when he says, "I said nothing
  in secret"?
- How does Jesus defend himself?
- Whom does Jesus suggest they question to find out
  about his teachings?

- Why did the official slap Jesus?
- How does Jesus respond?

WELCOME TO MY WORLD

- What ticks me off most about these interrogations?
- What would I have said to these religious leaders?
- Has a religious institution ever treated me unfairly?
- How did I deal with it?

Peter's Second and Third Denials

John 18:25-27

25 Meanwhile, Simon Peter was still standing there warming himself. So they asked him, "You aren't one of his disciples too, are you?"

He denied it, saying, "I am not."

26 One of the high priest's servants, a relative of the man whose ear Peter had cut off, challenged him, "Didn't I see you with him in the garden?"

27 Again Peter denied it, and at that moment a rooster began to crow.

Jesus continues to tell the truth, while Peter continues to tell lies. Peter is still standing with Jesus' enemies near the fire, and he's still denying Jesus. The other three Gospels tell us that Peter's denials took place in the courtyard outside Caiaphas's palace. John puts the three denials outside of Annas's home. This may be two different ways of referring to the same shared courtyard.

Several people engage Peter in conversation as he warms himself by the fire (Matthew 26:71; Mark 14:69; Luke 22:58). In verse 25, they ask Peter if he is one of Jesus' followers; for a second time, he declares, "I am not." The third denial comes in response to a question from one of the relatives of Malchus, the servant whose ear Peter cut off. A relative would have had great interest in the recent events. Although being a disciple of Jesus was not yet a crime, physically attacking a man with a sword was. The relative asks, "Didn't I see you with him in the garden?" Again, Peter denies being associated with Jesus. The other Gospel accounts tell us he got angry and cursed, and then he swore he didn't know Jesus (Matthew 26:74).

Immediately, the rooster began to crow. There was a regulation in Jewish law that said that fowl (roosters and hens) weren't allowed in Jerusalem, especially around the temple area, because the birds defiled holy things. Some have suggested this prohibition wasn't strictly obeyed. But there is another possible explanation for the rooster's crowing.

In the first century, the night was divided not into hours but "watches." Thus, there were four watches, each lasting three hours:

- First watch was from 6:00 to 9:00 P.M.
- Second watch was from 9:00 P.M. to midnight.
- Third watch was from midnight to 3:00 A.M.
- Fourth watch was from 3:00 to 6:00 A.M.

There was a changing of the guard between the third and fourth watch of the night in a place called the Fortress of Antonia. The dungeon where Barabbas was being kept (which becomes significant in a few verses) was likely inside this fortress. When the guards changed positions between the third and fourth watch, there would be two blasts from a trumpet (m. Sukk. 5.4). The term for this procedure was "cock crow" because that was the time of day when many live roosters would normally crow. But instead of live roosters, they had trumpets. If you awakened at the end of the third watch and lived near the palace, you'd hear the "cock crow" of the trumpets.

If this is what Peter heard, then that would mean that Jesus pinpointed the exact hour this denial would happen. Jesus had told Peter before "cock crow" you will have denied me three times—and it happened just as Jesus predicted. Whether it was a rooster or a trumpet, Peter knew exactly what the sound meant.

The Gospel of Luke weaves together the trials of Jesus and Peter's denials in a different way: "Peter replied, 'Man, I don't know what you're talking about!' Just as he was speaking, the rooster crowed. The Lord turned and looked straight at Peter. Then Peter remembered the word the Lord had spoken to him: 'Before the rooster crows today, you will disown me three times.' And he went outside and wept bitterly" (22:60-62). Imagine that scene: Jesus—beaten, bruised, and bloodied—turns and looks straight into the eyes of Peter, penetrating deep into his soul. Peter's heart must have been crushed. Realizing what he'd done, he went outside the courtyard and wept.

READ BETWEEN THE LINES

- Where was Peter standing?
- Who was there?
- Who asked the questions?
- Why did Peter respond as he did?
- Why are these denials recorded in Scripture?
- What is the significance of the rooster crowing?

WELCOME TO MY WORLD

- It would be easy to say to Peter, "Well, he told you so." But what do I think I would have done in those same circumstances?
- Have I ever denied being a follower of Jesus?
- What can I learn from Peter's experience?

John 18:25-27

Jesus Before Pilate

John 18:28-30

28 Then the Jewish leaders took Jesus from Caiaphas to the palace of the Roman governor. By now it was early morning, and to avoid ceremonial uncleanness they did not enter the palace, because they wanted to be able to eat the Passover. 29 So Pilate came out to them and asked, "What charges are you bringing against this man?"

30 "If he were not a criminal," they replied, "we would not have handed him over to you."

Jesus has already been betrayed by Judas, denied by Peter, interrogated by the high priests, and beaten by guards. But the worst is still to come. Some translations use the term "Jews" in verse 28 in place of "Jewish leaders." Again, it's important to remember that John isn't referring to the entire Jewish community, nor even all the Jewish religious leaders. He is referring to a specific group of religious leaders who were hostile toward Jesus.

These leaders bring Jesus to Pontius Pilate, the Roman governor in this region. Pilate had a permanent residence in Caesarea (Acts 23:33). However, when visiting Jerusalem during the feasts, Pilate lived in the Jerusalem residence of the procurator, which was called the *praetorium*. The praetorium was in the palace built by Herod the Great along the Western Wall of the city. Pilate had another residence and headquarters in the Fortress of Antonia (named after Mark Anthony), located northwest of the temple grounds. It was also built by Herod the Great.

Like the religious trial, Jesus' trial before the Roman officials had three distinct phases. Roman Court opened at sunrise and closed at sunset, but John's Gospel notes that the trial was rushed and completed in the early morning—before a lot of people could get wind of it.

John again reminds us that as Jesus appears before the Roman governor, it is Passover—the time when the lambs are being prepared for sacrifice in the temple. Jesus will be the final Passover Lamb. The Jewish leaders wouldn't enter a Gentile house because they would be defiled and considered unclean (4:9-11; Acts 10:28), which would have prevented them from celebrating the Passover (13:1). They are diligent in following these rules, yet seem to have no conscience when it comes to murdering a man who, even if he had not been the Messiah, was clearly innocent of any crime. This is religious hypocrisy. These guys were definitely whitewashed tombs (Matthew 23:27-29). But since the Jewish leaders won't enter Pilate's home, Pilate comes out to meet them. Their refusal to come into his home must have really ticked off Pilate.

All four Gospels acknowledge Pontius Pilate as the Roman governor of Judea (Matthew 27:1-2; Mark 15:1-14; Luke 23:1-6). He ruled from AD 26 to AD 36. In the past, some critical scholars questioned whether Pilate ever really existed, but that changed in 1962 when an Italian archaeologist, Antonio Frova, led an expedition at Caesarea Maritima. There, they discovered a stone slab with a Latin inscription that read: *Tiberium Pontius Pilate Prefect of Judea*. The title *prefect* is a military identification; *procurator* is a civilian title given to governors of lesser provinces like Judea. Pilate would have been considered one of the lower nobility compared to those of Roman senatorial rank.

These religious leaders don't really want a trial. They made the decision to kill Jesus back in John 11:47-53. They've reinforced that decision through their three religious interrogations. They simply want Pilate to follow their wishes and order that Jesus be executed. But they have no real charges to bring before Pilate. They couldn't offer a single truthful accusation that would have stood up in a Roman court. So they return a sarcastic reply to Pilate's question, insisting they wouldn't have brought Jesus to Pilate if he weren't guilty.

John 18:31-32

³¹ Pilate said, "Take him yourselves and judge him by your own law."

"But we have no right to execute anyone," they objected. ³² This took place to fulfill what Jesus had said about the kind of death he was going to die.

Notice how God's perfect timing is involved in the events that are unfolding. The Roman Empire was a patchwork collection of geographic areas the Romans had conquered. The Romans had established rules by which all of the conquered communities had to abide. One of these rules allowed for capital punishment only with final approval from Rome.

Before this rule the Jewish leaders would have been permitted to execute Jesus themselves, and they would have done so by stoning him. But an ancient Jewish document tells us that "jurisdiction over life was taken from Israel forty years before the temple was destroyed" (C. K. Barrett, 445; R. E. Brown, 850). This Roman decree upset many of the Jewish leaders.

In the year A.D. 30—two years prior to these events—the Romans took away the Jewish right of capital punishment. In response, the rabbis ripped their clothes, donned sackcloth, threw dirt on their heads, and said, "God has failed us. God has failed us," as they marched through the streets of Jerusalem. Why did they cry, "God has failed us"? Because in the Book

> of Genesis, the promise was given that the scepter would not depart from Judah until Messiah came (49:10). But the basic foundation of government was the ability to deal with law-breakers, so the scepter had, indeed, departed—with Messiah seemingly nowhere in sight. Oh, but Messiah *was* there—right in their midst. They just didn't recognize Him.
>
> —*Jon Courson's Application Commentary, New Testament,* 585

This decree would mean that around AD 30 the power was limited in Roman colonies, giving only Rome itself the right to execute criminals. That's why Jesus is tried by both religious and civil authorities, meaning that Jews and Gentiles share responsibility for his death. It also explains why Jesus isn't stoned but executed by the Roman method of crucifixion (as prophesied in Psalm 22 and Isaiah 53). When Stephen is killed by stoning in Acts 7 (becoming the first Christian martyr), it was an illegal act by a riotous mob.

Pilate gives the religious leaders the green light to judge Jesus, but they know they aren't permitted to execute him. Yet they're also aware that they have no accusations that would stand up in a Roman court. Eventually, according to Luke 23:1-2, they alter their charge of blasphemy, replacing it with three claims that would stand up in Roman court: "And they began to accuse him, saying, 'We have found this man subverting our nation. He opposes payment of taxes to Caesar and claims to be Messiah, a king.'" These three accusations—that Jesus was subverting Rome, opposing payment of taxes, and claiming to be king—would amount to treason, a crime punishable by death in Roman law.

John 18:33-36

33 Pilate then went back inside the palace, summoned Jesus and asked him, "Are you the king of the Jews?"

34 "Is that your own idea," Jesus asked, "or did others talk to you about me?"

35 "Am I a Jew?" Pilate replied. "Your own people and chief priests handed you over to me. What is it you have done?"

36 Jesus said, "My kingdom is not of this world. If it were, my servants would fight to prevent my arrest by the Jewish leaders. But now my kingdom is from another place."

Pilate may have been aware that the crowds wanted to make Jesus king. In the first century, kings were all-powerful and ruled according to their own impulses and desires. Pilate may be serious in asking Jesus whether he considers himself a king, yet Pilate also seems to know that Jesus isn't trying to be king (at least in the sense that Pilate understands). He asks—perhaps with a skeptical, bemused tone—if Jesus is planning on overthrowing the government. Jesus doesn't look like a king.

Pilate knows the religious leaders have a weak case against Jesus. When Jesus asks if the idea that he's a king is Pilate's own idea, Pilate responds in a mocking, sneering manner: "Am I a Jew?" He's being sarcastic. He's asking, "What do I know of Jewish dealings, bickering, and superstitions?" Pilate isn't interested in getting involved in local Jewish affairs. Pilate is similar to Gallio, the ruler whom Paul was brought before in Acts 18:12–17. Both Pilate and Gallio felt they were too busy to get involved with these local Jewish disagreements. But how could Pilate effectively govern when he doesn't take the time to know and understand the culture of the people he's leading?

Jesus tells Pilate that he isn't a politically minded king who seeks to challenge Rome or the emperor. His kingdom is altogether different. If he'd been interested in overthrowing the government, Jesus says, his servants (disciples? angels?) would have been creating riots in the streets.

His kingdom is in one sense otherworldly in nature. His rule does not come from the "world" that has rebelled against God. But this is not to say that his kingdom is only a spiritual or heavenly kingdom. Jesus instructed his disciples to pray, "Our Father in heaven, hallowed be your name, your kingdom come, your will be done, on earth as it is in heaven" (Matthew 6:9-10). His is a kingdom of Truth. When talking to Nicodemus, Jesus said, "Very truly I tell you, no one can see the kingdom of God unless they are born again" (3:3). When believers receive this new birth, they become a part of this kingdom—a kingdom that exists wherever God's rule is acknowledged. Wherever the king is in charge, that's where the kingdom is. The kingdom of God is in you, in the midst of you (Luke 17:21). The kingdom of God is where people seek to be one with God as the Son is one with the Father.

John 18:37-38

37 "You are a king, then!" said Pilate.

Jesus answered, "You say that I am a king. In fact, the reason I was born and came into the world is to testify to the truth. Everyone on the side of truth listens to me."

38 "What is truth?" retorted Pilate. With this he went out again to the Jews gathered there and said, "I find no basis for a charge against him."

Pilate still doesn't get it. Jesus didn't come into the world to rule over it in the same way that Judas Maccabaeus or Herod the Great or the emperor would. Jesus came into the world to testify to the Truth.

Pilate, with his seemingly flippant question—"What is truth?"—sounds a lot like twenty-first-century humans. People today have many different answers when asked

"What is truth?" A scientist might respond, "Truth is what you can see and touch." A philosopher may say, "Truth is relative; we can't know anything for sure." A mystic might declare, "I find truth within myself." In Pilate's day, and even more so in our own, people are very skeptical regarding any claims to absolute truth. All truth is believed to be relative— there is no black and white, only shades of gray. And even if absolute truth exists, how could we know what it is?

Think of how Jesus refutes such thinking throughout the Gospel of John:

- John 14:6—"I am the way and the truth and the life. No one comes to the Father except through me."
- John 17:17a—"Sanctify them by the truth."
- John 17:17b—"Your word is truth."
- John 16:13—"But when he, the Spirit of truth, comes, he will guide you into all the truth."

Some think Pilate's question is sarcastic, but it's possible he was a very disillusioned, bitter person. Pilate knows that history is written by the victors and that the powerful people are the ones who define truth in their time. Pilate may be thinking, *Truth is whatever Rome wants it to be, whatever works.* Pilate may not have realized it, but in that moment he was standing at the greatest crossroads of his life, the place where he could either choose Truth or deny it in pursuit of power and self-interest. Pilate was looking Truth in the eye, and he never realized it (14:6-7). On that day, Pilate set Truth aside.

Three times Pilate declares, "I find no basis for a charge against him" (18:38-39; 19:4, 6). Pilate believed Christ was innocent. Why, then, didn't Pilate dismiss this whole trumped-up case against Jesus?

A brief history lesson might prove helpful. When Herod the Great died, his three sons became tetrarchs. *Tetrarch* means "ruler of a fourth." After Herod the Great's death, two of his sons were each given a quarter of his kingdom, and the third, Herod Archelaus, ruled over the other half. Archelaus was such a terrible ruler that the Jewish leaders appealed to Rome to send someone else in his place. Eventually, Pontius Pilate was appointed governor-procurator over Palestine. But throughout his 10-year rule (AD 26–36), there was incredible tension between Pilate and the Jewish leaders.

The historian Philo of Alexandria described Pilate as "a man of a very inflexible disposition, and very merciless as well as very obstinate." Pilate brought images of Caesar into the city of Jerusalem, violating the Jewish law against "graven images" (Deuteronomy 4:15-18). The Jewish leaders asked Pilate to remove them during a huge meeting in Caesarea. When Pilate said no, the protestors "fell prone all around his house and remained motionless for five days and nights," as the first-century historian Josephus tells it. On the sixth day, Roman troops surrounded the protestors, and Pilate threatened "that he would cut them to pieces unless they accepted the images." The Jews refused to budge, and "as though by agreement fell to the ground . . . and bent their necks shouting that they were ready to be killed rather than transgress the Law." Pilate backed down and removed the statues, but it was a public-relations nightmare for him.

Pilate could also be an arrogant bully. He once robbed the temple treasury to build an aqueduct. The people rioted, and Pilate sent plainclothesmen into the crowds to stop the riot by killing their leader—another public-relations disaster. The Jewish leaders appealed to Emperor Tiberius—and Pilate nearly lost his position. As Chuck Swindoll, pastor and writer, would say, "Pilate suddenly found himself without a friend in the world." When the Jewish leaders brought Jesus before Pilate, Pilate knew that if he didn't do what they wanted, they would again appeal to the emperor. Pilate was basically being blackmailed. He knows that if he allows Jesus to live, his job is in jeopardy.

John's account doesn't mention the second phase of Jesus' civil trial, but Luke records it in Luke 23. Having found no basis for a charge against Jesus, Pilate tries to pass the buck. Herod Agrippa, the ruler of Galilee, just happens to be in Jerusalem at the time. So Pilate tries to pass the responsibility for Jesus off on Herod, a higher-ranking Roman authority. (Herod, as you will remember, is the one who beheaded John the Baptist.) According to Luke's account, Herod asks to see a few miracles, but Jesus doesn't respond to his questions. Herod's soldiers ridicule and mock Jesus. They dress him in an elegant robe, and then Herod passes him back to Pilate (Luke 23:6-12).

Imagine Pilate enjoying breakfast on his patio, thinking he's finished with Jesus. Then he looks up to see Jesus, with his hands still bound, being led back by Herod's soldiers. Pilate is again faced with the decision every person has to make: What do I do with Jesus?

John 18:39-40

39 But it is your custom for me to release to you one prisoner at the time of the Passover. Do you want me to release 'the king of the Jews'?"

40 They shouted back, "No, not him! Give us Barabbas!" Now Barabbas had taken part in an uprising.

There seems to be have been a custom of amnesty in which one prisoner was released at the time of the Passover (Matthew 27:15; Mark 15:6-8). The custom may have been started by Pilate himself (Mark 15:6) or one of his predecessors—its origin is uncertain. (The *Mishnah* may be referring to this tradition in *Pesachim* 8:6). Thinking this may be a way out of his dilemma, Pilate offers to release the "king of the Jews"—a title that meant nothing to Pilate. (This may be an example of Pilate's cynical humor, or perhaps it is the title Jesus is accused of having claimed for himself.) Even though many Jewish leaders hated Jesus, Pilate probably expects that the people who've gathered will want to free Jesus.

Barabbas was a notorious insurrectionist (Matthew 27:16; Luke 23:19) who was accused of both murder and plotting to overthrow the Roman government. Possibly he was one of the Zealots. Pilate never dreamed the people would want to set free this terrorist, a man who is a genuine threat to Rome. Evidently, Pilate wasn't accurately apprised as to how the people felt about being under Roman rule! Barabbas may have been a hero to many in the Jewish community who hated being under Roman rule and paying taxes to the detested Roman government. Pilate also may have misjudged the influence of the religious leaders and their loathing for Jesus, as they surely persuaded the crowd to ask for the release of Barabbas (Matthew 27:20; Mark 15:11).

When he heard the crowd's response, Pilate must have done a double take. He probably couldn't believe what he was hearing. Not only did his plan not relieve him of making a decision about Jesus, but now he was responsible for releasing a known treacherous criminal (Barabbas). Rome will not be happy!

Barabbas is an interesting name. *Bar* means "son" and *abba* means "father." That seems odd—"son of the father." But in those days, rabbis were frequently referred to as the "fathers" of the communities they served. It is possible, then, that Barabbas was a rabbi's son who had gone sour, rebelling against the very things his father stood for. It is also fascinating that John has continually presented Jesus as "the Son of the Father" who obeyed his Father in every detail.

This is a dramatic scene. Barabbas was in the Fortress of Antonia awaiting crucifixion. The fortress was located no more than 2,000 feet from the temple of Herod. Barabbas probably was too far away to hear the isolated voices, but he was close enough to hear the crowd's response. In Matthew 27:21, the governor asks, "Which of the two do you want me to release to you?" (Barabbas would not have heard this question.)

"Barabbas," they answered. (Barabbas would have heard his own name as the crowd called it out.)

"What shall I do, then, with Jesus who is called the Messiah?" Pilate asked. (Barabbas would not have heard this.)

They all answered, "Crucify him!" (Barabbas would have heard this.)

Imagine that you're Barabbas sitting there in your prison cell. You hear the crowds cry out your name, and then you hear these unmistakable words: "Crucify him!" Think how terrified Barabbas must have been as the prison guards came down to open his cell! Then imagine his great surprise when he hears the words, "You can go. You've been set free."

Jesus was crucified on a cross made for Barabbas. In *A Walk Thru the Book of John* we read, "But it's more than irony: it's a picture of our salvation. A perfectly righteous life was exchanged for our unrighteousness; he died in our place; and we've been set free. Caiaphas was right. It *is* expedient that one should die for the many."

READ BETWEEN THE LINES

- Why did the Jewish leaders take Jesus to the Roman governor, Pilate?
- Why are the religious leaders rushing this trial?
- Why does John mention that it was "early morning"?
- Why didn't the Jewish leaders enter Pilate's palace?

- Why did they not respond with any specific charges at first (18:29-30)?
- Why did the religious leaders change the crimes they accused Jesus of committing when appearing before Pilate?
- What kind of kingdom is Jesus talking about?
- What is truth?
- If Pilate finds Jesus innocent, why doesn't he set him free?
- Why would the crowd choose to release a known criminal?
- What kind of person is Pilate?
- How are Pilate and Peter similar? How are they different?

WELCOME TO MY WORLD

- How would I describe the kingdom of God?
- When have I been accused of something I didn't do? How did I handle it?
- How do I dodge having to make challenging choices?
- What would I have done in Pilate's place?
- What can I learn from Jesus' responses?
- In what ways am I like Peter or Pilate?

Jesus Sentenced to Be Crucified

John 19:1

¹ Then Pilate took Jesus and had him flogged.

Pilate ordered the flogging, but he wouldn't have actually done the flogging himself. Jesus would have been taken to the Roman garrison located in the Fortress of Antonia.

The Romans used three types of flogging, each with an increasing degree of severity (*fustigation*, *flagellation*, and *verberation*). The first (*fustigation*) required a few blows from the whip. The second (*flagellation*) required an increased number of blows. The third type (*verberation*) was extremely severe and was usually administered just before a crucifixion (19:16b).

Flogging was so brutal and hideous that it was never done to a Roman citizen (Acts 22:25-30). The man who did the flogging was called the *lictor*. The instrument he used was called a *flagrum*. It was a piece of wood between 14 and 18 inches long that had long leather thongs attached to it at various lengths. The leather thongs or straps could be tied at the ends. For greater damage during *verberation*, the straps could be embedded with pieces of metal or sharpened sheep bones.

In all three types of floggings, the prisoner was stripped of his clothing and either forced to lie on his stomach or strapped to a post with his ankles and wrists secure. The *lictor* would stand about six feet from the prisoner. The *flagrum* was brought back over the *lictor's* shoulder and then was brought forward.

There was a difference between Jewish flogging and Roman flogging. Jewish flogging is described in Deuteronomy 25:2-3—"If the guilty person deserves to be beaten, the judge shall make them lie down and have them flogged in his presence with the number of lashes the crime deserves, but the judge must not impose more than forty lashes." The Jewish leaders were afraid of breaking the law by accidentally miscounting, so they'd commonly beat a victim 39 times just to be safe. Roman flogging had no limit on the number of lashes.

Dr. C. Truman Davis, an Anglican bishop and ophthalmologist, has written about the crucifixion from a medical point of view. He describes the third type of flogging (*verberation*) in this way:

> The heavy whip is brought down with full force again and again across a person's shoulders, back and legs. At first the heavy thongs cut through the skin only. Then, as the blows continue, they cut deeper into the subcutaneous tissues, producing first an oozing of blood from the capillaries and veins of the skin, and finally spurting arterial bleeding from vessels in the underlying muscles. The small pieces of lead first produce large, deep bruises, which are broken apart by subsequent blows. Finally, the skin on the back is hanging in long ribbons and the entire area is an unrecognizable mass of torn, bleeding tissue.

Severe flogging could cause bare bones to poke through the skin. It was the equivalent of being skinned alive. Eusebius, a third-century historian stated, "The sufferer's veins were laid bare, and the very muscles, sinews, and bowels of the victim were open to exposure." It was not uncommon for a person to die during this whipping. Invariably the prisoner would pass out due to the pain and would be revived by having salt water thrown on the open wounds. Those who did not die immediately would often die a few days later from infection. That's why flogging was also called the "halfway death."

Some scholars believe the writer of the fourth Gospel may have misplaced the flogging by describing it here. In John's Gospel the flogging comes earlier in the chain of events leading to the crucifixion than it does in Matthew (27:26) or Mark (15:15). Other scholars suggest that John isn't following a strict chronological order of the events. Additional scholars say it's possible there were two floggings.

If Jesus was flogged twice, then perhaps Pilate may have had the *lictor* use the least severe form of flogging (*fustigation*) in this initial whipping. Perhaps Pilate is hoping he can pacify the religious leaders by simply roughing up Jesus a bit. If there were two floggings, the second would likely have taken place immediately before the crucifixion (19:16b), and it would have been the most severe type of flogging (*verberation*).

John 19:2-3

2 The soldiers twisted together a crown of thorns and put it on his head. They clothed him in a purple robe 3 and went up to him again and again, saying, "Hail, king of the Jews!" And they slapped him in the face.

The soldiers are mocking Jesus by creating a crown of thorns and placing it on his head. The crown was most likely made from the thorny date palm or another thorn bush common in that area. Its thorns may have been up to several inches in length. These plants were normally cut, dried, and stored in a bucket to use as kindling to start a fire. These soldiers probably snatched a few from a bucket and formed them into a crown that resembled the crowns of leaves worn by the rulers of that day, which can be seen on many Roman coins. The crown was pushed down on Jesus' head, forcing the thorns deep into his skin.

Matthew 27:28-29 tells us they put a mock scepter in his hands. Mark 15:19-20 say, "Again and again they struck him on the head with a staff and spit on him. Falling on their knees, they paid homage to him. And when they had mocked him, they took off the purple robe and put his clothes on him." The Greek words translated "slapped him in the face" (John 19:3) and "struck him on the head" (Mark 15:19) indicate a continuous action. The soldiers mocked Jesus by dressing him as a king, possibly placing a soldier's purple cloak (the color of royalty) over his open, bleeding wounds—and then ripping it from his skin later on.

By the time the soldiers were finished, Jesus would have been a bloody mess—much different from the museum paintings of the crucifixion, where Jesus has small drops of blood on his head, hands, and feet. Isaiah 53:2 declares, "He had no beauty or majesty to attract us to him, nothing in his appearance that we should desire him."

John 19:4-6

4 Once more Pilate came out and said to the Jews gathered there, "Look, I am bringing him out to you to let you know that I find no basis for a charge against him." 5 When Jesus came out wearing the crown of thorns and the purple robe, Pilate said to them, "Here is the man!"

6 As soon as the chief priests and their officials saw him, they shouted, "Crucify! Crucify!"

But Pilate answered, "You take him and crucify him. As for me, I find no basis for a charge against him."

Pilate must have been hoping that the religious leaders and angry mob would be satisfied when they saw that Jesus had been humiliated and severely beaten. But they show no pity. Pilate tells the crowd he's found no basis for a charge against Jesus. The case should have ended here. But once again Pilate doesn't act on his own convictions.

In both 18:38 and 19:4, Pilate declares that he finds no basis for a charge against Jesus. We find similar words declaring Jesus' innocence on the lips of others throughout the various Gospel accounts of Jesus' trial and crucifixion:

- Matthew 27:4—Judas says, "I have sinned, for I have betrayed innocent blood."

- Matthew 27:19—Pilate's wife writes in a note to her husband, "Don't have anything to do with that innocent man."

- Matthew 27:54—Those guarding Jesus at the cross exclaim, "Surely he was the Son of God!"

- Luke 23:14-15—Pilate says that both he and Herod find no crime in Jesus: "I have examined him in your presence and have found no basis for your charges against him. Neither has Herod, for he sent him back to us; as you can see, he has done nothing to deserve death."

- Luke 23:41—One of the thieves being crucified with Jesus says, "We are punished justly, for we are getting what our deeds deserve. But this man has done nothing wrong."

- Luke 23:47—"The centurion [near the cross], seeing what had happened, praised God and said, 'Surely this was a righteous man.'"

Pilate may have emphasized the word *man* when he said, "Here is the man!"—suggesting that Jesus didn't look like a king. The blood from his head would have been dripping down from his crown of thorns and onto his cheeks, mingling with the blood on his back, chest, and sides. Isaiah prophesied in Isaiah 52:14, "Just as there were many who were appalled at him—his appearance was so disfigured beyond that of any human being and his form marred beyond human likeness." But the religious leaders and crowd remain unsatisfied and demand again and again that Jesus be crucified. They wanted more blood. They were like sharks when there is blood in the water. They were a mob out of control.

Pilate then sarcastically dares the religious leaders to crucify Jesus themselves. Yet he knows full well that the Jewish leaders don't have the authority to impose the death penalty.

John 19:7-9

7 The Jewish leaders insisted, "We have a law, and according to that law he must die, because he claimed to be the Son of God."

8 When Pilate heard this, he was even more afraid, 9 and he went back inside the palace. "Where do you come from?" he asked Jesus, but Jesus gave him no answer.

The law they are referring to may be Leviticus 24:16—"Anyone who blasphemes the name of the LORD is to be put to death." Claiming to be God was blasphemy, a crime punishable by death. In this case, the charge is accurate. Jesus had claimed to be God. If he'd been a mere man, then the law specified that he would deserve death. But the irony is that Jesus wasn't violating the law when he said these things; what Jesus said was true.

The statement "he claimed to be the Son of God" must have caught Pilate by surprise. These religious leaders had been unsuccessful in convincing Pilate that Jesus should be crucified for treason, so now they return to the real reason they want Jesus crucified. They believe he broke religious law. They don't really care which accusation Pilate believes just as long as Jesus is crucified.

"Son of God" was a title that Caesar Augustus took for himself because he was the heir to Julius Caesar who'd been declared a god. Romans and Greeks had numerous myths about the gods coming to earth as men (Acts 14:8-13). Pilate may now be putting "Son of God" together with Jesus' earlier statement, "My kingdom is not of this world" (18:36). Pilate is alarmed, perhaps wondering, *Is Jesus a god who came to earth?*

Pilate asks Jesus, "Where do you come from?" Jesus has been questioned about his origin previously (7:27-28; 8:14; 9:29-30). And Pilate already knows that Jesus is a Galilean (Luke 23:6-7); he wasn't asking Jesus for his local address. He seems to be unsure about who Jesus really is. Did he come from heaven or some other world? Is he really God's Son?

Jesus gives Pilate no answer; there is only an eerie silence. Jesus is now finished with Pilate and stops responding to him. It's a terrible day when Jesus is silent. His silence brings to mind the suffering servant mentioned in Isaiah 53:7—"He was oppressed and afflicted, yet he did not open his mouth; he was led like a lamb to the slaughter, and as a sheep before its shearers is silent, so he did not open his mouth."

John 19:10-11

10 "Do you refuse to speak to me?" Pilate said. "Don't you realize I have power either to free you or to crucify you?"

11 Jesus answered, "You would have no power over me if it were not given to you from above. Therefore the one who handed me over to you is guilty of a greater sin."

Pilate is ticked off by Jesus' lack of respect for his authority. It's as if Pilate is saying, "Don't you realize who you're talking to?" And Jesus could have answered, "No, *you're* the one who doesn't realize who he's talking to!"

Pilate brags about having the power to set Jesus free or crucify him. But the spineless Pilate doesn't have the courage to do either. Jesus makes it clear that God has permitted Pilate to have this power only because of the necessity of getting Jesus to the cross (18:36).

Pilate was merely a pawn in a very elaborate plan. Pilate did all of this in ignorance. The greater sin is knowing what's true and rejecting it. "The one who handed me over to you" may refer to Judas or the religious leadership or the high priest Caiaphas. This verse seems to suggest there are degrees of sin (9:40-41). But Pilate's ignorance doesn't get him off the hook. He's still guilty of playing a key role in the crucifixion of Jesus.

John 19:12-13

12 From then on, Pilate tried to set Jesus free, but the Jewish leaders kept shouting, "If you let this man go, you are no friend of Caesar. Anyone who claims to be a king opposes Caesar."

13 When Pilate heard this, he brought Jesus out and sat down on the judge's seat at a place known as the Stone Pavement (which in Aramaic is Gabbatha).

Pilate continues to try to set Jesus free. In John's account, Pilate comes off looking better than he does in the Synoptic Gospels or in the writings of Jewish historian Josephus, who was harsh in his descriptions of Pilate's early years of service. Pilate seems eager to find a way to release Jesus. But the Jewish leaders have one more trick up their sleeves: They claim Pilate would be "no friend of Caesar" if he were to set Jesus free.

"Friend of Caesar" was a term reserved for senators, knights, and administrators who served as Caesar's agents. A Roman official who lost this title would be not only removed from his job, but also cut off from all Roman life. Sejanus, a Roman official who may have helped Pilate get his job, was later found guilty of a plot against the emperor and executed for not being a "friend of Caesar." These religious leaders now threaten to report to Emperor Tiberius that Pilate is releasing a person who is a threat to the Empire and who claims to be a king.

Pilate is now seated; Jesus is standing next to him. The judgment seat (*bema*) was a high platform or bench from which official decrees, proclamations, and judgments were given. John tells us the seat was located in a place called the Stone Pavement, also known as Gabbatha. (Josephus, the Jewish historian, says *Gabbatha* means "hill.") It was part of the Fortress of Antonia, which bordered the northwest corner of the temple complex.

Matthew 27:19 tells us, "While Pilate was sitting on the judge's seat, his wife sent him this message: 'Don't have anything to do with that innocent man, for I have suffered a great deal today in a dream because of him.'" This message must have added to the pressure Pilate is feeling. He may have been thinking, *What if I've just beaten up the Son of God?*

The religious leaders' threats get to Pilate. It seems Pilate valued his neck more than his soul. But someday Pilate will come in front of Christ's judgment seat. Pilate sat down to judge, but the irony is that he will be judged on the basis of how he responds to Jesus Christ. Jesus is the King of Kings, regardless of what Pilate decides.

John 19:14-16a

14 It was the day of Preparation of the Passover; it was about noon.

"Here is your king," Pilate said to the Jews.

¹⁵ But they shouted, "Take him away! Take him away! Crucify him!"

"Shall I crucify your king?" Pilate asked.

"We have no king but Caesar," the chief priests answered.

¹⁶ Finally Pilate handed him over to them to be crucified.

John notes that it was "about noon" on "the day of Preparation for the Passover" (see 13:1-2) when Jesus was to be crucified. Mark 15:25, however, tells us Jesus was crucified at "nine in the morning." Perhaps both times are approximations. In either case, this would be the time when the temple priests were slaughtering the Passover lambs. Jesus will be hanging on the cross as the lambs are being slaughtered. Jesus is the final Passover Lamb.

Pilate must have lost his breath when the chief priests said, "We have no king but Caesar." How hypocritical and pathetic! The Jewish people hated Caesar. In claiming Caesar as their rightful king, the priests are ignoring their entire national heritage (Isaiah 26:13). These religious leaders are willing to trade Barabbas for Jesus, and Caesar for God. In the heat of the moment and their blind insistence on seeing Jesus killed, they have discarded everything they've believed, ignoring a thousand years of songs, Scripture, and slogans. They've abandoned all pretense of devotion to God. But you know something, they were right. They didn't have any other king but Caesar (1 Samuel 8:6-9).

Pilate hands Jesus over to the chief priests. But Roman soldiers will carry out the crucifixion. According to Greek historian Herodotus, crucifixion began in Persia around 1000 BC. The Persians believed the ground where they lived was pure, holy, and sacred. They had a god called Ormuzd who was the god of the earth (or ground). They thought a criminal's body should not defile and contaminate the ground. Out of allegiance to Ormuzd, they would lift a criminal off the ground on a pole and keep the unlawful person there, letting the body decay or be consumed by wild animals and vultures. The body was never taken off the pole and buried. This torturous form of execution was passed on to the Phoenicians and Carthaginians and then on to the Romans, who developed it into an art. They had tested other methods, including stoning, drowning, burning, boiling in oil, strangulation, and flaying; but they found crucifixion to be the most effective. There were even different types of crosses; in addition to the shape we traditionally associate with the cross, there were also T-shaped, Y-shaped, I-shaped, and X-shaped crosses.

The ancient Roman philosopher Cicero called crucifixion "the cruelest and most horrifying death possible." Roman historians said, "It was a despicable death." Being crucified was worse than being beheaded, gored, eaten by animals, or even burned alive. It remains one of the cruelest and most tortuous forms of execution in human history. It was humiliating, tormenting, slow, and always terminal. Crucifixion was so horrible that the Romans almost never crucified a Roman citizen (with a few exceptions). It was a punishment set aside for the lower classes, slaves, foreigners, criminals, and soldiers found guilty of some treasonous act.

Unlike modern-day U.S. executions, which take place in private, first-century crucifixions were intended to be public spectacles for all to see. The cross served as a warning to others that if you break the law, there is a price to pay. It was also the Romans' way of saying to all, "See what happens if you oppose us?"

Have you ever wondered if young people today consider these realities when they buy and wear gold, silver, or jeweled crucifixes? Today, the cross is considered a symbol of glory and victory. But people in the first century would have gasped at the thought of wearing a cross. It would be similar to having a miniature hangman's noose, electric chair, or guillotine attached to your ear or hanging from your neck. (Some students I know would have no problem with this!)

> Somewhere along the line, we have lost the horror of the Crucifixion scene. Maybe we don't want to frighten the little children in the Easter pageants at church. But the scene was gruesome and frightening, and we trivialize the suffering of Christ when we forget that fact.
>
> —Bruce Bickel and Stan Jantz, *John: Encountering Christ in a Life-Changing Way*, 140

READ BETWEEN THE LINES

- If Pilate believed Jesus was innocent, why did he have him whipped?
- What charges were brought against Jesus?
- What were the soldiers' responses to Jesus?
- Explain the crown of thorns and purple robe.
- What kind of response was Pilate hoping for when he presented a flogged Jesus to the mob?
- Describe what you think Jesus may have been feeling physically, mentally, and emotionally during these events.
- Why does the term "Son of God" alarm Pilate?
- What does Pilate fear?
- Why does Pilate ask, "Where do you come from?"
- Why doesn't Jesus answer Pilate's question?
- Are there degrees of sin (19:11b)?
- What does it mean to be a "friend of Caesar"?

- What are Pilate's options in this situation? What consequences are likely for each choice?
- Why is it significant that the crucifixion occurs around the Passover?
- Why would the chief priests say, "We have no king but Caesar"?

WELCOME TO MY WORLD

- Have I ever been in a mob or crowd situation that felt out of control? What happened? How did I feel?
- How is crucifixion different from modern forms of capital punishment?
- How much of my life is designed by God and how much is designed by me?
- How do I make decisions?
- How am I similar to Pilate?

The Crucifixion of Jesus

John 19:16b

So the soldiers took charge of Jesus.

The first half of verse 16 says that Pilate handed Jesus over to be crucified. But Romans 8:32 informs us that God handed him over. This tells me God and Pilate are working together—only Pilate doesn't know it! Pilate meant it for evil, but God meant it for good (Genesis 50:20). What Pilate did was illegal—there was supposed to be at least a day between trial and execution. But this fulfills the Scripture, which says, "He was taken from prison and from judgment" (Isaiah 53:8, NKJV). This was not the normal order of events. Usually it was prison, judgment, prison, and then death.

The soldiers typically took the prisoner to the *lictor* to be flogged just before the crucifixion (Matthew 27:26; Mark 15:15). If Jesus were flogged twice (see commentary on 19:1), then the second and more severe flogging would have occurred at this time. The severity of the flogging could determine how long a person would survive on the cross.

John 19:17

17 Carrying his own cross, he went out to the place of the Skull (which in Aramaic is called Golgotha).

Prisoners typically didn't carry the entire cross, just the horizontal crossbeam called the *patibulum*. It weighed about 75 pounds and would have been carried on the prisoner's back and shoulders. He would be chained at his feet and neck. According to the Synoptic Gospels, Jesus carried his own cross at first, but eventually a man named Simon, a visitor from the North African city of Cyrene (which would be part of Libya today), was forced to carry the cross for Jesus (Matthew 27:32; Mark 15:21; Luke 23:26).

Jesus carrying the wooden cross reminds us of how Isaac carried the wood for his own sacrifice in Genesis 22:6. Centuries ago, the early church father John Chrysostom once pointed out that Abraham's trip up the mountain to where Isaac was nearly sacrificed occurred on Nisan 15, which would later mark the date of the Passover.

The passage says Jesus "went out." He was taken out of Jerusalem. Jewish stoning had to be done outside the city or camp (Numbers 15:36). The same was true of crucifixions. According to Jewish law, sin offerings were to be burnt outside the camp (Exodus 29:14; Leviticus 4:12; 16:27) In Hebrews 13:11-12, we read, "The high priest carries the blood of animals into the Most Holy Place as a sin offering, but the bodies are burned outside the camp. And so Jesus also suffered outside the city gate to make the people holy through his own blood." Jesus was the ultimate sin offering; and like the Passover lamb, his sacrifice needed to take place outside the camp.

Evidently, the place where Jesus was crucified has the appearance of a skull when viewed from a distance. In Aramaic it would be called *Golgotha*; in Latin it would be *calvaria*—which we translate as "Calvary." The exact location is uncertain. The traditional site is either west of Jerusalem at the Church of the Holy Sepulcher or at Gordon's Calvary north of the city.

John 19:18

18 There they crucified him, and with him two others—one on each side and Jesus in the middle.

When they arrived at the location of the crucifixion, the vertical beam or post (*stipe*) may have already been in the ground. The person to be crucified would lie on his back, and his arms would be stretched out and attached to the crossbeam. In some cases, the hands were nailed to the crossbeam; in others, they were tied to the crossbeam with a rope, which was less expensive and also caused the time on the cross to be lengthened. Jesus was attached by nails (20:25-27). The nails were several inches long and were driven through the base of the palm or between the wrist bones so the hand wouldn't rip away when the cross beam was lifted up by four executioners and attached to the vertical beam.

The force applied on the arms in this position not only rips the flesh, but also may have caused dislocation of both shoulders and possibly both elbows. It has been calculated by engineers that the force on each arm could equal the pressure of one ton structurally. The arms could be stretched up to six inches longer than normal. This could be similar to the effects of the medieval torture rack.

The feet were attached to the cross with the knees slightly flexed. The right foot was placed over the left foot, and a single nail was driven through either the heels or ankles. A small board would be attached below the feet to step on and another small board to sit on, to prolong the suffering.

Crucifixions could last for hours and sometimes days. Every movement was painful, and the wounds gradually gangrened. However, death usually came about by suffocation. To catch a breath, the person being crucified would push up on the board beneath his feet, which tore his flesh. But he could hold that position only for a few seconds. It is exhausting, but the crucified person must breathe. Carbon dioxide would build up in the blood, and there was an increasing drive to breathe in more air. The arms, legs, and torso scream with pain. The lungs begin to collapse as the heart beats faster to drive more blood through the lungs. Toward the end, the heart can no longer keep up and it begins to fail.

Jesus died just like a common criminal among other criminals. Isaiah 53:9, 12 says, "He was assigned a grave with the wicked . . . and [he] was numbered with the transgressors."

Psalm 22:16 states, "Dogs surround me, a pack of villains encircles me; they pierce my hands and my feet." The psalmist had never heard of crucifixion, yet he wrote about it.

In Luke 23:39-43 we read the dialogue between Jesus and the two criminals crucified on either side of him. They are referred to as revolutionary bandits, the same term used to describe Barabbas. Perhaps they were his acquaintances, and the very cross on which Jesus died was intended for Barabbas.

Luke tells us:

> One of the criminals who hung there hurled insults at him: "Aren't you the Messiah? Save yourself and us!"
>
> But the other criminal rebuked him. "Don't you fear God," he said, "since you are under the same sentence? We are punished justly, for we are getting what our deeds deserve. But this man has done nothing wrong." Then he said, "Jesus, remember me when you come into your kingdom."
>
> Jesus answered him, "Truly I tell you, today you will be with me in paradise."

John 19:19-20

19 Pilate had a notice prepared and fastened to the cross. It read: JESUS OF NAZARETH, THE KING OF THE JEWS. 20 Many of the Jews read this sign, for the place where Jesus was crucified was near the city, and the sign was written in Aramaic, Latin and Greek.

Those who were about to crucify Jesus would parade him along as many roads as they could (traditionally Jerusalem's *Via Dolorosa*, which is Latin for "Way of Grief" or "Way of Suffering"). And a man would walk in front carrying a *titulus*—a placard or notice that gave the name of the person to be crucified and his crimes. The sign was sometimes hung around the neck of the one to be crucified. This practice was meant to warn others that crime doesn't pay and serve as a deterrent for the people. The walk was also done so that if anyone had any evidence that would justify a new trial, they could present it at that time. Once the group arrives at the crucifixion spot, the placard is attached to the cross.

The wording of Jesus' placard may have been Pilate's attempt to get back at the Jewish leaders for blackmailing him. Nazareth (1:45) was an insignificant town; to say that the Jews' king came from there was meant as an insult. Also, Pilate thought it was clever to present this humiliated, bloody, weak-looking human as the King of the Jews. But the placard was true in a way that Pilate didn't realize. Jesus was coming into his kingdom.

To add insult to injury and further express his resentment of the Jewish leaders, Pilate orders that the sign be written in the three major languages that were spoken in that world: Aramaic (the language of the Jews), Latin (the official language of the Roman Empire), and Greek (the "universal" language of the time). That way, everyone (Jews and non-Jews) would get the message.

Pilate doesn't believe Jesus is the King of the Jews any more than the religious leaders do. But what Pilate meant in jest is actually true: Jesus is the "King of the Jews." And he's not just the King over Israel, but also the Gentiles and the entire world—as the multiple languages used on that sign would indicate. We know from John 10:16 that Jesus has other sheep outside of Israel. Jesus is King of the whole universe.

John 19:21-22

21 The chief priests of the Jews protested to Pilate, "Do not write 'The King of the Jews,' but that this man claimed to be king of the Jews."

²² Pilate answered, "What I have written, I have written."

The chief priests seem to use the term "this man" in a derogatory way here. Yet Pilate refuses to change the wording of the notice. It's ironic that Pilate stands firm on something that matters so little, yet he is a coward when it comes to standing for things that really matter. It may have been this inscription that caused the thief on the other cross to respond as he did to Jesus.

This is the last mention of Pilate in this Gospel. Whatever happened to him? According to Matthew 27:24, "When Pilate saw that he was getting nowhere, but that instead an uproar was starting, he took water and washed his hands in front of the crowd. 'I am innocent of this man's blood,' he said. 'It is your responsibility!'" In the year AD 36 or 37, Pilate was deposed and sent to Rome to face charges in front of Emperor Tiberius who was going to banish him. It seems Pilate had sent troops to attack some Samaritans who'd climbed Mt. Gerizim searching for golden objects supposedly hidden by Moses. Many Samaritans died in the attack, and the rest complained to Rome.

As Pilate was on his way to appear before Tiberius, Tiberius died and Pilate never faced the charges. Some have suggested Pilate was eventually banished anyway; others say he was executed; still others suggest he committed suicide. Pilate may have washed his hands, but he could never get rid of the stain of his guilt. Like Lady Macbeth in Shakespeare's tragedy, Pilate can't ever wipe the guilt from his hands. Billy Graham once said that Pilate will spend all of eternity trying to wash the blood off his hands.

John 19:23-24

²³ When the soldiers crucified Jesus, they took his clothes, dividing them into four shares, one for

each of them, with the undergarment remaining. This garment was seamless, woven in one piece from top to bottom.

24 "Let's not tear it," they said to one another. "Let's decide by lot who will get it."

This happened that the scripture might be fulfilled that said, "They divided my clothes among them and cast lots for my garment."[a]

So this is what the soldiers did.

Romans would typically crucify people naked. The Romans occasionally made an exception, allowing the criminal to wear undergarments in deference to the Jewish aversion to nudity. But it's possible that Jesus was humiliated even further by dying naked, unlike many of the paintings that depict him on the cross.

Here, as was common, the soldiers divide up Jesus' clothes. According to D. A. Carson, the clothes probably included sandals, a coat, a belt, and a head covering. The soldiers throw dice for Jesus' seamless undergarment. This may simply have been a nice piece of clothing. However, in the Old Testament the garment of the high priest had to be one piece of material (Exodus 28; Leviticus 16). The priest's job was to be the mediator between God and humans. (The word for *priest* in Latin, *pontifex*, means "bridge-builder.") Here, we see Jesus, the final high priest, building a bridge as no other priest before him. Jesus is both the high priest and the ultimate sacrifice.

John quotes a prophecy from Psalm 22:18, a Davidic messianic passage, "They divide my clothes among them and cast lots for my garment." These guys fulfilled Scripture and didn't realize it. You can be sure they didn't have a scroll of the Hebrew Scriptures in their hands. Yet it almost seems like they are following a script unawares.

a John 19:24 See Psalm 22:18

John 19:23-24

In this chapter we've looked at several Old Testament prophecies that were fulfilled by Christ. According to one scholar, the Old Testament includes 322 prophecies that were fulfilled in Jesus' life, many of which concerned events surrounding his crucifixion.

John 19:25

25 Near the cross of Jesus stood his mother, his mother's sister, Mary the wife of Clopas, and Mary Magdalene.

Where are the "courageous" disciples now? They're scattered and hiding in fear—except John! Tom Wright has suggested that the reason why John wasn't arrested was because he may have been very young, perhaps still a mere lad, and the Roman soldiers didn't recognize him as a potential revolutionary.

But some of Jesus' followers stand with him to the end. At the foot of the cross are four brave women. They loved the Lord and were willing to pay any price to be with Jesus. Although the twelve disciples are all men, it's clear that Jesus treated women far differently than others did in that culture, always treating them with dignity and recognizing their value. Women played key roles throughout Jesus' ministry. By the time we get to the early church depicted in Acts 8:3, we learn that both men and women were subject to persecution: "But Saul began to destroy the church. Going from house to house, he dragged off both men and women and put them in prison."

The following four women were standing at the foot of the cross:

- **"His mother"**—John doesn't call her "Mary" anywhere in this Gospel. Thirty-plus years before the crucifixion, Simeon told her that her soul would be pierced (Luke 2:25-35). Imagine her great pain in seeing the son she raised and loved now dying on the cross.

- **"His mother's sister"**—This may be Salome, the wife of Zebedee and the mother of James and John (which would make them Jesus' cousins; Matthew 27:56). If Jesus and John were cousins, this would explain why Jesus would entrust his mother to John after his death (19:26-27).

- **"Mary, the wife of Clopas"**—We know very little about her. Perhaps she is the "other Mary" who sat alongside Mary Magdalene across from the tomb of Jesus (Matthew 27:61). She may have been among the women who tried to tell the disciples that Jesus had risen (Luke 24:10). She may also be the mother of James the younger and of Joseph (Mark 15:40).

- **"Mary Magdalene"**—Mary was from the village of Magdala, on the west shore of the Sea of Galilee. She was the one from whom Jesus cast out seven demons (Mark 16:9; Luke 8:2). Some have suggested that she may have been the "sinful woman" in Luke 7:37-50 who wet Jesus' feet with her tears, wiped them with her hair, and then kissed them and poured perfume on them. Mary Magdalene will play a prominent part in the next chapter, as she becomes the first person to see Jesus after his resurrection.

John 19:26-27

26 When Jesus saw his mother there, and the disciple whom he loved standing nearby, he said to her, "Woman,b here is your son," 27 and to the disciple, "Here is your mother." From that time on, this disciple took her into his home.

We've already discussed that "the disciple whom he loved" may be John's way of referring to himself (13:23). If we assume this is true, here we have John sharing in this

b John 19:26 The Greek for *Woman* does not denote any disrespect.

intimate exchange between son and mother at the foot of the cross. Jesus calls his mother *woman*, recalling his first miracle of turning water into wine at a wedding in Cana. That night Jesus addressed Mary using this same term (2:1-11). Here, Jesus gives Mary a new son.

Mary had other children besides Jesus (John 7:3-5). Perhaps Jesus was reluctant to place Mary in the care of these men because they did not yet believe in him. However, by the time you get to the book of Acts, the whole family believes (Acts 1:14). Mary may have been in her late forties or early fifties at this time. Evidently, her husband Joseph had died years ago.

How amazing that in the midst of his excruciating pain, Jesus expresses concern, tenderness, and love for his widowed mother. John receives her as if she were his own mother. What a great example for us on how to care for our families—and especially our aging parents.

READ BETWEEN THE LINES

- How were God and Pilate working together?
- Why would Jesus carry his own cross?
- Why was Jesus taken outside the city?
- What would cause the different responses from the two criminals?
- What was the purpose of the notice (placard)? Why was it written in three different languages? What would the words mean to Pilate, the soldiers, the Jewish leaders, and Jesus?
- Why did the Jewish leaders object to the placard?
- Why did Pilate refuse to change the wording of the placard?

- What is the significance of the soldiers dividing up Jesus' clothes?
- Where were the disciples during the crucifixion?
- Describe those who stood by Jesus near the cross.
- Do you think Jesus' mother expected these events, or did they catch her by surprise?
- Why would Jesus turn the care of his mother over to "the disciple whom he loved"?
- How does Jesus show kindheartedness at the cross?

WELCOME TO MY WORLD

- What does it mean to "take up my cross" (Matthew 16:24)?
- How do I feel knowing that nothing can stop God's plans?
- Have I ever had to stand up to a crowd or an individual?
- Have I ever had to defend a friend against others?
- What group of people is the hardest for me to stand up against?
- Is Jesus King of my life?
- If I were alive at the time of the crucifixion, would I have been near the cross or hiding someplace?

The Death of Jesus

John 19:28-29

28 Later, knowing that everything had now been finished, and so that Scripture would be fulfilled, Jesus said, "I am thirsty." 29 A jar of wine vinegar was there, so they soaked a sponge in it, put the sponge on a stalk of the hyssop plant, and lifted it to Jesus' lips.

Those dying by crucifixion are often desperately thirsty. Certainly, this was true of Jesus. However, John's wording here suggests that Jesus may have requested a drink primarily to fulfill the Scriptures more than to quench his thirst. Jesus knew there was one more thing he had to do as he died on the cross to fulfill Scripture. Years ago, God had prompted the psalmist to write, "They . . . gave me vinegar for my thirst" (69:21). Similarly, Psalm 22:15 reads, "My mouth is dried up like a potsherd, and my tongue sticks to the roof of my mouth; you lay me in the dust of death." So, Jesus makes this statement, perhaps out of the desire to stay within the Father's will.

This wine vinegar Jesus receives differs from the wine mixed with myrrh, a sedative, that Jesus refused to drink as he walked to Golgotha (Mark 15:23). Jesus chose to be fully conscious throughout the torturous experience. The soldiers didn't have to respond to Jesus' request, but they did so as an act of kindness. This wine vinegar was a cheap, common, watered-down, sour wine that soldiers would drink. Perhaps it was given to those hanging on crosses to moisten their parched throats so their final words could be heard.

The sponge was placed on a stalk of the hyssop plant, which is significant because the same plant was used to brush the blood of the Passover lambs on the doorposts of the Israelites' homes (Exodus 12:22). John offers another reminder that Jesus is the Passover sacrifice.

> They took this wine vinegar, and they put it basically in a sponge on a stick, and then they shoved it in his mouth. . . . A few years ago, I had the privilege of going to Israel with my family, my wife and five kids, and as we were touring the ancient city of Ephesus, we came across what was an ancient public restroom, a number of toilets made out of marble. And the way those work is that you would sit on the toilet because there wasn't necessarily plumbing in all the homes, but more centrally located for the very affluent and rich. And as you would sit down, there would be a trough of water that would pass in front of you to cleanse yourself, and underneath the toilet there was an open place to put your hand.
>
> Well, those who were very rich, they didn't want to clean themselves, so they hired the slaves. What the slaves then would do, they would take a stick with a sponge on it, and then they would clean you after you went to the bathroom. They would use this same sponge for multiple patrons, until they figured out that actually causes disease and infection among those who were using the public toilet. . . . And so they decided to sanitize it. They would dip it in sour wine, so as to kill bacteria and germs.
>
> And it became fairly common for soldiers to carry this stick with this sponge, as part of their gear, to cleanse themselves when they went to the bathroom, and that's what they shoved in the mouth of God.
>
> —Mark Driscoll, Sermon notes

Although the statement isn't included in John's Gospel, the words Jesus spoke from the cross as they're recorded in Matthew 27:46 deserve particular attention. Matthew tells us: "About three in the afternoon Jesus cried out in a loud voice, *'Eli, Eli, lema sabachthani?'* (which means 'My God, my God, why have you forsaken me?')." This is the only time recorded in the Gospels in which Jesus prays using the formal, distant word *God* instead of *Abba* or *Father*. We know Jesus was quoting the beginning of the messianic Psalm 22, which would have confirmed to his listeners who he is. But there is so much more here.

In *The Jesus I Never Knew*, Philip Yancey wrote that Jesus was "expressing a grave sense of estrangement. Some inconceivable split had opened up in the Godhead. The Son felt abandoned by the Father. . . . All we have is a cry of pain from a child who felt forsaken. . . . We are not told what God the Father cried out at that moment. We can only imagine."

In Galatians, Paul writes that the Son became a "curse for us" (3:13). Paul expresses a similar idea in 2 Corinthians 5:21—"God made him who had no sin to be sin for us, so that in him we might become the righteousness of God."

John 19:30

30 When he had received the drink, Jesus said, "It is finished." With that, he bowed his head and gave up his spirit.

"It is finished" is a single word—*tetelestai*—in the original language. It's the word people would write on a bill after it had been paid in full. Jesus victoriously proclaims that he has completed the work of redemption. He has finished the mission the Father gave him to do. God has accomplished everything he designed to do in the life of his Son. Jesus paid the price of sin; the debt is cancelled. Therefore, our salvation cannot be anchored in our own religious performance. Dietrich Bonhoeffer put it in the terms of our own intense personal crisis: "We cannot confer forgiveness upon ourselves." But what was needed to satisfy God ought to satisfy us as well. Jon Courson writes, "We can't do anything to get right with God or closer to God except to realize it has already been done."

Compared to most crucifixions, Jesus died fairly quickly (in three to six hours). John says he bowed his head—this means Jesus laid his head down, but not with a sudden jerk or slump. Jesus died in full control; he was no victim. As he said in John 10:18, "No one takes [my life] from me, but I lay it down of my own accord." Jesus had no sickness, disease, or sin; but it was time to die, so he chose to do so.

Jesus finishes his work and dies on the afternoon of the sixth day of the Passover Festival. He is at rest. This echoes Genesis 2:2, "By the seventh day God had finished the work he had been doing; so on the seventh day he rested from all his work."

> If salvation indeed comes from God, and is entirely His work, just as creation was, it follows, as a matter of course, that our first and highest duty is to wait on Him to do the work that pleases Him.
>
> **—Andrew Murray, *Waiting on God*, 4**

The phrase "gave up his spirit" may simply mean to give up his life. This Greek phrase, *paradidomi*. is often used to describe death. But the verb here also seems to suggest that Jesus was "handing over" his spirit, as one might pass on something to a successor in a promissory way. This may refer to the gift of the Spirit (Ezekiel 36:25-28; Acts 20:22). And John may want us to see both meanings.

Luke 23:44-45 tells us, "It was now about noon, and darkness came over the whole land until three in the afternoon, for the sun stopped shining." Each of the three Synoptic Gospels adds that at the moment of Jesus' death, "the curtain of the temple was torn in two [from top to bottom]" (Matthew 27:51; Mark 15:38; and Luke 23:45b).

John 19:31-34

31 Now it was the day of Preparation, and the next day was to be a special Sabbath. Because the Jewish leaders did not want the bodies left on the crosses during the Sabbath, they asked Pilate to have the legs broken and the bodies taken down. 32 The soldiers therefore came and broke the legs of the first man who had been crucified with Jesus, and then those of the other. 33 But when they came to Jesus and found that he was already dead, they did not break his legs. 34 Instead, one of the soldiers pierced Jesus' side with a spear, bringing a sudden flow of blood and water.

The Passover meal was eaten on Thursday evening; Friday was the day of the Preparation; and the Sabbath came on Saturday (beginning Friday evening at sunset). This is a special Sabbath, a very high holy day because it's the Sabbath of the Passover week. Evening is approaching (Mark 15:42), which marks the beginning of the Sabbath, so the religious leaders want the legs of the men hanging on the crosses to be broken (to quicken death and put the men out of their misery). Both the Greek wording and history indicates that a large mallet was used, and those hanging on the crosses were hit repeatedly until their legs were shattered completely. This would increase the loss of blood and would eliminate the person's ability to rise up to breathe, so suffocation and death would come more quickly.

The Jewish leaders also want to assure that death comes quickly so the bodies can be removed from the poles, because it was against the Jewish law to leave a dead body exposed overnight. Deuteronomy 21:22-23 says, "If someone guilty of a capital offense is put to death and their body is exposed on a pole, you must not leave the body hanging on the pole overnight." Romans typically would leave a corpse hanging on a cross for several days to serve as further warning to potential criminals. Josephus tells us the Romans made an exception in the case of the Jews.

Jesus was already dead, so they did not break his leg bones. The other Gospels report that the centurion who stood in front of Jesus said, "Surely he (this man) was the Son of God!" (Matthew 27:54; Mark 15:39). Notice that he used the word *was* not *is*, indicating that Jesus was dead. If Jesus had not already died, his legs would have been broken, too. Numbers 9:12, written centuries earlier, tell us that when dealing with Passover lambs, "They must not . . . break any of its bones." Referring to the coming Messiah, Psalm 34:20 states, "he protects all his bones, not one of them will be broken."

Even though the soldiers knew Jesus was dead, they decided to verify it by stabbing him with a spear. This would eliminate any further doubt.

John's noting that blood and water flowed from Jesus' body was a slap at the docetists who sought to deny Jesus' humanity. Jesus did not simply appear to die, as they would claim. The death of Jesus is as real as his life.

There is a medical debate as to what would cause "blood and water" to flow. Yet none of the medical explanations brings complete satisfaction. Did the water and blood flow from his chest, heart, stomach, and sac around the heart—or all of the above? There are those who point to deeper and more symbolic meanings:

- The blood and water from his side serve as a reminder that Eve was created from a rib from Adam's side (Genesis 2:21). Jesus is the new Adam; the church is the new bride bursting forth.
- Some say Jesus is also dying of an emotionally ruptured heart.
- Tertullian and Aquinas speculated that the water represents baptism and the blood represents martyrdom.

- Others have suggested the blood is the Eucharist.
- Some understand the water to be the Living Water of the Spirit being poured out (7:38-39); as Jesus' life flees, the Spirit is no longer restricted.
- Others see this as a reminder of when Moses struck the rock at Meribah and water flowed out of it, giving life (Exodus 17:5-7).
- Still others point out that the blood of the Passover lambs in the Old Testament wasn't congealed (as it would be if the animal were already dead) but flowed at the moment of sacrifice.

But it is equally possible that John was simply describing how brutal all of this was and verifying the fact that Jesus is clearly, really, undeniably dead. Four executioners had to sign his death warrant before he could be taken down from the cross.

John 19:35-37

35 The man who saw it has given testimony, and his testimony is true. He knows that he tells the truth, and he testifies so that you also may believe. 36 These things happened so that the scripture would be fulfilled: "Not one of his bones will be broken,"c 37 and, as another scripture says, "They will look on the one they have pierced."d

Here, the author is letting us know that he is giving an eye-witness account. He's also making it clear that his purpose in writing this is so all will believe. He then retells what he's mentioned previously, quoting Psalm 34:20, Numbers 9:12, Zechariah 12:1, Isaiah 53:5, and Isaiah 53:10.

---

c John 19:36 See Exodus 12:46; Numbers 9:12; Psalm 34:20
d John 19:37 See Zechariah 12:10

READ BETWEEN THE LINES

- Why did Jesus say, "I am thirsty"?
- Why did he not drink the wine offered to him earlier (Mark 15:23)?
- What is the significance of the hyssop plant?
- What are Jesus' final words?
- Explain "It is finished." *What* is finished?
- What does "gave up his spirit" mean?
- Why did the Jewish leaders want the bodies removed from the crosses?
- Why would the soldiers break the legs of the criminals?
- How do we know Jesus was dead?
- Why was Jesus' death necessary?
- How was Jesus' death voluntary?
- What is the significance of blood and water coming out of the wound?
- How was Jesus' death both heartbreaking and victorious?
- What prophesies does the writer of this Gospel reference in verses 35-37?

WELCOME TO MY WORLD

- Have I ever seen someone in their final days of life, just before the person died? How did I feel?
- How has Jesus' death on the cross changed how I live?
- How would I have felt if I'd been standing at the cross with John and Mary?
- How do I feel when I consider my own death?

The Burial of Jesus

John 19:38

38 Later, Joseph of Arimathea asked Pilate for the body of Jesus. Now Joseph was a disciple of Jesus, but secretly because he feared the Jewish leaders. With Pilate's permission, he came and took the body away.

All four Gospels mention that Joseph of Arimathea took responsibility for burying Jesus (Matthew 27:57-61; Mark 15:42-47; Luke 23:50-56). Archeologists have never been able to confirm the location of Arimathea, but Joseph likely lived in Jerusalem. He was a prominent member of the Council, and he was rich. Luke tells us Joseph was "waiting for the kingdom of God" and that he had not consented to the Sanhedrin's "decision and action" (23:51). John adds that Joseph was "secretly" a disciple of Jesus because he feared the Jewish leaders. John 12:42-43 offers a somewhat critical description of these secret disciples: "Yet at the same time many even among the leaders believed in him. But because of the Pharisees they would not openly acknowledge their faith for fear they would be put out of the synagogue; for they loved human praise more than praise from God."

Joseph has always kept his faith a secret. But here he counts the cost, summons up his courage, and steps out boldly to ask Pilate for the body of Jesus. Pilate probably agreed because he wanted to avoid offending any more Jewish leaders. He was eager to distance himself as far as possible from this tragedy of justice. Joseph's burial of Jesus fulfills another Old Testament prophecy: "He was assigned a grave with the wicked and with the rich in his death" (Isaiah 53:9).

Around the fifth century, legends began popping up regarding Joseph of Arimathea, suggesting that he may have been a brother of Jesus' mother Mary, and therefore an uncle of Jesus. The legends also say that Joseph, a tin merchant, took Jesus to Britain during his youth, where Jesus supposedly founded a church in the town of Glastonbury. Another legend suggests that Joseph went back to Britain with the cup from the Last Supper. The cup became the object of innumerable quests by the Knights of the Round Table who served under King Arthur.

In 1345, King Edward III is said to have permitted a search for Joseph of Arimathea's body in Glastonbury. In 1367, a monk named R. de Boston was quoted as saying "The bodies of Joseph of Arimathea and his companions were found in Glastonbury." In 1577, Holinshed's *Chronicles* also indicated that Joseph's tomb was at Glastonbury. In 1928, the remains of Joseph of Arimathea were said to have been transferred to St. Catherine's Chapel, also in Glastonbury.

It must be noted that nothing in the Gospels give any type of hint that Jesus or Joseph of Arimathea ever traveled anywhere outside of Palestine. These legends are among the many stories that make claims about what Jesus did as a youth. (Other stories claim that Jesus visited India at a young age.) While such tales are curious and can be interesting, there is no solid historical evidence for what Jesus did as a youth besides the witness of the New Testament Gospels (Luke 2:40-52; John 2:11; 7:14-16).

John 19:39-42

39 He was accompanied by Nicodemus, the man who earlier had visited Jesus at night. Nicodemus brought a mixture of myrrh and aloes, about seventy-five pounds.[e] 40 Taking Jesus' body, the two of them wrapped it, with the spices, in strips

e John 19:39 Or about 34 kilograms

of linen. This was in accordance with Jewish burial customs. ⁴¹ At the place where Jesus was crucified, there was a garden, and in the garden a new tomb, in which no one had ever been laid. ⁴² Because it was the Jewish day of Preparation and since the tomb was nearby, they laid Jesus there.

Nicodemus has been a memorable minor character in our story, one whom we've encountered twice before (3:1-21; 7:50-51). He was Israel's teacher and a member of the Sanhedrin. Some time after his first meeting with Jesus in John 3, he seems to have received Jesus as Lord—although it's possible he simply feels guilty about the death of an innocent man. (We prefer the former explanation.)

"And I, when I am lifted up from the earth," Jesus had declared, "will draw all people to myself" (12:32). Now we see this beginning to be fulfilled in Joseph and Nicodemus stepping out. This act took remarkable bravery. Also, these law-abiding Jews were possibly handling the dead body of Jesus, which would have made them ritually unclean and prohibited them from participating in any of the Passover Festival ceremonies. This could have damaged, if not destroyed, their political and religious careers. (It's also possible, and perhaps more likely, that these men directed their servants to do the work of preparing Jesus' body for burial.)

While Romans would have allowed the body to rot on the cross or be eaten by animals, the Jews normally would have buried the body of an executed criminal in a common grave outside the city walls. Instead, Joseph and Nicodemus bury Jesus with dignity, placing him in Joseph's new garden tomb nearby. (Joseph didn't realize Jesus would need to borrow the tomb for only a few days!) The Old Testament records that kings of Israel were buried in garden tombs (2 Kings 21:18, 26).

Nicodemus brought approximately 65 to 80 pounds of aromatic spices to counteract the smell of decomposition. This is a large amount—far more than what Mary poured over Jesus in Bethany (12:3)—and similar to what might be used in a royal burial. (At the funeral of Herod the Great, there were 500 servants carrying spices.) Nicodemus and Joseph wrap Jesus' body in strips of linen cloth in the limestone tomb, using spices (including myrrh). Thirty-plus years earlier, another Joseph wrapped a baby Jesus in a linen cloth and placed him in a stone manger, then watched as he was presented with myrrh as a gift. (For more information on the preparation of a body and the burial process, see the commentary regarding Lazarus in John 11:38-44.)

Perhaps the women who come to the tomb to anoint Jesus on Sunday weren't aware of what Joseph and Nicodemus had already done (Mark 16:1). Or maybe, with the Sabbath beginning at sundown on Friday, Joseph and Nicodemus only had time to put on one layer of linen and spices, and they were intending to come back on Sunday to finish the job before sliding the body into one of the tomb's burial niches.

The tomb would have had a single entrance (about 3 to 4 feet high by 2 to 3 feet wide) that would be covered by a heavy wheel or stone (Mark 16:4) that was rolled down an incline and set in a trough to keep out grave robbers and wild animals. A Georgia Tech geologist has estimated that such stones may have weighed as much as two tons—which would require several people to move it. The "rolling" stone wasn't typical, according to A. Klooner, who notes, "Of 900 second temple burial tombs found in Judea, only four had rolling stones."

According to Matthew 27:62-66, guards were placed around the tomb at the request of the Jewish leaders, in order to prevent Jesus' disciples from stealing the body and claiming he had risen. Roman guard units consisted of 16 men who protected 36 square feet of space each. They slept in eight-hour shifts, and each soldier carried five weapons at all times. (This was like our SWAT teams today.) If a soldier was found asleep during his watch, he would be set on fire immediately and left to burn at the exact spot where he was caught sleeping.

Matthew also notes that a seal was placed over the stone (27:65-66). It consisted of two crossed pieces of rawhide, with a clay pack in the center featuring the seal of Rome. The imprint of Caesar would be pressed into the seal. Break the seal and the Roman authorities would seek you out (and *not* to give you the key to the city).

In Leviticus 16, it is prescribed that on one day each year—Yom Kippur, the Day of Atonement—the high priest was to trade his beautiful priestly robes for the simple linen robes worn by his fellow priests. And what did the high priest do on the Day of Atonement? He went through the veil into the Holy of Holies to sprinkle blood on the lid, or mercy seat, of the ark of the covenant—the two-foot-by-three foot box that held the Ten Commandments. If he were defiled, he would stay in that place as a dead man and would later have to be pulled out with a rope. But if he wasn't defiled, he would walk out into the courtyard of the temple to the jubilant cries of the people who knew they were forgiven for another year.

Here, our great High Priest, Jesus Christ, is inside the tomb. Would He emerge? Did the sacrifice work? Are we free? Only if He came out among the people as He had prophesied could there truly be celebration and could we know our sins are forgiven—not just for one year, but forever.

—*Jon Courson's Application Commentary: New Testament*, 590

READ BETWEEN THE LINES

- What is known about Joseph of Arimathea?
- What does it mean to be a "secret disciple"?
- What motivated Joseph and Nicodemus to bury Jesus' body? Would there be a cost for doing what they did?
- Why didn't the other disciples do this?
- Why did they use such a huge amount of myrrh and aloes?
- Why doesn't John record the fact that the tomb was sealed and guarded by soldiers?

WELCOME TO MY WORLD

- Am I a secret believer? Do I hide my faith from my friends, fellow students, or coworkers?
- How do I need to step up for Jesus?
- What fears do I need Jesus to remove before I can do this?

The Empty Tomb

John 20:1-2

¹ **Early on the first day of the week, while it was still dark, Mary Magdalene went to the tomb and saw that the stone had been removed from the entrance.** ² **So she came running to Simon Peter and the other disciple, the one Jesus loved, and said, "They have taken the Lord out of the tomb, and we don't know where they have put him!"**

Dawn is breaking as Mary Magdalene and other women approach the tomb (Matthew 28:1; Mark 16:1; Luke 24:1; also notice the "we" in John 20:2). Mark's Gospel tells us they are bringing spices to anoint Jesus' body. Mary Magdalene had been at the crucifixion (19:25), and then she stayed to see where Jesus was to be buried (Matthew 27:58-61). The women may not have been aware that Joseph of Arimathea and Nicodemus had already anointed Jesus' body (19:38-40), or perhaps the women came to finish that job. Notice that women are the first ones to discover Jesus Christ's victory over death and the first to preach the gospel message to the world. These women would not have been permitted to stand before the Jewish council and testify on behalf of Jesus. But they took advantage of the opportunities given to them to serve Christ and proclaim the gospel.

In the Synoptic Gospels, the tomb of Jesus serves as a prelude from which we await the resurrection. The tomb is shut and sealed, a guard is posted, and everyone awaits as angels arrive and an earthquake breaks open this grave that cannot contain its occupant.

As Matthew, Mark, and Luke envision the tomb, it is theologically linked to Easter Sunday, becoming a vital part of the early

> Christian apologetic for Jesus' resurrection. John of course, employs the tomb of Jesus in the resurrection story (20:1-10). But there is no account of guards or seals or heavy stones rolled in front. The tomb is the resting place for the great King, the culmination of his work on the cross, the terminus of his journey through the hands of Caiaphas and Pilate. The resurrection for John is not a solution to a problem (Jesus' death and burial), but another step along the way, as Jesus moves from earth to heaven ... The tomb thus is not a place of depressing, exhausting defeat. It too, like the cross, is a place of glory and victory.
>
> —Gary M. Burge, *The NIV Application Commentary: John*, 520–521

Matthew 27:51-53 tells us, "The earth shook, the rocks split and the tombs broke open. The bodies of many holy people who had died were raised to life. They came out of the tombs after Jesus' resurrection and went into the holy city and appeared to many people." Matthew goes on to inform us that an angel rolled back the stone in front of the tomb (28:2). However, the stone was removed from the entrance so others could get in, not so Jesus could get out.

Mary Magdalene thinks someone may have stolen Jesus' body. She leaves the other women and runs to find Peter and the other disciple, the one whom Jesus loved.

> The biggest fact about Joseph's tomb was that it wasn't a tomb at all—it was a room for a transient. Jesus just stopped there a night or two on his way back to glory.
>
> —Herbert Booth Smith

Skeptics have advanced a number of different theories about what might have happened to Jesus' body:

Theory One: The Disciples Stole the Body. According to Mark, moving that huge stone would have required someone to roll it up an incline. And according to Luke, that stone was moved away from not just the opening, but from the entire sepulcher. If the disciples were going to steal the body, then why would they move the stone so far? According to John 20, the stone wasn't rolled away but picked up. Even if the guards had been sleeping, this action should have woken them up. The shaking of the ground would have registered on the Richter scale. And, yes, the soldiers would have been killed for falling asleep on guard duty.

Also, the disciples had no reason to steal the body. They were discouraged. They'd scattered. And they certainly would have known that if they'd been caught breaking the government seal on the tomb, then the equivalent of the FBI in those days would have hunted them down for the rest of their lives. And why would they steal the body? At the time, no one believed the Messiah would die and then be raised from the dead. The current belief was that the Messiah would be a conquering military ruler. That's why John says the disciples didn't realize Jesus would rise from the dead—even though he'd told them so many times (20:9).

Finally, if the disciples had stolen the body, why would they live so boldly and be willing to die for something they all knew to be a lie?

Theory Two: The Romans or Jewish Leaders Stole the Body. The Romans had no reason to steal the body. They'd posted guards at the tomb to make sure the body wasn't stolen. Why would they cause problems for themselves? The same is true of the Jewish leaders. They were the ones who requested the Roman guards so the disciples couldn't steal the body. (Apparently they remembered what the disciples had forgotten about Jesus claiming he would rise from the grave on the third day.) If the religious leaders had stolen the body, they could have ended Christianity simply by producing the dead body. Find the body of Jesus, and Christianity would crumble. The silence of the Jewish religious leaders speaks as loudly as the Christians' verbal witness.

Theory Three: Jesus Was Really Thrown into a Common Pit. If this were the case, why did the Romans seal and guard this tomb? And why would the Jewish leaders and Romans concoct a stolen-body story if Jesus were just lying in a common pit?

Theory Four: Hallucination. Some have suggested that the disciples were so grieved by Jesus' death that they hallucinated, only thinking they saw him. However, the disciples weren't expecting to see Jesus, and hallucinations don't start and stop suddenly. The other problem is that more than 500 different people—at different times and locations—reported they'd seen Jesus in the days shortly after the resurrection. Did hundreds of people in dozens of different settings all have the same hallucination?

Theory Five: Swoon Theory. Some have claimed that Jesus didn't really die on the cross; he just passed out because of a great loss of blood. If this is true, then the four Roman executioners must have been mistaken when they declared Jesus was dead. This is unlikely; Roman soldiers knew when someone was dead.

According to this theory, Jesus would also have to survive the huge spear wound in his side. He'd have to breathe through the heavy cloth and spices he was wrapped in inside the tomb. Then he'd have to jump up off the preparation table (after being flogged and crucified), hobble over to the very heavy stone blocking the tomb's exit, and push the massive stone away with his bionic arms. Once that was done, he must have tied up the Roman guards and gone back inside the tomb to lay out his grave clothes in two neat piles. Then he hobbled two miles (with nail wounds in his feet) to get to the upper room and be with his disciples. This theory was introduced 1,600 years after the resurrection. (Yes, it took someone that long to think it up.)

Theory Six: Wrong Tomb. This theory proposes that the women went to the place where they *thought* Jesus was buried, but they actually went to the wrong tomb. With all of their tears, you see, they probably couldn't see very clearly. In order to accept this idea, we'd have to assume the disciples, Jewish leaders, Romans, and Joseph of Arimathea (who owned the garden tomb) had also gone to the wrong tomb.

Theory Seven: Jesus Just Evaporated. It's been suggested that the body of Jesus disintegrated through normal processes, simple evaporating into natural gases in only three days. While decay certainly would have begun during those three days, a complete chemical decomposition isn't possible. To believe that the body of Jesus would evaporate into gases within three days of his death takes more "faith" than belief in the resurrection itself.

Can you believe the extremes people have gone to in trying to discount the truth of the resurrection? But the reality is that Jesus rose from the grave and appeared to more than 500 people at 14 different times and locations:

- Mary Magdalene (Mark 16:9; John 20:11-14)
- The women returning from the tomb (Matthew 28:8-10)
- Peter later in the day (Luke 24:34; 1 Corinthians 15:5)
- The Emmaus disciples (Luke 24:13-33)
- The apostles, with Thomas absent (Luke 24:36-43; John 20:19-24)

- The apostles, with Thomas present (John 20:26-29)
- The seven by the Lake of Tiberias (John 21:1-14)
- A multitude of 500-plus believers on a Galilean mountain (1 Corinthians 15:6)
- James (1 Corinthians 15:7)
- The Eleven (Matthew 28:16-20; Mark 16:14-20; Luke 24:33-52; Acts 1:3-12)
- Saul/Paul on the Damascus Road (Acts 9:3-6; 1 Corinthians 15:8)
- Paul in the temple (Acts 22:17-21; 23:11)
- Stephen (Acts 7:55)
- John on Patmos (Revelation 1:10-19)

The early Christians staked everything on the resurrection. If Jesus were not resurrected, then today he would merely be admired as a great teacher in the same way that Confucius or Socrates are revered. The apostle Paul acknowledged the centrality of the resurrection in 1 Corinthians 15:17 when he wrote, "And if Christ has not been raised, your faith is futile; you are still in your sins."

John 20: 3-10

3 So Peter and the other disciple started for the tomb. 4 Both were running, but the other disciple outran Peter and reached the tomb first. 5 He bent over and looked in at the strips of linen lying there but did not go in. 6 Then Simon Peter came along behind him and went straight into the tomb. He saw the strips of linen lying there, 7 as well as the cloth that had been wrapped around Jesus' head. The cloth was still lying in its place, separate from the linen. 8 Finally the other disciple, who had reached the tomb first, also went inside. He saw and believed. 9 (They still did not understand from

**Scripture that Jesus had to rise from the dead.)
¹⁰ Then the disciples went back to where they
were staying.**

Luke 24:11 tells us the disciples did not believe the women at first because their words "seemed to them like nonsense." But John makes it clear that at least two of the disciples were intrigued enough to want to check out the women's story. Again, the "other disciple" is presumably John, and he wants to make it clear that he ran faster than Peter to the gravesite. (Peter may have been older.) In verse 5, John bends over (the opening may have been only three or four feet high) and takes a quick look (*blepo*) without entering the tomb. When Peter gets there, he runs right past John and goes into the tomb, carefully observing all of the details inside.

Jesus seems to have floated right out of those linen grave clothes. (Lazarus, when he arose, was still wearing his grave clothes.) The linen strips remain right where Jesus' body had been. The cloth (handkerchief) that had been tied around Jesus' head to prevent the mouth from falling open, is folded (neatly arranged) in a place separate from the other cloth.

In verse 8 John says he "saw." The Greek word here is *eidon*, from which we get our word *idea*. This may indicate that John puts it all together in this moment and realizes that Jesus has risen. Maybe he concludes that grave robbers—or anyone else—would not have taken the time for such precise placement of the linen cloth and handkerchief.

John believes, although he still doesn't understand completely. He still hasn't made the connection between what he sees in this moment and Jesus' earlier statements or the many Old Testament Scriptures that say Jesus would rise. For example, Psalm 16:9-11 is a prophecy of the resurrection of Jesus "Therefore my heart is glad and my tongue rejoices; my body also will rest secure, because you will not abandon me to the realm of the dead, nor will you let your faithful one see decay." (See also Psalm 110; 118; Isaiah 53; and Hosea 6.) In Matthew 12:40 Jesus told them, "For as Jonah was three days and three nights in the belly of a huge fish, so the Son of Man will be three days and three nights in the heart of the earth."

Some have suggested that the physical resurrection is relatively insignificant. For example, the famous New Testament scholar Rudolf Bultmann argued that in John's Gospel the point is for Jesus to reveal the glory of God, and this he does in the signs and miracles throughout John's account. So, Bultmann said, in the resurrection Jesus merely does what he's been doing all along—revealing God's glory. But this misses a vital point both within John's theology and in biblical theology generally. We would certainly agree with Gary Burge who writes, "Interpreters who say that [the resurrection] is a mere postscript to the story are clearly wrong." There is something unique about the resurrection. Only because of the resurrection can the Spirit come to dwell within (see John 14:17 and John 20:22). Only because of the resurrection can we dwell in the will of the Father. Only because of the resurrection can we be saved from the power and the penalty of our sins.

Apparently, the two disciples didn't know what to do in response to what they'd just experienced. They must have been overwhelmed. John tells us they went back to the place they'd been staying. Later, the disciples would meet in the upper room as a group behind locked doors (20:19).

READ BETWEEN THE LINES

- Why did Mary go to the tomb early in the morning?
- How did Mary react to the empty tomb?
- Why did she go to Simon Peter and the other disciple?
- Why is everyone running in these verses (20:2-4)?

- What do Mary and the disciples think has happened to Jesus' body?
- Why does John mention that he beat Peter to the tomb?
- What did John believe—and why?
- Why did the disciples go back to their homes?

WELCOME TO MY WORLD

- Why is the resurrection so important to Christians?
- What evidence of the resurrection is most helpful to me?
- How does the resurrection of Jesus make me feel about a loved one's death? How does it affect my thinking about my own death?
- Have I gone to a cemetery to visit the grave of someone I loved? How did that go?

Jesus Appears to Mary Magdalene

John 20:11-12

11 Now Mary stood outside the tomb crying. As she wept, she bent over to look into the tomb 12 and saw two angels in white, seated where Jesus' body had been, one at the head and the other at the foot.

Mary Magdalene must have returned to the tomb after Peter and John left. Crying profusely, she approaches the tomb and stoops down to peek inside once more. She is in for a real surprise. Where did those angels come from? They weren't there a few moments earlier when Peter and John were inside the tomb.

The two angels look like humans, dressed in white and situated at either end of the burial-preparation shelf where Jesus' body had been laid. This would bring to mind the scene around the ark of the covenant and the blood-splattered mercy seat described in Exodus 25:10-22, with the two carved angels facing each other. God would meet humankind between these two angels.

John refers to Mary here using the Greek form of her name (*Maria*); however, when Jesus (the new Moses) meets her in 20:16, he uses the Hebrew form of her name: *Miriam*. In Exodus 2:1-10, the infant Moses is placed in a floating bed (made of papyrus, tar, and pitch) that becomes a coffin and a tomb from which the child is raised to life and avoids death. Moses' sister, Miriam, watches carefully to ensure the baby's safety, and later she becomes a prophetess who brings a message to Israel. Now, in the New Testament, another Miriam becomes a caretaker of the new Moses, Jesus, and will bring a prophetic message to the disciples (20:18).

John 20:13-15

13 They asked her, "Woman, why are you crying?"

"They have taken my Lord away," she said, "and I don't know where they have put him." 14 At this, she turned around and saw Jesus standing there, but she did not realize that it was Jesus.

15 He asked her, "Woman, why are you crying? Who is it you are looking for?"

Thinking he was the gardener, she said, "Sir, if you have carried him away, tell me where you have put him, and I will get him."

Mary didn't recognize that the ones inside the tomb were angels. Mark and Luke tell us they looked like men; plus, Mary was crying. The angels ask Mary why she is crying. Her tears are flowing not so much because Jesus died, but because his body is missing. However, the angels know something Mary doesn't know. They know this is not the time for crying: Jesus has been raised! Mary thinks Jesus' body has been taken away. She doesn't realize Jesus is standing just a few feet away from her.

Then Mary turns around and sees Jesus—but she doesn't recognize him. She thinks he is a gardener, and in one sense he is. He's the new Adam, a Gardener who will grow order out of chaos. Some have explained that Mary failed to recognize Jesus at first because she wasn't expecting to see him. Others suggest that her hair fell in front of her eyes or her tears made it hard to see. Others propose that Mary didn't even look up, or else she took just a quick look at Jesus and then turned away, because verse 16 indicates that she turns back to him after he calls her name. Perhaps Jesus was in a supernatural resurrected body that made it harder for someone to recognize him immediately (Luke 24:15-16). He was in that in-between stage where it was neither his same earthly body, nor his fully glorified heavenly body.

Isn't it cool that Jesus appears first to this woman whom the culture deemed insignificant? The text indicates that Mary was crying or wailing a great deal. But this is about to change. As Jesus told them in John 16:20, "Your grief will turn to joy."

Jesus asks her the same question the angels had asked, and then he adds an additional question. She thinks maybe this gardener is the one who took Jesus' body away. Mary seems to be only half-listening to him, as she's still focused on solving the riddle of the empty tomb.

The first garden was Eden (where death entered and paradise was lost). Here, at this garden tomb, Jesus has reversed the curse of death by conquering it.

John 20:16

16 Jesus said to her, "Mary."

She turned toward him and cried out in Aramaic, "Rabboni!" (which means "Teacher").

Jesus calls her by name. That was all it took. When someone you love calls your name, you know who it is. With just one word, Jesus breaks through Mary's wall of grief and despair. John 10:3 declares, "He calls his own sheep by name and leads them out." In her great joy, she greets him as "Teacher."

Mary's experience is a lesson for all of us. We should never get so wrapped up in our grief that we don't recognize Christ. He is there for us in our time of sorrow. That's when He wants to comfort us. We should be expecting to see Him.

—Bruce Bickel and Stan Jantz, *John: Encountering Christ in a Life-Changing Way*, 154

John 20:17

17 Jesus said, "Do not hold on to me, for I have not yet ascended to the Father. Go instead to my brothers and tell them, 'I am ascending to my Father and your Father, to my God and your God.'"

Jesus' words here suggest that Mary may have embraced him. She doesn't want to lose him again. At first glance it seems odd that Jesus would say, "Do not hold on to me." Some have pointed out the apparent contradiction that Jesus tells Mary not to hold on to him, but later he invites Thomas to touch his hands and side (20:27)—even though it seems Thomas didn't follow through on Jesus' invitation (20:28-29).

There are many opinions about why Jesus says this, none of which feel particularly convincing. Some suggest that Jesus' wounds were still sore or that he didn't want Mary to defile herself by touching a "dead" body. Another questionable explanation quotes Hebrews 7:26 and suggests that as our high priest, Jesus must remain unstained and separate from sinners. Since the Scriptures say that Jesus' grave clothes were still in the tomb, some have even suggested that he may have been naked, which would have made an embrace inappropriate. Still others have taken issue with the wording of the passage, suggesting that a scribe may have made a mistake and intended to use a similarly spelled Greek phrase meaning "do not fear" instead of "do not hold on to me." You may want to check out the paintings of Giotto, Fontana, Fra Angelico, Titian, and Rembrandt to see their interpretations of this scene.

Perhaps the simplest solution is that this is a transition before "the hour" when Jesus would ascend to the Father and the glorification process would be complete. Mary may be thinking that Jesus is resuming his physical presence with them, but he is not. Jesus will be present physically for only forty days before he ascends to the Father (Acts 1:3).

Jesus is telling her not to try to hold on to him because he hasn't returned to the Father.

Jesus' resurrected body is unique. It isn't the same kind of flesh-and-blood body that Lazarus had when he came back to life. Jesus' body isn't subject to the same laws of nature that it was before his death. He could suddenly appear inside a locked room (20:19); yet he wasn't a ghost or disembodied spirit because he could be touched (20:27), and he could eat (Luke 24:41-43). Jesus' resurrection was literal and physical—but his body was not the same as it had been before the crucifixion.

Jesus seems to be letting Mary know that he won't remain with them in this new glorified body, but in the form of the Holy Spirit (14:18). Jesus desires to enter his disciples' lives in a way they were unable to grasp; he wants to live in them completely by the indwelling Holy Spirit. Jesus wants to see his disciples before he fulfills his promise by ascending (16:19-22). For these early disciples, the indwelling of the Spirit is still to come (20:22; Acts 2:1-12).

In speaking with Mary, Jesus refers to his disciples by a new name. He has called them servants and friends (15:15), but here for the first time he calls them brothers. Romans 8:29 uses similar language—"that he might be the firstborn among many brothers and sisters." Hebrews 2:11 affirms that Jesus isn't ashamed to call us brothers and sisters as well: "Both the one who makes people holy and those who are made holy are of the same family. So Jesus is not ashamed to call them brothers and sisters."

Jesus is making it clear that his Father is also our Father. His God is our God. God is the Father both of Jesus and of believers, but in different ways. The death and resurrection of Jesus puts believers in a new relationship with God the Father. Because of what Jesus accomplished, we can enter into a new richness of life—the life God originally intended for all of us, but which we humans walked away from when our first parents sinned in the garden of Eden.

John 20:18

[18] Mary Magdalene went to the disciples with the news: "I have seen the Lord!" And she told them that he had said these things to her.

Mary obeyed Jesus' command; she did what Jesus asked her to do. John was the first to believe in Jesus' resurrection; but Mary was the first to see the risen Lord, and she was the first to be entrusted by Jesus to testify about him to others. This is quite a contrast from the traditional rabbinic teaching on the restrictions placed on women's witness in the first century. Jesus turns that way of thinking and acting upside down. Who but Jesus would give Mary Magdalene the starring role in this narrative? She becomes the first missionary to share the full story. Andrew Lincoln points out that Mary Magdalene has been called the "apostle to the apostles."

Jesus' resurrection is absolute proof of who he is. Paul wrote in Romans 10:9—"If you declare with your mouth, 'Jesus is Lord,' and believe in your heart that God raised him from the dead, you will be saved."

READ BETWEEN THE LINES

- Why was Mary crying?
- What significance is there regarding the two angels in the tomb?
- Why did the angels ask her why she was crying?
- Why didn't Mary recognize Jesus at first?
- What caused Mary to realize she was talking to Jesus?
- Why does she call him "Teacher"?

- Why did Jesus appear to Mary first after the resurrection?
- Why does Jesus say, "Do not hold on to me"?
- What did Mary tell the disciples?
- What would Christianity be like without the resurrection?

WELCOME TO MY WORLD

- What excites me the most about Jesus' rising from the dead?
- Have I ever had an experience when Jesus became real to me?
- How have I felt immediately after someone I love dies? Describe.
- How have I experienced God's presence during difficult times? What happened?
- How has my life changed since I met Jesus?
- What kind of a resurrected body will I have (1 Corinthians 15:35-58)?
- What dead person would I want to visit me?

Jesus Appears to His Disciples

John 20:19-21

19 On the evening of that first day of the week, when the disciples were together, with the doors locked for fear of the Jewish leaders, Jesus came and stood among them and said, "Peace be with you!" 20 After he said this, he showed them his hands and side. The disciples were overjoyed when they saw the Lord.

21 Again Jesus said, "Peace be with you! As the Father has sent me, I am sending you."

Sunday, the first day of the week, is the day Jesus Christ rose from the dead. Most Jews continue to worship on the seventh day of the week (Saturday), the Sabbath, commemorating God's finished work of creation (Genesis 2:1-3). On the other hand, most Christian groups now worship on the first day of the week, the Lord's Day (Sunday), commemorating Christ's finished work of redemption. God the Father worked for six days and then rested. God the Son suffered on the cross for six hours and then rested.

The "disciples" here may refer to only ten of the twelve apostles chosen by Jesus at the beginning of his ministry (minus Judas, who committed suicide, and Thomas, who wasn't in attendance). Or the group may be a larger circle of Jesus' followers who are now holing up in this private room. The doors of the room were locked (probably bolted) in case the Jewish leaders, or perhaps even the Romans, would try to arrest them. Despite the locked doors, Jesus appears to them unexpectedly. Luke 24:37 tells us, "They were startled and frightened, thinking they saw a ghost." Jesus promised the disciples in Matthew 18:20, "For where two or three gather in my name, there am I with them." Even today whenever we gather together in Jesus' name, he is in our midst.

In his glorified body, Jesus could pass through solid substances like locked doors or walls (20:19). But he still had a physical body and could be recognized as the same person they'd known all along. Some have suggested that Jesus entered the room by climbing through a second-story window or climbing down from the roof, or that he'd sneaked into the room before the meeting and hid. Such speculation seems unfounded. If Jesus could walk on water and pass through his grave clothes, he could pass through walls. We don't know how Jesus materialized in their midst, but he was clearly there.

The first words out of Jesus' mouth are "Peace be with you!"—a common Jewish greeting (Judges 6:23) with a special meaning to these disciples. Notice that Jesus doesn't criticize them for not being at the cross or for pretending they didn't know him when they were questioned. Jesus greets them in peace and shows them his side and his hands (the Greek word used here includes the wrists and forearms). Seeing the scars of his suffering and victory would have eliminated any lingering doubts the disciples had and filled them with joy. Jesus tells them not to be concerned; he is still in control. Before his crucifixion, Jesus had promised them peace and joy (14:27; 15:11; 16:19-24; 17:13); now he delivers on that promise. Then he commissions the disciples by sending them into the world in the same way he'd been sent by the Father. Jesus is God's agent, and they are to be Jesus' agents. We are to continue the ministry of the Christ.

John 20:22-23

22 **And with that he breathed on them and said, "Receive the Holy Spirit. 23 If you forgive anyone's sins, their sins are forgiven; if you do not forgive them, they are not forgiven."**

Jesus then gives the Holy Spirit to his disciples, just as he received the Holy Spirit after John the Baptist baptized him in the Jordan River (1:33). Jesus is filling them with his own Spirit and life. As Jesus is about to depart, he places into their lives the Holy Spirit that is within him. The miracle of our becoming children of God happens only because the Holy Spirit enters and transforms our lives.

As Jesus breathes on the disciples, it's a reminder of Genesis 2:7 where God breathed life into Adam and he became a living soul. Some have suggested that this event in the upper room is perhaps a pledge—a partial, symbolic anointing in anticipation of the time when believers would receive the Holy Spirit in full (Acts 2). God had dwelt *among* them in the person of Jesus Christ, but now the Holy Spirit will dwell *in* them (14:17).

These words about the disciples' forgiving (and not forgiving) others' sins have caused a great deal of confusion and division within the church. This brings to mind the story from Mark 2:5-7, where Jesus heals a paralyzed man who'd been lowered through the roof by his friends. Mark writes, "When Jesus saw their faith, he said to the paralyzed man, 'Son, your sins are forgiven.' Now some teachers of the law were sitting there, thinking to themselves, 'Why does this fellow talk like that? He's blaspheming! Who can forgive sins but God alone?'" The teachers of the law in Mark's story are correct: Only God can forgive sins. So what do we make of Jesus' words here in John? They raise several questions: Is God's forgiveness really somehow dependent on the disciples' forgiveness? Is this ability to forgive sins given just to these disciples, or to church leaders? Or is it given to all Christians down through the centuries and to the present? How much authority has Jesus given his followers?

Some have suggested these disciples became the first bishops of the church and had the authority to remit or retain sin as the people confessed their sins to them. Traditionally, these spiritual leaders also told people what penance they must do in order to obtain remission of sins. However, in Acts 10:23b-48 when Peter goes to the household of Cornelius and then Cornelius falls at Peter's feet in reverence, Peter makes it very clear that he is only a man, just like Cornelius. And in his speech Peter says it isn't through any other human being but only through Jesus that forgiveness comes—"everyone who believes in [Jesus] receives forgiveness of sins through his name" (10:43).

We know that all Christians are to do the work of baptizing and making disciples. In the final words of Matthew's Gospel, Jesus says:

> "Therefore go and make disciples of all nations, baptizing them in the name of the Father and of the Son and of the Holy Spirit, and teaching them to obey everything I have commanded you. And surely I am with you always, to the very end of the age."
> (28:19-20)

We know Christians don't provide forgiveness from sin (only Jesus forgives), but we can proclaim it. As Jesus' ambassadors we can tell new believers who receive Jesus' work on the cross that their sins are forgiven. And to those who reject Jesus, we can say their sin remains and judgment awaits them (9:39; 12:48; Mark 16:16), because only the blood of Jesus can wash sin away.

The significance of the word *anyone* can be overlooked easily. Jesus is talking about the forgiveness of the sins of "anyone"—no exceptions. No sinner has traveled so far from the Lord that there is no longer any hope for him or her. Our job is to extend Christ's love and forgiveness to everyone.

READ BETWEEN THE LINES

- What day is the first day of the week?
- Why were the disciples in a locked room?
- Why did Jesus choose "Peace be with you" to be the first words out of his mouth instead of explaining the resurrection? What are his priorities?
- What are the disciples' fears?
- Why were the disciples overjoyed to see the Lord?
- What does it mean to be sent by Jesus?
- How is verse 22 reconciled with Acts 2:1-13?
- How do you explain verse 23?

WELCOME TO MY WORLD

- When I was a kid, where would I hide? Where would I hide now?
- What are the locked doors in my life? How will Jesus get inside?
- What would peace look like to me at this time in my life?
- What do I need Jesus to whisper to me?
- What does it mean to have the Holy Spirit in me?
- How would I explain my faith to a person who doesn't believe?
- "I am sending you" or "so send I you" (ASV) is a famous missionary verse. Where is God sending me?

Jesus Appears to Thomas

John 20:24-25

²⁴ Now Thomas (also known as Didymus[a]), one of the Twelve, was not with the disciples when Jesus came. ²⁵ So the other disciples told him, "We have seen the Lord!"

But he said to them, "Unless I see the nail marks in his hands and put my finger where the nails were, and put my hand into his side, I will not believe."

Thomas wasn't with the other disciples on the night of Jesus' resurrection. Perhaps he'd gone back to his home in Galilee. But Thomas missed Jesus' appearance in the upper room. See what happens when you miss church! Hebrews 10:24-25 affirms the importance of believers gathering together: "And let us consider how we may spur one another on toward love and good deeds, not giving up meeting together, as some are in the habit of doing, but encouraging one another—and all the more as you see the Day approaching."

Thomas was skeptical and expressed doubts about the reality of Jesus' resurrection. His words also show a lack of confidence in his fellow disciples. It is a tribute to the other disciples that they didn't toss him out of the group for his doubts. But it's also a tribute to Thomas that he was willing to express his doubts honestly, yet remain in the company of the other disciples. Both Thomas and the disciples had integrity in this matter. Thomas issues a challenge indicating he wants not only a sign (4:48), but also hard evidence.

The Gospel of John tells us more about Thomas (Jewish name) than does any other book of the Bible. In the Synoptic Gospels, Thomas is mentioned only when the list of disciples is given. His Greek name, Didymus, means "twin." At times, Thomas reminds me of the pessimistic donkey

---

a John 20:24 *Thomas* (Aramaic) and *Didymus* (Greek) both mean *twin*.

named Eeyore in the *Winnie the Pooh* stories. From these verses we know him as "doubting Thomas," but other passages portray him differently. In John 11:16 he is *fatalist* Thomas—his love for Jesus is so strong that he would die for him; his faith is so weak that he knows he will die. In John 14:5 he is *honest* Thomas, telling Jesus that he and the rest of the disciples don't know what they'll do after his death.

But we should cut Thomas a little slack. The other disciples were no better when you consider the way they ridiculed the initial reports about Jesus' resurrection (Mark 16:10-13; Luke 24:9-11). With the possible exception of John, none of the other disciples believed until they saw Jesus face to face. Elisabeth Elliot, missionary and author, has been quoted as saying that during difficult, faith-crushing times, Christians often move from denial to doubt to devotion.

John 20:26-29

26 A week later his disciples were in the house again, and Thomas was with them. Though the doors were locked, Jesus came and stood among them and said, "Peace be with you!" 27 Then he said to Thomas, "Put your finger here; see my hands. Reach out your hand and put it into my side. Stop doubting and believe."

28 Thomas said to him, "My Lord and my God!"

29 Then Jesus told him, "Because you have seen me, you have believed; blessed are those who have not seen and yet have believed."

One week later (the next Sunday), the disciples are gathered in the same room with the doors locked (evidently still fearing the Jewish and Roman leaders). This time Thomas is with them. Jesus appears again and repeats the greeting from the previous week. Perhaps this second appearance is for Thomas alone. Jesus comes to Thomas in a sympathetic, compassionate, loving manner and invites Thomas to live out the ultimatum he'd made earlier: He challenges Thomas to reach out and touch his wounds. Jesus seems to have supernatural knowledge of what Thomas said (2:24).

John doesn't tell us if Thomas acts on Jesus' invitation. But it doesn't appear as though Thomas feels the need to follow through with his test. Maybe he realized the inappropriateness of his demand. Jesus gives credit to Thomas's "seeing" (not "touching") as the cause for his faith.

Have you ever wondered why Jesus' resurrected body has scars? Maybe they serve as a reminder to the disciples (and to us) of Jesus' suffering in our place, as well as a reminder to Jesus of his confinement in a limiting, pregnable, vulnerable human body while on this earth.

Notice that Thomas says, "*My* Lord and *my* God,"—not *the* Lord and *the* God. Thomas offers his confession of heartfelt belief in Jesus as Lord and God in the flesh (1:1, 14, 18), and Jesus doesn't challenge Thomas' statement. In Revelation 4:11 the elders fall before the throne of God and utter similar words, "You are worthy, our Lord and God, to receive glory and honor and power." The title Thomas gives to Jesus is also how the Roman Emperor Domitian (AD 81–96) wished to be addressed. This may be John's way of opposing the worship of any Roman emperor.

Jesus wasn't hard on Thomas for his doubts. Despite his skepticism, Thomas was still loyal to the believers and to Jesus himself. Some people need to doubt before they believe. If doubt leads to questions, questions lead to answers, and the answers are accepted, then doubt has done good work. It is when doubt becomes stubbornness and stubbornness becomes a life-style that doubt harms faith. When you doubt, don't stop there. Let your doubt deepen your faith as you continue to search for the answer.

—*Life Application Bible Studies, John*, 399

Thomas gets a gentle rebuke when Jesus says, "Blessed are those who have not seen and yet have believed." That's us! We have all the proof we need in the words of the Bible and the testimony of believers.

READ BETWEEN THE LINES

- Why wasn't Thomas with the disciples when Jesus first appeared to them?
- What was Thomas's response to the disciples telling him they'd seen the Lord?
- What might the relationship and interactions between Thomas and the other disciples have been like in the week between Jesus' two appearances?
- Why does Jesus wait a week in between the two appearances?
- How did Jesus know what Thomas had said after his first appearance?
- How does Thomas's reaction differ from Mary's and John's?
- How does Jesus respond to the doubts of Thomas?
- Why does Jesus keep the scars from his crucifixion in his resurrected body?
- What was Thomas's response to Jesus? What does he call Jesus?
- What does it mean to be blessed?
- Who is Jesus talking about in verse 29?
- Why might Jesus have appeared only to believers after the resurrection? (The apostle Paul in Acts 9 and Jesus' brother James in 1 Corinthians 15:7 are the only exceptions.)

WELCOME TO MY WORLD

- Has there been a big event in the life of my family or friends that I missed out on because I wasn't there? How did that feel?

- Would I have reached out and touched Jesus' wounds?

- How have I wrestled with spiritual doubts?

- What's been the most helpful way I've found to deal with my doubts?

- How do I feel about my doubts after reading Jesus' response to Thomas's doubts?

- What am I struggling with spiritually right now?

- How do I feel knowing that Jesus was referring to me in verse 29?

The Purpose of John's Gospel

John 20:30-31

[30] Jesus performed many other signs in the presence of his disciples, which are not recorded in this book. [31] But these are written that you may believe[b] that Jesus is the Messiah, the Son of God, and that by believing you may have life in his name.

Many scholars believe these two verses originally concluded this Gospel. John is letting us know that he purposely included some of the signs Jesus did and left out others. (In other words, John was aware of the other signs and didn't merely overlook them.)

John recorded seven signs as evidence to encourage non-Christian readers to "believe" and/or to challenge Christian readers to continue to "believe." The existing early manuscripts of John record two different spellings for the word *believe*. A simple Greek *s* (sigma) separates them, hence the two possible meanings.

Some have pointed out that the noun *faith* is not found even once in many English translations of the Gospel of John, while the verb *believe* appears 95 times. (In the NIV translation, the word *faith* does appear once—in John 12:42.) On the other hand, the verb *believe* appears a total of only 36 times in the three Synoptic Gospels. John seems more interested in the action of believing than in the possession of faith. John also commonly follows the verb *believe* with the preposition *in* (or *into*), indicating that we aren't simply to believe for the sake of belief. Our belief needs to be placed in someone powerful and trustworthy—and that's Jesus.

The purpose of John's Gospel is that people would believe Jesus is the Messiah, the Son of God. (Other titles in

---

b John 20:31 Or *may continue to believe*

the Gospel of John include Rabbi, Prophet, Son of Man, the King of Israel, Lord, and God.) John wants people to believe so they might receive life—life that begins now and continues into the kingdom of God to come.

READ BETWEEN THE LINES

- Why didn't John include all of the signs that Jesus did in the presence of his disciples?
- Why did John select these particular signs and leave out others?
- What is the purpose of John's Gospel?
- What does it mean to "believe"?
- Is this Gospel intended for non-Christians, Christians, or both?
- What does it mean to "have life in his name" (v. 31)?

WELCOME TO MY WORLD

- What convinced me to put my faith in Jesus?
- What three signs described in this Gospel are the most significant to me?

Jesus and the Miraculous Catch of Fish

The Gospel seems to close with 20:30-31, but here we encounter another chapter. This is not uncommon; the apostle Paul wrote something similar in Romans 15:33, "The God of peace be with you all. Amen." He then writes 34 more sentences (27 verses), which we know as Romans 16.

Some scholars have noted certain stylistic differences in chapter 21 and have suggested that it may have been a later edition to the Gospel. They point particularly to John 21:24-25, which at first glance seems to have been written after the death of the beloved disciple. They suggest that a member of the Johannine school (or circle) tacked on the final chapter as an appendix or supplement, including other stories recorded by the beloved disciple that weren't found in John 1:1–20:31. At the time, this sort of thing wasn't uncommon, nor would it have been considered dishonest in any way for the followers of a certain school of thinking to write material under their teacher's name.

However, as Gary Burge points out, "There is no evidence in the manuscript tradition that this Gospel ever circulated without this final chapter." Burge continues, "There are twenty-eight words in chapter 21 that do not appear in chapters 1–20, yet in chapter 21 we have a new subject (fishing), which alone demands new vocabulary."

Apart from the addition of "fishing" language, chapter 21 doesn't differ significantly from the rest of the Gospel. The majority of words and images in chapter 21 complement what has already appeared in the Gospel. For example, the charcoal fire (18:18 and 21:9), drawing all people (12:32 and 21:8), and the image of a shepherd (10:1-42 and 21:15-19) all echo themes that appeared earlier in the Gospel.

Most scholars believe John included an epilogue as his final chapter, just as he included a prologue as the first chapter of the Gospel. The two serve as bookends for John's account of Jesus' life. Andreas Köstenberger writes, "The presence of an epilogue seems required by the opening prologue in order to preserve balance and symmetry of structure. . . . Hence, both prologue and epilogue frame the Gospel in such a way that they form an integral part of the theological and literary fabric of the entire narrative."

Some have proposed that only John 21:20-25 was added by another writer or editor; they believe the writing in the rest of John 21 comes from the same pen as John 1–20. But others suggest that John 21:20-25 simply reflects John's unique style of writing, and is similar to John 19:35.

The material in chapter 21 offers not only further proof of the resurrection of Jesus, but also an explanation of details that were left unanswered or in need of clarification at the end of John 20. Fortunately, the Holy Spirit leaves no loose ends dangling. The epilogue answers two questions in particular:

1. What happens to Peter who, according to Acts 3:1, becomes John's partner in ministry? John 21 offers an explanation of how Peter went from denying Christ to being a leading partner in ministry.
2. What about that first-century rumor that said John wouldn't die before Jesus returns?

John 21:1-3

1 Afterward Jesus appeared again to his disciples, by the Sea of Galilee.[a] It happened this way: 2 Simon Peter, Thomas (also known as Didymus[b]), Nathanael from Cana in Galilee, the sons of

---

a John 21:1 Greek *Tiberias*

b John 21:2 *Thomas* (Aramaic) and *Didymus* (Greek) both mean *twin*.

Zebedee, and two other disciples were together. ³ "I'm going out to fish," Simon Peter told them, and they said, "We'll go with you." So they went out and got into the boat, but that night they caught nothing.

The setting of this scene is by the Sea of Galilee, sometime after Jesus' appearance to Thomas, and no more than a month after the resurrection. This area was very familiar to Peter and the sons of Zebedee (James and John). It's where they began following Jesus and where he told them he would make them "fishers of people" (Mark 1:17). After the resurrection, it seems the disciples don't know what to do with themselves. According to Matthew 28:16, Jesus had asked the disciples to wait at an appointed place on or near a mountain in Galilee (see also Matthew 26:32; Matthew 28:5-7; Mark 14:28). But apparently, they must have grown tired of waiting. So they decide to go back to their old ways of fishing (Mark 1:16-20).

Impatient, impetuous, and perhaps still depressed by his denial of Jesus, Peter announces, "I'm going out to fish" (21:3). And like baby ducks following their mother, the rest of this little group of seven disciples (including two who aren't named) follow him. Fishing must have given them a sense of normalcy and comfort. It may have been a way to kill time while waiting for Jesus. Or maybe they were just hungry. But it doesn't appear as though they ever considered asking God what they should do. God wants them to fish—but for people (Matthew 4:19; Mark 1:17).

Not only that, but Jesus told them, "No one who puts a hand to the plow and looks back is fit for service in the kingdom of God" (Luke 9:62). If you want another example of what happens when we start looking back at our old life, check out Lot's wife in Genesis 19:26.

These men are professional fishermen. They fish in the late evening, which was a great time to catch fish because they could then turn around and sell the fresh fish to the markets in the morning. W. M. Thompson offers a wonderful description of night fishing in *The Land and the Book*: "It is a beautiful sight. With blazing torch, the boat glides over the flashing sea, and the men stand gazing keenly into it until their prey is sighted, when, quick as lightning, they fling their net or fly their spear." The torches along with chum (bait thrown overboard) would normally attract the fish to the surface.

But this passage is a classic illustration of the futility of trying to do it all ourselves. These expert fishermen caught nothing. Perhaps Peter and the others thought they could rely on their own strength, but God rerouted every fish so they couldn't catch even one. Sometimes we have to see our own weakness before God gives us his strength.

John 21:4-5

4 Early in the morning, Jesus stood on the shore, but the disciples did not realize that it was Jesus.
5 He called out to them, "Friends, haven't you any fish?"

"No," they answered.

Jesus is on the shore about 100 yards away from the disciples (21:8). They don't know it's Jesus. He greets them as "friends," but this word might also be translated "children" or "fellas" or "lads" or "guys." It's not the way one would normally greet a close friend, although it's still kinder than what Jesus could have called them. The writer of the Gospel may be suggesting that whenever we go on our own path, we risk missing out on the warmth and intimacy of Jesus Christ. If they had obeyed Jesus, they'd still be waiting on that mountain like he asked them to do (Matthew 28:16).

Jesus asks if they've caught any fish. Of course, he already knows the answer. These frustrated fishermen respond with the strongest Greek word for *no*. Evidently, the old life wasn't bringing them the satisfaction it once did.

John 21:6

6 He said, "Throw your net on the right side of the boat and you will find some." When they did, they were unable to haul the net in because of the large number of fish.

The disciples aren't using fishing poles. They used large ten-foot nets that they'd cast onto the water in places where they could see fish swimming. Sinkers attached to the edges of the net would cause the net to trap the fish. Then the net and fish would be pulled into the boat. A typical boat of this period is on display at the Beit Yigal Allon Museum in Ginosar, along the western banks of the Sea of Galilee. It is 26.5 feet long and 7.5 feet wide.

These fishermen must have thought this man was crazy: "Right, buddy! All the fish are hiding just a few feet away from us on the other side of the boat." But the man onshore must have had an authoritative and commanding voice because they don't argue. Instead, they toss the net over their heads, and it lands on the water like a parachute before the sinkers take it down. The net is immediately so full that the men can't haul it in. Evidently, obedience brings blessing. In Genesis 22:18, God tells Abraham, "Through your offspring all nations on earth will be blessed, because you have obeyed me." An abundant catch of fish was also seen as a sign of God's favor and blessing in Judaism (*T. Zebulon*, 6:1-8).

This scene has strong similarities to the one described in Luke 5:1-11, where Jesus first called his disciples. Maybe that's why the disciple whom Jesus loved responds as he does in the next verse.

John 21:7-11

7 Then the disciple whom Jesus loved said to Peter, "It is the Lord!" As soon as Simon Peter heard him say, "It is the Lord," he wrapped his outer garment around him (for he had taken it off) and jumped into the water. 8 The other disciples followed in the boat, towing the net full of fish, for they were not far from shore, about a hundred yards.[c] 9 When they landed, they saw a fire of burning coals there with fish on it, and some bread.

10 Jesus said to them, "Bring some of the fish you have just caught." 11 So Simon Peter climbed back into the boat and dragged the net ashore. It was full of large fish, 153, but even with so many the net was not torn.

The disciple whom Jesus loved immediately knew who was responsible for this incredible catch of fish. And the minute Peter realizes it's Jesus, he acts impulsively. As usual, John is fast to perceive, and Peter is fast to act. Peter puts on his outer garment (perhaps used to ward off the morning chill) and jumps into the water. This seems a little odd at first. Perhaps Peter was naked or wearing only a loin cloth, yet it still seems unusual to put on a shirt, coat, or smock when getting ready to jump into the water. Peter may have wanted to be more properly dressed to meet Jesus. (Some suggest he may have been tucking his outer garment between his legs and around his waist.) In any case Peter dives into the water and swims to shore as the rest of the guys row the boat in, towing the overloaded net of fish.

---

c John 21:8 Or about 90 meters

On the shore is a fire of burning coals (18:18). Charcoal fires have a distinct smell. Different smells bring back different memories. This smell must have brought back to Peter the events from just a few days earlier, when he'd denied Jesus three times while standing around a similar fire in the high priest's courtyard.

Peter drags the net ashore—the same net that a few minutes earlier was too heavy for the disciples to haul into the boat (21:6). Either Peter is a very strong man, or the other disciples joined him in pulling in the net.

The mention of a specific number of fish indicates an eyewitness account. Some scholars believe the number 153 may have deeper symbolic meanings. Several have suggested there were only 153 types of fish in the sea at that time, meaning that Jesus' followers should reach out to all people—but there is no historic proof of this. Others have noted that according to the numeric value of the Greek and Hebrew letters, the words *Simon* and *fish* total 153, as does *church of love*. Gary Burge in *The Application Commentary* and C. S. Keener in *The Gospel of John* have offered even more possibilities—and there may be some complex mathematics going on here. But we should be cautious; there's a danger in that focusing on ideas about the possible significance of the number 153 can trivialize what's going on in the narrative and draw our attention away from it.

At the purely historical level, it is unsurprising that someone counted them, either as part of dividing them up amongst the fishermen in preparation for sale, or because one of them was so dumbfounded by the size of the catch that he said something like this: "Can you believe it? I wonder how many there are?"

—D. A. Carson, *The Gospel According to John*, 672

The fact that they hauled in so many fish may point to two miracles. First, they catch an overabundance of fish, which must have been a shocker given the futility of the previous night's fishing. Second, they didn't lose a single fish due to a broken net. These disciples will soon begin fishing for people, and the numbers "caught" then will also be staggering.

John 21:12-14

12 Jesus said to them, "Come and have breakfast." None of the disciples dared ask him, "Who are you?" They knew it was the Lord. 13 Jesus came, took the bread and gave it to them, and did the same with the fish. 14 This was now the third time Jesus appeared to his disciples after he was raised from the dead.

Jesus is cooking breakfast on the shore. Feeling compassion for these tired, hungry disciples, Jesus feeds them. Think about that: The Creator of the Universe, God in the flesh, is making breakfast for a few fishermen on this isolated beach. Here again, Jesus is being a servant. Imagine what breakfast made by God would taste like; it would be heavenly. Do you know how God makes breakfast? *Poof!* Here's breakfast! (Well, he *could* have done it that way!)

Jesus didn't need anyone's help. But he invites the disciples to put some of the fish they've just caught on the fire, thus involving them in the preparation of the meal.

How dreadfully easy it is for Christian workers to get the impression that we've got to do it all. God, we imagine, is waiting passively for us to get on with things. If we don't organize it, it won't happen. If we don't tell people the good news, they won't hear it. If we don't change the world, it won't be changed. "He has no hands but our hands," we are sometimes told.

> What a load of rubbish. Whose hands made the sun rise this morning? Whose breath guided us to think, and pray, and love, and hope? . . . Neither the institutional church nor its individual members can upstage him. Jesus welcomes Peter's catch. He asks him to bring some of it. But he doesn't, in that sense, *need* it.
>
> —Tom Wright, *John for Everyone, Part Two: Chapters 11–21*, 160

"None of the disciples *dared* ask him 'Who are you?' They knew it was the Lord." These words sound odd. It almost seems as if they're afraid to ask Jesus a question. These resurrection appearances sound both weird and wonderful. The disciples have been with Jesus for two or three years—24/7—yet here they don't dare ask him a question.

This makes sense only if they recognize that Jesus is somehow different. But how is he different? He's gone from death to life. This is not a mere resuscitation of his body, but a resurrection. This physical body was recognizable, yet it was different; it would no longer suffer decay. He wasn't going to have to die again. This is no sleight-of-hand or magic trick; it is real.

The disciples may also still be feeling the pain of having deserted Jesus at the cross. Yet, in this area of the world, eating a meal with someone who's wronged you is an expression of forgiveness.

It's interesting that they'd spent all night looking for some fish, and Jesus had them grilled and ready to eat on the shore all along. Sometimes we go off doing our own thing, only to discover later that Jesus had what we needed all along.

Jesus providing a meal of fish and bread: Wouldn't that bring back fond memories (6:5-15)?

READ BETWEEN THE LINES

- Who wrote chapter 21?
- "Afterward" refers to what? (21:1)
- Why were these disciples at the Sea of Galilee?
- Why are they fishing at night?
- Is there any significance in the fact that they caught nothing all night long?
- Why didn't the disciples realize it was Jesus standing on the shore?
- Why does Jesus call them "friends"?
- Why did Jesus ask whether they'd caught anything? Didn't he know the answer?
- Why did Jesus tell them to throw their net on the other side of the boat?
- How did the disciple whom Jesus loved know it was Jesus?
- Why did Peter put on an outer garment before jumping in the water?
- What is the significance of a fire of burning coals?
- Why does Jesus invite them to bring some of their fish for part of the meal?
- This was the third time Jesus appeared to his disciples. Is this significant?
- What memories of eating a similar meal of bread and fish (prepared by Jesus) would this event bring back to these disciples' minds?

WELCOME TO MY WORLD

- What would it be like to eat breakfast prepared by Jesus?

- Describe a time when I was impatient while waiting on God's prompting, which then resulted in my doing something unwise. What lessons did I learn from that experience?

- Describe a time in my life—after I came to know Jesus—when I realized my old life was no longer satisfying.

- What qualities of good fishermen are desirable in my reaching out to people with the message of Jesus?

- When have I found that obedience to God brings blessing?

- Have I ever found myself getting carried away with meaningless speculation about a passage of Scripture?

- When have I felt God's presence?

- What would I talk to Jesus about over a meal?

- How does it feel to know that Jesus doesn't need my help, but he allows me to participate in his work?

Jesus Reinstates Peter

John 21:15

¹⁵ **When they had finished eating, Jesus said to Simon Peter, "Simon son of John, do you love me more than these?"**

"Yes, Lord," he said, "you know that I love you."
Jesus said, "Feed my lambs."

John may have told the story about the disciples catching the fish simply to set the scene that now unfolds. This conversation between Jesus and Peter takes us back to an earlier conversation in which Peter tells Jesus, loudly and emphatically, "I will lay down my life for you" (13:37). Peter was certain he'd never let Jesus down. The rest of the disciples might fall away, but Peter would not. Yet his good intentions fell apart as he denied being a follower of Jesus three times (18:15-18, 25-27). After the third denial, a rooster began to crow. Since that moment, we've not heard a word from Peter. His mouth has been shut; his voice has been silent. This would have been very unusual for Peter.

Even as the disciples eat an entire meal on the beach with Jesus, it appears that Peter doesn't speak. In fact, no one does. It may have been an eerie, uncomfortable silence. Have you ever experienced a similar silence? Maybe as a teenager you did something you knew would get you in trouble, and your parents found out about it. But then they didn't discuss it with you right away. And so you sat through an entire meal with them, keeping your eyes focused on your plate and not wanting to make eye contact with either parent. I think maybe the disciples were experiencing that kind of silence here.

In this passage who makes the first move? Who always makes the first move? First John 4:19 tells us, "We love because he first loved us." Jesus always makes the first move. Long before we knew Jesus, he loved us.

Jesus breaks the silence. Peter's heart must have been racing as Jesus speaks directly to him. There is some unfinished business that needs to be taken care of, and Jesus does it publicly. Peter will need authority as the leader of the disciples and the early church, so his situation needs to be dealt with publicly. (His denials of Jesus were also public.) Jesus asks Peter three questions. This, too, has got to bring back painful memories of his denial. At some point in their conversation, Jesus may have taken Peter aside, perhaps walking along the shoreline with him, because verse 21 says, "the disciple whom Jesus loved was following them."

In Mark 16:5-7 as the women enter the tomb, they meet a young man dressed in white. "Don't be alarmed," he said. "You are looking for Jesus the Nazarene, who was crucified. He has risen! He is not here. See the place where they laid him. But go, tell his disciples and Peter, 'He is going ahead of you into Galilee. There you will see him, just as he told you.'"

What catches my attention here is the phrase "go, tell his disciples and Peter." This seems odd. Wouldn't it be sufficient just to say, "go tell his disciples"? Wouldn't that include Peter? Why make a point of making sure Peter gets this message? Could it be that God in his kindness and forgiveness wants to ensure that Peter knows he is still part of the group in spite of what he's done by denying Jesus?

—Les

Jesus calls him by his formal name—"Simon, son of John." That must have hurt. Jesus has called him Simon before (Matthew 17:25; Mark 14:37; Luke 22:31). Perhaps Jesus calls Peter by his old name here because he's been acting like his old self. Jesus now gently leads Peter through a process of restoration.

Jesus asks Peter present-tense questions. (Perhaps Jesus has already taken care of Peter's past failures in his appearance to Peter recorded in Luke 24:34.) At any rate, Peter may be focused on his past failures, but Jesus is focused on the present moment. Peter denied Jesus three times; now he will affirm his love for Jesus three times.

Jesus asks Peter, "Do you love me?" Love is the compelling force behind true obedience. We obey those we love. If Peter doesn't love Jesus, he will never be effective in ministry.

John's Gospel uses two words that can be translated as "love"—*agapao* and *phileo*. John uses these words somewhat interchangeably, although they have slightly different meanings. The term *agapao* (found in 3:16; 3:19; 3:35; and 11:4-5) is a self-sacrificing kind of love that puts the other before oneself. The term *phileo* (found in 5:20; 11:3; and 20:2) refers to a compassionate, affectionate, deep bond of friendship. (Philadelphia, "the city of brotherly love," traces its name back to this same Greek term.)

Although John tends to use these words almost interchangeably in most of the Gospel, some scholars say this present passage is the one place where the specific meaning of each term takes on greater significance. Others believe that, even here, John uses the terms as synonyms. I tend to think the meaning of the story is enhanced if we look closely at the terms John chooses.

Here in verse 15, the Greek word Jesus uses is *agapao*. But what does "more than these" refer to? Is Jesus asking if Peter loves Jesus more than any other disciple loves Jesus? Peter had said as much earlier, "Even if all fall away on account of you, I never will" (Matthew 26:33). Or is Jesus asking if Peter's love for Jesus is greater than Peter's love for the other disciples? Or is Jesus talking about Peter's love for his old life of fishing—the daily routine of boats, nets, and fish? Perhaps his question includes all of these possibilities:

"Peter, do you love me more than anyone or anything?" In any case Jesus is asking Peter to examine himself.

Peter responds that he does love Jesus, but he uses the other Greek word for love—*phileo*. If Peter had used the world *agapao*, he would have been a hypocrite because his recent denial did not reflect such a sacrificial love. It seems Peter is now a humble man, no longer a braggart.

Jesus accepts Peter where he's at spiritually and tells him, "Feed my lambs." This brings to mind the shepherd image found throughout the Scriptures. Shepherds who love God will care for God's sheep and carry out God's will (Ezekiel 34). Jesus is telling Peter to get involved in service, to take care of the needs of others. Jesus is giving Peter an assignment, a command, a challenge. The lambs may be referring to children or youth. Hey, maybe Jesus is telling Peter to be a youth worker!

John 21:16

16Again Jesus said, "Simon son of John, do you love me?"

He answered, "Yes, Lord, you know that I love you."

Jesus said, "Take care of my sheep."

The second time Jesus leaves off the "more than these" but still uses *agapao*. Jesus perhaps is cutting out the peer pressure. Peter again responds using the Greek word *phileo*. And Jesus tells Peter to feed his sheep. Jesus is telling Peter to be a pastor and take care of his people.

John 21:17

17 The third time he said to him, "Simon son of John, do you love me?"

Peter was hurt because Jesus asked him the third time, "Do you love me?" He said, "Lord, you

**know all things; you know that I love you."
Jesus said, "Feed my sheep."**

This third time Jesus uses the word *phileo*. Peter was hurt because it was the third time Jesus had questioned him about his love. Perhaps he was also disappointed to hear Jesus use the word *phileo* for love. Jesus seems to be questioning every level of Peter's commitment: "Peter, do you even *phileo* me?" Peter responds by appealing to Jesus' omnipotence. "Jesus, you know everything. You know the state of my heart." And then, a third time, Peter affirms to Jesus that he loves him—again using the word *phileo*.

It's encouraging that Jesus knows everything about us, because there are days when our lives don't always show that we love him. We must be humbly aware of our own limitations. Clearly, God can use even our failures for his purposes. Jesus gives Peter—and each of us—a second chance. Sins can be forgiven; we must not quit. Remember that God is always eager to receive us when we seek him, like the father from Jesus' parable who spends his days waiting for his lost son to come home (Luke 15:11-31).

John 21:18-19

[18] **"Very truly I tell you, when you were younger you dressed yourself and went where you wanted; but when you are old you will stretch out your hands, and someone else will dress you and lead you where you do not want to go."** [19] **Jesus said this to indicate the kind of death by which Peter would glorify God. Then he said to him, "Follow me!"**

Here, Jesus may have been quoting a well-known proverb of the time. Jesus is telling Peter that even though he might have done his own thing and went wherever he wanted as a young man, it will be different when Peter is old. Jesus uses an expression that writers of the ancient world used in reference to crucifixion ("stretch out your hands"). Also, the verb *dress* can mean to bind or fasten—as hands and feet are attached to a cross. Jesus is telling Peter that he will die the same way Jesus did. This brings to mind John 13:36 where Jesus tells Peter, "Where I am going, you cannot follow now, but you will follow later."

This may not appear to be good news, but it's good news to Peter. Jesus is telling Peter he'll have another chance to show his faithfulness to Christ, and this time he won't deny Jesus. This gives Peter confidence. Peter's death will glorify God (12:27-28; 13:31-32; 17:1).

For several years I lived in the San Francisco Bay area, home of the Golden Gate Bridge. The bridge was built in two stages and was completed in 1937. The first stage of work went very slowly, while the second went very quickly. In the first stage, several men fell to their deaths, and work ground to a halt because fear paralyzed the workers who'd seen their companions plummet from the structure to the water far below. Finally, an ingenious person suggested building a net under the bridge as it was being constructed. They built the net at a cost of more than $100,000. It was the largest net ever built. The net saved 10 workers who fell into it, and the work proceeded 25 percent more quickly than before. The job was completed. When we know we are secure in Jesus' love, we can move forward with confidence and strength.

—Les

By the time John wrote his Gospel, Peter would already have died. Tradition says that both Peter and his wife were imprisoned under Nero's reign (AD 64–66). According to Clement of Rome, Tertullian, and Eusebius of Caesarea, Peter was crucified—after first being forced to watch his wife be crucified. Peter was crucified upside down because he felt he was unworthy to die as Christ had.

In John 12:26, Jesus said, "Whoever serves me must follow me; and where I am, my servant also will be. My Father will honor the one who serves me." Jesus' call to "Follow me!" seems like a fairly simple and straightforward command, but here at the end of John's Gospel, it takes on new meaning.

READ BETWEEN THE LINES

- Why does Jesus call Peter by his given name, Simon?
- Is there any significance in John's use of the two Greek words for love (*agapao* and *phileo*)?
- Who or what are the "more than these"?
- What does it mean to "feed my lambs," "take care of my sheep," and "feed my sheep"?
- Why does Jesus delete the phrase "more than these" the second time he asks Peter if he loves Jesus?
- Why does Jesus ask three times if Peter loves him?
- How is Peter feeling by the third question?
- What is Peter appealing to in his third response to Jesus' question?
- What is Jesus referring to when he says, "you will stretch out your hands" and "someone else will dress you"? Would this encourage or discourage Peter? Why?
- What does Jesus mean when he tells Peter, "Follow me!"

WELCOME TO MY WORLD

- Have I ever eaten a meal in silence because I knew there was an awkward or troubling conversation that I needed to have with someone?
- Where do I go to get away with God?

- Do my parents or other family members have a way of calling my name that lets me know I'm in trouble?
- How would I have responded to Jesus' questions?
- Have I ever felt beyond forgiveness? How do I feeling after reading this passage?
- How should I respond to those who've hurt me?
- Is there anyone or anything I love more than Jesus?

The Fate of the Disciple Jesus Loved

John 21:20-21

20 Peter turned and saw that the disciple whom Jesus loved was following them. (This was the one who had leaned back against Jesus at the supper and had said, "Lord, who is going to betray you?") 21 When Peter saw him, he asked, "Lord, what about him?"

Near the end of his conversation with Jesus, Peter possibly hears some footsteps behind them. It's "the disciple whom Jesus loved"—which many scholars believe is John's way of referring to himself. This same disciple was identified as the one who'd leaned back against Jesus at the Last Supper and said, "Lord, who is going to betray you?" (13:23-25).

John and Peter are often paired up in the Gospel accounts. John is the younger of the two. At times, he almost seems like Peter's kid brother. Is Peter's question an expression of genuine concern about his younger friend? Or is Peter wondering if John is going to get to do something better than him? Peter has just been told he's going to be crucified; he may want to know if John will also die as a martyr for Christ.

This mild rivalry between Peter and John comes to a head in this passage. This only confirms the humanity of the disciples. They are made of flesh and blood, cut from the same human cloth. They aren't perfect models or escapees from wax museums. Like us, each of them is a work in progress.

In previous chapters we've read of John sitting close to Jesus and having an intimate conversation with him in the upper room (13:21-30), while Peter has to ask questions through John. John is known to the high priest (18:15). John is at the cross and takes care of Jesus' mother (19:26-27). John beats Peter to the tomb (20:4) John is the first to believe (20:8) and the first to recognize Jesus on the beach (21:7). John remains in the boat to row the huge catch of fish to shore, while Peter jumps out of the boat and swims to shore (21:7-8).

Peter's question in verse 21 brings the rivalry out in the open. He is comparing. Many of us know this tendency all too well. We compare children, grades, ministry sizes, salaries, and jobs. We let jealousy take hold of us. Not a good idea. If we know we are in God's will and following Jesus, we can be content in whatever situation we find ourselves. And the good news is that God can use all of us—from the impulsive Peter to the thoughtful John.

In *The Horse and His Boy*, the fifth book of C. S. Lewis's Chronicles of Narnia, the boy Shasta finally meets the great lion, Aslan. Shasta learns from Aslan the amazing story of his own young life and Aslan's part in it. Aslan tells Shasta of the boy's beginnings and his journeys, and he helps Shasta understand what it all means. At that point Shasta asks Aslan to explain the meaning of some of the experiences of his traveling companion, Aravis. Aslan answers: "I am telling you your story, not hers. I tell no one any story but his own."

—Les

John 21:22

²²Jesus answered, "If I want him to remain alive until I return, what is that to you? You must follow me."

Jesus doesn't give Peter an answer to his question. In fact, he sounds a bit ticked. Instead, Jesus gives Peter a loving rebuke, saying, "If it's my will that John remains physically alive until I return, what's that to you?" This is the only reference to the second coming in John's Gospel. Jesus is telling Peter to focus on his own journey. He doesn't need to worry about John; Peter has only one duty and that is to follow Jesus (both physically and spiritually).

Of course, we know that Peter and John, empowered by the Holy Spirit, will both go on to make amazing contributions to the beginnings of the Christian church. Peter will offer the first sermon on Pentecost (in which he recognizes that Gentiles could become Christians without first becoming Jews). He will write two letters that will become part of the New Testament, encouraging believers to have patience as we wait for the second coming. And he will die as a martyr because of his faith. John will write not only this Gospel, but also three New Testament letters and the book of Revelation.

New Testament scholar Raymond Brown has written about the tension between the Johannine and Petrine Christian communities in the late first century. There seems to have been some strain between those who adored Peter and those who adored John concerning which disciple was the greatest. Perhaps this last chapter was written in part to help bring harmony between these two groups.

John 21:23

23 Because of this, the rumor spread among the believers that this disciple would not die. But Jesus did not say that he would not die; he only said, "If I want him to remain alive until I return, what is that to you?"

As an eyewitness to these events, John would have heard exactly how Jesus responded to Peter's question. Here, he acknowledges that some early believers misunderstood

Jesus' words, believing Jesus had said John would remain alive until the second coming. This misunderstanding could have led to confusion among early believers when John died. And then people outside the church would have jumped all over this, calling Christianity a lie. So the writer corrects this false rumor to clear up the confusion.

John 21:24-25

24 This is the disciple who testifies to these things and who wrote them down. We know that his testimony is true.

25 Jesus did many other things as well. If every one of them were written down, I suppose that even the whole world would not have room for the books that would be written.

Verse 24 could indicate that John has died and his trusted friends or disciples (notice the "we") are placing the finishing touches on his Gospel. Some scholars think these final verses may have been penned by elders from the Ephesian church. But others dismiss this possibility, believing that John wrote this statement in the first person plural ("we") as an editorial device or as a way of including those present with him as he completed the manuscript.

Some early church historians believe John spent several years in exile on the island of Patmos (Revelation 1:9) and then returned to Ephesus where he died an old man, near the end of the first century. We can be certain that he's given us an intimate account of Jesus' life and ministry, and that his account is true. John is the last observer in a long line of witnesses. Gary M. Burge writes, "This Gospel is no fanciful speculation, no whimsical, inspired redrawing of Jesus' portrait. It is a record of what happened, given by a man who had seen it." The "these things" in verse 24 refers not only to this chapter, but to the entire Gospel.

The final verse seems to have come from the hand of John himself. Earl Palmer has written, "Perhaps, like Paul, he dictated the letter to a secretary and now takes the pen into his own hand to place a personal autograph at its close." In words that echo the close of chapter 20, John affirms that there is much more that could be said about Jesus' life. Statements like this were somewhat common in John's day. For example, consider these words from the first-century Rabbi Johanan ben Zakkai: "If all heaven were a parchment, and all the trees produced pens, and all the waters were ink, they would not suffice to inscribe the wisdom I have received from my teachers: and yet from the wisdom of the wise I have enjoyed only so much as the water a fly which plunges into the sea can remove" (*Soperim* 16.8).

John acknowledges that he's been selective regarding what he's included (20:30-31), but he closes by noting that all the books in the world couldn't contain Jesus' entire story. This isn't mere exaggeration; there is so much to tell about Jesus. But all who follow Christ will be forever indebted to John for sharing his own faithful account of Jesus' life, death, and resurrection.

READ BETWEEN THE LINES

- Why did Peter ask, "Lord, what about him?" (21:21).
- Why didn't Jesus answer the question?
- Why is Jesus so concerned about Peter comparing himself to the other disciples?
- What is the significance of the rumor about John that was spreading among the believers? Why was it important for John (or his followers) to squelch this rumor?
- Who are the "we" in "we know that his testimony is true"?

- What parts of the life of Jesus did the writer include in this Gospel? What incidents in Jesus' life aren't included in the Gospel of John?

WELCOME TO MY WORLD

- When have I fallen into the trap of comparing myself with others? What makes me do that?

- What do I know about Jesus' return (the second coming)?

- Have I ever been part of a rumor or misunderstanding that got out of control and hurt someone?

- Have I ever gotten into a heated discussion about who is the better Christian speaker or recording artist? What's the danger in engaging in these types of conversations?

BIBLIOGRAPHY

Arnold, Christian E., editor. *Zondervan Illustrated Bible Backgrounds Commentary: New Testament, Volume 2*. Grand Rapids, MI: Zondervan, 2002.

Barclay, William. *The Gospel of John, Vol. 1*. Philadelphia, PA: The Westminster Press, 1956.

Barclay, William. *The Gospel of John, Vol. 2*. Philadelphia, PA: The Westminster Press, 1956.

Barker, Kenneth, ed. *The NIV Study Bible: Gospel of John*. Grand Rapids, MI: Zondervan, 1985.

Barnhouse, Donald Grey. *The Love Life: A Study of the Gospel of John*. Glendale, CA: Regal Books, 1973.

Barrett, C. K. *The Gospel According to St. John*. London: Society Promoting Christian Knowledge, 1962.

Barrett, C. K., "'The Father is Greater than I' (John 14:28): Subordinationist Christology in the New Testament," *Neues Testament und Kirche. Für Rudolf Schnackenburg. Edited by* J. Gnilka. Freiburg: Herder, 1974.

Barton, Bruce B., Phillip Comfort, David Veerman, and Neil Wilson. *The Life Application Bible Commentary: John*. Wheaton, IL: Tyndale House, 1993.

Bickel, Bruce, and Stan Jantz. *John: Encountering Christ in a Life-Changing Way*. Eugene, OR: Harvest House Publishers, 2003.

Bishop, Jim. *The Day Christ Died*. New York: Harper, 1957.

Blomberg, Craig L. *Jesus and the Gospels*. Nashville, TN: Broadman & Holman, 1997.

Borgen, P. "God's Agent in the Fourth Gospel," *Religions in Antiquity*, Edited by J. Neusner. *New Testament Studies* 16 (1969): 288–295.

Brown, Raymond E. *The Gospel According to John, XIII–XXI*. New Haven, CT: Yale University Press, 1970.

Brown, Raymond E. *An Introduction to the Gospel of John*. New Haven, CT: Yale University Press, 2003, 2010.

Bruce, F. F. *The Gospel and Epistles of John*. Grand Rapids, MI: Eerdmans, 1983.

Bruns, J. Edgar. "The Use of Time in the Fourth Gospel," *New Testament Studies* 13 (1967): 285–290.

Bryant, Beauford H., and Mark S. Krause. *The College Press NIV Commentary: John*. Joplin, MO: College Press Publishing Company, 1998.

Burge, Gary M. *The NIV Application Commentary: John*. Grand Rapids, MI: Zondervan, 2000.

Butler, Paul T. *The Gospel of John*. Joplin, MO: College Press, 1961.

Carroll, Lewis. *Alice's Adventures in Wonderland*. London: MacMillan, 1865.

Carroll, Lewis. *Through the Looking Glass*. London: MacMillan, 1871.

Carson, D. A. *The Gospel According to John, Pillar New Testament Commentary*. Grand Rapids, MI: Eerdmans, 1991.

Cook, G. "Seeing, Judging and Acting: Evangelism in Jesus' Way According to John 9," *Evangelical Review of Theology* 16, no. 3 (1992): 251–261.

Cosgrove, C. H. "The Place Where Jesus Is: Allusions to Baptism and Eucharist in the Fourth Gospel," *New Testament Studies* 35 (1989): 522–539.

Courson, Jon. *Jon Courson's Application Commentary: New Testament*. Nashville, TN: Thomas Nelson, Inc., 2003.

Crossan, John Dominic. *Jesus: A Revolutionary Biography*. New York: Harper Collins. 1994.

Driscoll, Mark. Sermons delivered at Mars Hill Church in Seattle, Washington. http://marshill.com/media/sermons.

Foxe, John. *Foxe's Christian Martyrs of the World*. Chicago, IL: Moody Press, 1960.

Fredrikson, Roger L. *The Communicator's Commentary: John*. Waco, TX: Word Books, 1985.

Gordon, Ernest. *To End All Wars*. Grand Rapids, MI: Zondervan, 2002.

Harvey, A. E. "Christ as Agent" in *The Glory of Christ in the New Testament*. Edited by L. D. Hurst and N. T. Wright. New York: Oxford University Press, 1987.

Hendriksen, William. *New Testament Commentary: Exposition of the Gospel According to John*. Grand Rapids, MI: Baker Book House, 1953.

Hughes, R. Kent. *John: That You May Believe*. Wheaton, IL: Crossway Books, 1999.

Ironside, H. A. *Addresses on the Gospel of John*. Neptune, NJ: Loizeaux Brothers, 1976.

Jackson, H. M. "Ancient Self-Referential Conventions and Their Implications for the Authority and Integrity of the Gospel of John." *Journal of Theological Studies* 50:1–34.

Jordan, Clarence. *The Cotton Patch Version of Matthew and John*. New York: Association Press, 1970.

Keener, Craig. S. *The Gospel of John: A Commentary (Two-Volume Set)*. Peabody, MA: Hendrickson, 2003.

Keller, W. Phillip. *A Shepherd Looks at Psalm 23*. Grand Rapids, MI: Zondervan, 1970.

Koester, Craig R. *Symbolism in the Fourth Gospel: Meaning, Mystery, Community*. Minneapolis, MN: Fortress Press, 2003.

Korb, Scott. *Life in Year One*. New York: Riverhead Books, 2010.

Köstenberger, Andreas. "Jesus as Rabbi in the Fourth Gospel," *Bulletin for Biblical Research 8* (1998): 97–128.

Köstenberger, Andreas. *John: Baker Exegetical Commentary on the New Testament*. Grand Rapids, MI: Baker Academic, 2004.

Kysar, Robert. *Augsburg Commentary on the New Testament: John*. Minneapolis, MN: Augsburg Publishing House, 1986.

Lamott, Anne. *Bird by Bird: Some Instructions on Writing and Life*. New York: Random House, 1995.

Lamott, Anne. *Plan B: Further Thoughts on Faith*. New York: Riverhead Books, 2005.

Lamott, Anne. *Grace (Eventually): Thoughts on Faith*. New York: Riverhead Books, 2007.

Lee-Thorp, Karen, ed. *LifeChange Series: A Life-Changing Encounter with God's Word from the Book of John*. Colorado Springs: NavPress, 1987.

Lenski, R. C. H. *The Interpretation of St. John's Gospel*. Minneapolis, MN: Augsburg Publishing House, 1943.

Levine, Lee I. *Jerusalem: Portrait of the City in the Second Temple Period (538 b.c.e.–70 c.e.)*. Philadelphia, PA: The Jewish Publication Society, 2002.

Lewis, C. S. *Chronicles of Narnia: The Horse and His Boy*. New York: Harper Collins. 1954, 1994.

Lewis, C. S. *Miracles*. New York: Harper Collins, 1947, 2001.

Lincoln, Andrew. *Black's New Testament Commentary: The Gospel According to Saint John*. Peabody, MA: Hendrickson Publishers, 2006.

Lipscomb, David. *A Commentary on the Gospel of John*. Nashville, TN: Gospel Advocate Company, 1939.

MacArthur, John. *The MacArthur New Testament Commentary: John 1–11*. Chicago, IL: Moody Publishers, 2006.

MacArthur, John. *The MacArthur New Testament Commentary: John 12–21*. Chicago, IL: Moody Publishers, 2008.

Metzger, Paul Louis. *The Gospel of John: When Love Comes to Town*. Downers Grove, IL: InterVarsity, 2010.

Morris, Leon. *The Gospel According to John*. Rev. ed. Grand Rapids, MI: Eerdmans, 1995.

Murray, Andrew. *Waiting on God*. 1896.

Ortlund, Anne. *Up With Worship: How to Quit Playing Church*. Nashville, TN: Holman Publishers, 2001.

Palmer, Earl F. *The Intimate Gospel: Studies in John*. Waco, TX: Word Books, 1978.

Pate, C. Marvin. *The Writings of John*. Grand Rapids, MI: Zondervan, 2011.

Pollard, T. E. "The Exegesis of John 10:30 in the Early Trinitarian Controversies," *New Testament Studies 3* (1957): 334–349.

Ridenour, Fritz. *Tell It Like It Is: How Not to Be a "Witless Witness."* Glendale, CA: Regal Books, 1968.

Ryle, J. C. *Ryle's Expository Thoughts on the Gospels, Volume Three.* Grand Rapids, MI: Baker, 1977.

Sanders, Oswald J. *Spiritual Leadership.* Rev. ed. Chicago, IL: Moody Press, 1980.

Schaeffer, Francis A. *The Mark of the Christian.* Downers Grove, IL: InterVarsity Press, 1970.

Sloyan, Gerard. *Interpretation—A Bible Commentary for Teaching and Preaching: John.* Louisville, KY: John Knox Press, 1988.

Smalley, Stephen S. *John Evangelist and Interpreter.* Downers Grove, IL: InterVarsity Press, 1978.

Smith, Woodrow W. *The Twelve Who Walked in Galilee.* Old Tappan, NJ: Revell, 1974.

Swindoll, Charles R. *Swindoll's New Testament Insights: John.* Grand Rapids, MI: Zondervan, 2010.

Tenney, Merrill C. *The Expositor's Bible Commentary, Vol. 9: John and Acts.* Grand Rapids, MI: Zondervan, 1981.

Walk Thru the Bible. *A Walk Thru the Book of John.* Grand Rapids, MI: Baker Books, 2009.

Watkins, H. W. *The Gospel According to St. John.* London: Cassell & Company, Limited, 1890.

Watson, F. "Is John's Christology Adoptionist?" in *The Glory of Christ in the New Testament.* Edited by L. D. Hurst and N. T. Wright. New York: Oxford University Press, 1987.

Whitacre, Rodney A. *The IVP New Testament Commentary Series: John*. Downers Grove, IL: InterVarsity Press, 1999.

Wiersbe, Warren W. *Be Transformed*. Wheaton, IL: Victor, 1986.

Wiersbe, Warren W. *The Bible Exposition Commentary: New Testament, Volume 1*. Wheaton, IL: Victor, 1994.

Wiersbe, Warren W. *The Wiersbe Bible Study Series: John*. Colorado Springs: David C. Cook, 2010.

Wills, Gary. *What the Gospels Meant*. (New York: Viking Penguin, 2008).

Wilson, Marvin R. *Our Father Abraham: Jewish Roots of the Christian Faith*. Grand Rapids, MI: Eerdmans, 1989.

Wright, Tom. *John for Everyone, Part 1, Chapters 1–10*. Louisville, KY: Westminster John Knox, 2004.

Wright, Tom. *John for Everyone, Part 2, Chapters 11–21*. Louisville, KY: Westminster John Knox, 2004.

A Youth Worker's Commentary on John, Volume 1

Les Christie and David Nystrom

When a youth pastor is preparing a lesson, it's sometimes challenging to find a curriculum that really offers depth into the Scripture passages and goes beyond a cursory look at the text.

A Youth Worker's Commentary on John is the first in a new series of commentaries developed with youth workers in mind. An in-depth, yet readable approach to the gospel of John, this first volume includes commentary, word studies, personal and historical stories, and discussion questions that will help get students thinking and talking.

The gospel of John is the most personal and revealing of all the portraits of Jesus in the New Testament. This commentary has the entire NIV biblical text printed alongside a rich, deep look into the meaning of this gospel. Youth workers will find this to be an invaluable aid for message and lesson preparation. They'll get a solid understanding of the gospel of John, including its historical context, rationale, and meaning, to see how to apply what they uncover to the needs and issues the teens in their group are dealing with.

Available in stores and online!

ZONDERVAN®
.com

Share Your Thoughts

With the Author: Your comments will be forwarded to
the author when you send them to *zauthor@zondervan.com*.

With Zondervan: Submit your review of this book
by writing to *zreview@zondervan.com*.

Free Online Resources at
www.zondervan.com

Zondervan AuthorTracker: Be notified whenever your favorite
authors publish new books, go on tour, or post an update
about what's happening in their lives at www.zondervan.com/
authortracker.

Daily Bible Verses and Devotions: Enrich your life with daily
Bible verses or devotions that help you start every morning
focused on God. Visit www.zondervan.com/newsletters.

Free Email Publications: Sign up for newsletters on Christian
living, academic resources, church ministry, fiction, children's
resources, and more. Visit www.zondervan.com/newsletters.

Zondervan Bible Search: Find and compare Bible passages in
a variety of translations at www.zondervanbiblesearch.com.

Other Benefits: Register yourself to receive online benefits
like coupons and special offers, or to participate in research.

■ ZONDERVAN®

ZONDERVAN.com/
AUTHORTRACKER
follow your favorite authors